THE WILD GOOD

The Wild Good

LESBIAN PHOTOGRAPHS

and

WRITINGS ON LOVE

Edited by

Beatrix Gates

Anchor Books   Doubleday

NEW YORK LONDON TORONTO SYDNEY AUCKLAND

⚓

AN ANCHOR BOOK
PUBLISHED BY DOUBLEDAY
a division of Bantam Doubleday Dell Publishing Group, Inc.
1540 Broadway, New York, New York 10036

ANCHOR BOOKS, DOUBLEDAY, and the portrayal of an anchor
are trademarks of Doubleday, a division of Bantam Doubleday
Dell Publishing Group, Inc.

Book Design by Terry Karydes.

Acknowledgments for individual works appear on pages 265–270.

Library of Congress Cataloging-in-Publication Data
The wild good: lesbian photographs and writings on love / edited by
Beatrix Gates.
p.   cm.
1. Lesbians—Literary collections.   2. Lesbians' writings,
America.   3. Love—Literary collections.   4. Lesbians—Pictorial
works.   I. Gates, Beatrix.
PS509.L47W54   1996
810.8'09206643—dc20   96-15994
                                                                CIP

ISBN 0-385-48172-1
Copyright © 1996 by Beatrix Gates

for Joan Larkin

Contents

II. *Many Houses:* Body & Spirit

III. *Drinking the Rain:* Friendship

IV. *Against Silence:* FAMILY

V: *Praisesongs:* COMMUNITY & LEGACY

Acknowledgments

First thanks go to Roz Parr and Barbara Smith for early support of this project and steadfast follow-through during this past year. I am deeply grateful to Sydelle Kramer, my agent, for her support and intelligence throughout, and to Frances Goldin for her generosity. Thanks also go to Charles Flowers, my editor at Anchor Books, for his openness and intelligent feedback; to Jennie Guilfoyle for her help in bringing it to a close and to Terry Karydes for her design. Rachel Cohen also offered invaluable assistance at an important time. Special thanks to: Madelyn Arnold, Jane Cooper, Betsy Crowell and Louise Fishman, Anna Dembska and Andrea Hawks, David Geates and Alice Brock, Morgan Gwenwald, Keith Kayla, Eva Kollisch, Bea Kveloff and Edith Isaac-Rose, Richard La Bonte and Tommy Aviacolla Mecca, Joan Larkin, Jan Heller Levi, Andrea Lockett, Becket Logan, Jaime Manrique, Elena Martinez, Carol O'Donnell, Diana O'Hehir, Grace Paley, Nora Paley, Gerry Gomez Pearlberg, Bessy Reyna, Vita C. Shapiro, Shelly Smith and Meredith Tredeau, and Lucy Winer. I would also like to thank Bill Rukeyser for generously agreeing to the use of his mother's—Muriel Rukeyser's—words for the title of this book. Particular thanks also go to Helaine Pardo at Commerce Graphics; Chris Casilli and Mindy Farber at the Video Data Bank; Barry Swimar at Dancing Girl Productions; Lucien Terras at The Paula Cooper Gallery; the staff at A Different Light Bookstore, New York City; the women at the Lesbian Herstory Archives; Carol Seajay and Feminist Bookstore News for providing the list of independent and feminist bookstores for $1; and the Office of Special Collections of The New York Public Library. I am grateful to Ann Stokes at Welcome Hill, The PEN Writers Fund, The Author's League and the North Fork Women for Women Fund for support during the completion of this book. Lastly, there is a debt to the feminist and progressive small presses who have published Lesbians in mixed genre anthologies for over twenty years. I would like to thank them here for that work and commitment.

About the Editor

Beatrix Gates has published two books of poetry, *native tongue* and *Shooting at Night*, and her work has been widely published in periodicals and anthologies, including *The Women's Review of Books, The Nation, Gay & Lesbian Poetry in Our Time* and *The Key to Everything*. Her dramatic monologues appeared in *The Kenyon Review* Theatre Issue, and she is working on an original libretto called "The Singing Bridge." She has been awarded fellowships at The MacDowell Colony and The Millay Colony. As Founder of Granite Press (1973–1989), where she published feminist and lesbian titles, she designed and printed hand-made letterpress editions as well as trade paperbacks of poetry. She holds an MFA from Sarah Lawrence College and has taught creative writing, literature, Women's Studies, Gay and Lesbian Studies, and Book Arts at Goddard College, Hampshire College, The New School and The Writer's Voice. For the last three years, she has run the Lesbian & Gay Poetry Series at A Different Light Bookstore in New York City, and served on the Transition Team for Kitchen Table: Women of Color Press.

Introduction

I have thought of *The Wild Good: Lesbian Photographs & Writings on Love* as a lively conversation—charged connections, contrast, laughter, some fighting and a certain uneasiness that can signal attraction. I have sought beauty too, beauty in a clear-sightedness that cuts swiftly to the real bones of our lives. The photographs do that work as powerful and singular images, not necessarily as illustrations. The artists here pay deep attenion, and they capture a varied and forceful awareness of the worlds we inhabit. Lesbians do not just take photographs of each other, nor do the stories in this anthology prescribe purely sexual definitions or linear associations.

In a word, I have tried to put together something real. Playing off each other, the five sections—Friendship, Body & Spirit, Romance & Sex, Family and Community & Legacy—address many aspects of love. I have let themes of separation, loss and distrust read next to discovery, joy and long-held loyalties. How to describe the complex constellations we inhabit? What does it mean to experience love when we live with the very real daily threats to our existence? We handle many forms of violence and oppression—whether this violence comes in the form of poverty, racism, woman hatred, classism, homophobia, hatred of the body, anti-Semitism, disdain for aging, ableism or, more often for Lesbians, some combination of the above. These deep-rooted forces are a living history of which we are a part. It takes a lot of guts to arrive at the possibility of pleasure, understanding and joy given what we face, and I think Lesbians have developed unusual strength and flexibility in relation to love—by necessity.

To name the ways we survive and help each other out is to see how we share childcare, draw on the tangled and rich roots of our family histories, use the ways adversity or bigotry has informed our relationship to others. There is power in who has gone before, and in who follows, in the stories that mark our different identities—Mabel Hampton dancing at the Garden of Joy, coming up next to Alberta Hunter and Ethel Waters; grandfathers working as Pullman porters; sons who have grown up respecting Lesbian mothers; and bisexuals marking long friendships among ex-lovers. I doubt a day goes by without Lesbians praising and damning the contradictions that we embody as we seek to live our human lives openly. It is no accident that the Muriel Rukeyser poem from which I took the title for this anthology opens:

> Waking this morning,
> a violent woman in the violent day
> Laughing.

There is power, too, in the ways Lesbians enter the world on a daily basis—and it's important to see and report the bonds forged with any number of people as a way to get past the insular and unreal images of our lives. In this spirit, I chose not only to include bisexuals in this book, but also have stories where women deeply drawn to each other aren't calling any names yet—just making direct answer through action. We are expert navigators, and we have to have a sense of humor *and* an edge in order to maintain integrity, often with no reward but the thing itself. It is no small thing.

Most of all, I see this anthology is a gesture of respect toward the effort we continue to make to love. There is a way the title, *The Wild Good*, provides a sense of justice and delight, a natural order for Lesbians. To turn again to the Rukeyser poem, "Waking This Morning":

> . . . I want strong peace, and
>   delight,
> the wild good.
> I want to make my touch poems:
> to find my morning, to find you entire
> alive moving among the anti-touch people.

> I say across the waves of the air to you:
> today once more
> I will try to be non-violent
> one more day
> this morning, waking the world away
> in the violent day.

—Beatrix Gates,
May 1996

THE WILD GOOD

I

Acts of Love

R o m a n c e   &   S e x

Untitled photograph by Colleen McKay

Eileen Myles

Rut

I feel like a baby reading
a paper, an enormous
stranger pounding
between my legs.
She flies, a wolf,
she is green
sizzling, remarkable
she talks my
sex talk
she blows bubbles

the very chair
I sit upon
vibrates

at all the
issues in the world
she yawns
she is my baby

reading a paper
she turns me
red & brown
every creature
has its
smell for her
an easy violence
immense, stormy
waves rushing
over the
deck of
my rolling
ship

its little importances
my life. To her
it is nothing,
my pounding
goddess
drum beat,
no name

a furious dance
until I slip
into the
oblivion
of my
weeks & days

she sucks
the breath
from my
bones
she is water
underground

gooey
light

a cross
a spinning
stick

a treasure
commotion
the message
delivered
slowly

an ache
a stab
the lips of
the volcano
soft and
huge, the
lava flows
& she rolls
on hungry
turning
her head
seeking more
than the
building, people
hands, world
can give,
she caves
in, a monstrous
new &
holy
song.

"Indian Summer, Black Slip Hollow" by Morgan Gwenwald

Gale Jackson

the precision of the embrace.
the last chapter.

the jazz was back. when she opened the door it greeted her, wrapped lovin' weary arms around her, and pulled her past hesitation into the room. a home-coming embrace. it was the first thing she felt, hearing deep and resonantly felt, though she instinctively removed her shoes, took off her hat, put down the duffel bag and searched for a light before she let her mind drift out to meet the music the woman the home she had left so long ago behind. the jazz was back and it was a welcomed relief though she had just recently found the words to say why.

jazz. and over these years she had found herself getting into the avant garde young musicians as well as every female vocalist from the very blues beginnings. seem like some of those young players was reaching to wrap their legs around her sky and, now that she understood why, she could even hear it in the old-timey stuff—the crisp big bands, the glove tight rhythms of respect, the metronome of time clicking through a master drum. swinging. blowing. riffing. taking it down or out and out. they spoke to her many moods now that she had become moody. she had become moody and introspective and the last ten years had given her plenty of time, too much time, she thought, to think. and then the music had just swept in. and it thought. and it helped. billie and miles and min-gus and coltrane and sarah and nina, sweet hard nina, felt and thought and talked to her in some of those lonely places in her life. made a patch in the quilt she covered herself with at night. she had always loved music. always made it a part of the fluid stuff in the air to breathe and keep alive. she had collected hundreds, maybe thousands, of sides and delighted in all the technologies of sound. she had records on 78's, 33's, and 45's, discs and tapes of every medium size and sound. sound. gospel. finger popping. rhythm and blues. every single all girl group. every single disco side. and every love song. but the jazz was a new thing on her mind since she'd gone. maybe it was working on the docks that left the dissonant roar in her ear and tugged her spirit towards distant shores. all that jazz. she'd been learning a lot about love and improvisation and about living on the road and somehow that all came together to bring her back here, to this place, and to challdice singular song.

with challdice there had always been music. she remembered her first glance of challdice walking in her high narrow heels as though something very danceable was playing in her head. how she'd dance all night. disco. merengue. hustle. latin. calypso. jamaica ska. and in the dorm room where she stayed there had been the too soft european classical music playing, dancing its way through the hallway and teasing you towards the place where challdice studied slept and made love at the corner of the roof.

and challdice had been strange and familiar that winter in her memory. she had watched herself and the snow fall in love and was amazed at the world of child feelings she then remembered having forgotten growing up in the city. she had watched challdice writing or reading late into the night seeing something new and different become a comforting sight. she had watched the nights purple and wide just above uptown in a way she hadn't seen them from the streets that marked her life and her running buddies would tease her about the pretty young dancer so unlike the femmes uptown. different in texture. different in sound.

and then she was young enough to have both. this one and the other ones uptown. and then there was one in particular. beau. a girl then now a woman named beau who was losing her mind not so much from "the life" but from the contradictions in her own.

the thought of beau stopped her. she was still standing in the warm kitchen but the picture of beau, standing on the corner of 135th and amsterdam, was stamped on her eyes. beau, who usta run like clear water when they was kids, in an old man's hat and thick soled shoes selling *the watchtower* with the vision of the end in her smile. she shook her head. she sat down, cross legged, on the rug.

yea those days there was the block people and the scrambling and the clubs and the cab rides downtown leaned back in a woman's perfume. they had it like that. but challdice was another thing again. drawing her up above uptown through the winter and into spring when she decided, they decided, that together was the way they should stay.

and then, soon after, the jazz began and played so constant in that cellar room, whether or not challdice was at home, that anything that could have been before was all forgotten. the cacophony of sound began to move them together and, beyond the laughing crying jazz, beau's voice, the disappointment at city college, the medical degree she now knew she'd never have, all the shit was drowned out by the fluid music which wasn't asking anything of her but that she come for the ride. jazz was the strut and surrender of this new lover. the puzzle fit of their sex. the wings they came.

she stood and walked, for the first time, towards the front room where, she saw now, candles burned. candles and incense burned a path across the wall-length work desk. she looked for herself in the flames. would challdice still be expecting her she wondered before, laughing, she dismissed the thought. it *had* been too long. but it did seem as though challdice had been expecting someone. or to be right back. on the desk were more unlit candles, stick matched and, in a copper tray, a smoke. as if nothing had changed. as though the jazz had never left to be replaced by the undecipherable reggae chants, the matted hair, the strange churchy ways. when she left it was because challdice had become a riddle too difficult or too tiring to solve. when chad was no longer a lover and the pieces didn't fit. she remembered thinking, frightened and packing, heading for this other woman's easier arms, that chad too might be losing her mind. but now, she thought, blowing a heady column of smoke rings, it was as if that time had never been only the continual flowing of frankincense and the gentle passing of time in the candle flame. scented candles among the votives. the kind she loved.

she lowered herself to a squat and then again sat. the aroma of lemon wax rose from the wood below the hand-loomed rugs and she laughed aloud. she had taught that child from a house of indulgent women how to wash and wax a floor and even how to cook a pan of bread. and this, she announced to herself, running her fingers along the rugs' intricate weave, this she had gotten in a trade for two small bottles of scotch whiskey when they didn't have a dime between them or the pot to piss in. she was in the war and the war had her and she never made no bones about using it to her own advantage. she and her greek partner mikalis ran a brisk and lucrative business in whiskeys and rugs and, of course, american cigarettes. and like any good dealer she never touched the stuff. smoked greek cigarettes drank greek liquor. when in rome. this got to be worth more than a few grand she thought. she could use a drink but she was sure challdice wouldn't have one.

she remained still for a moment in the near dark. moonlight through the window. candlelight from the desk. this may have been the first time in her life when she felt so singularly complete. not needing noise and company. not necessarily lonely when alone. it had been a long time coming to this place. difficult times. a second marriage. a second divorce. jobs and relationships and parting with uncle sam along the way. there was a lot she wanted to talk about with challdice who would understand. even after all this time. she was sure about that too. challdice scent filled up the room around her. she looked at her watch. 12:15. after midnight. where was she? fifteen years had passed since she'd last turned her key in that lock. keys held. to a lock to a door to a room in all these years unchanged. the music. the light. the scent. jazz. and after hundreds of days and hundreds of nights what did she want from her now? she lay her head back against the wall. yea i do need a drink she thought standing.

she puttered in the direction of the kitchen with her hands pressed in her pockets and her eyes taking a million detours to caress the surfaces of things. to note what new picture new shelves new books new magazines. in a kitchen cabinet she found an unopened bottle of red wine. she opened it poured and drank quickly. deeply. "she has changed" she mouths to the stove trying to visualize the moment when challdice will break the silence of the closed door. pouring herself a second glass she heads for the audio system. though she doesn't expect challdice to have anyone with her the thought does cross her mind. "i'll just say i'm her cousin" she laughs looking through the tapes. she click one in and lay back on the rug. miriam makeba's voice swelled into the darkness around her. she loved music. did she love challdice? the dancing candles and the incense continued to burn.

"Kim/Clare" by Jean Weisinger

Cynthia Lollar

Tell Me Something
I Don't Know

There's not much sense in the way I feel about this, I know. I'm happy and steamed all at once. My friends in the fellowship say God doesn't give you more than you can handle. But the way I figure it, that's fear talking. That's stepping out onto the overpass without looking down at the traffic rushing by fast enough to kill you. Seems a lousy way to live, or anyway, I don't know how to do it. Nick does. He just keeps chugging along like the engine on our old Ford Ranger. I'm like the oil filter. I need a change now and again.

It's not like I don't have enough to deal with, going to work sober every day. I told my sponsor my first week dry, *"You* collate a year's worth of some candyassed lawyer's whining memos without a drink and see what happens." The agency pulled me from that job after one day; said my editorial suggestions to the senior partner hadn't been appreciated. With the liquor, I'd always managed to keep my lips on a glass instead of flapping around where they weren't welcome. I could go to work wherever the agency sent me, collate until the cows came home, and feel it all like someone punching me through pillows. It was enough to make you laugh, really. I'd tell Nick in the evening over a few brews on the front stoop and he'd skrinch up his face and imitate me so I could see how ridiculous I was making myself sound. Then we'd stumble inside and he'd try to hitch up my skirt from behind, like that's just what I wanted, and maybe it was or maybe I'd let him do it anyway, but finally it all felt the same.

Carolyn's calmer about it than I am. I think it's because she's a dog groomer.

Every day it's a different parade of middle-class mutts—the schnauzers, the chow chows, the god-awful giant poodles like hair balls on hormones. The ladies who drop them off go into the shop next door for their manicures and hairdos. Mutts in one door, matrons in the other, and it's a point of pride for Carolyn to see that *her* client comes out looking best, which to my mind isn't much of a standard to set. Carolyn is short and black, and the ladies treat her like she's the maid or something. But Carolyn knows who she is. That's one of the things I like about her. The pooch will be dancing and writhing and leaving sweaty little paw prints on the dark tile floor while its owner coos good-bye, but as soon as the leash is in Carolyn's hands something snaps to attention in the dog and it calms right down. Like inside the dog is this collapsible metal structure, all hinges and steel, and Carolyn is the power that pops it into place.

When I saw her the first time she reminded me of one of those little storybook creatures, her body all compact and sort of cozy. She wears her hair cut tight to her head so that her face looms out, lightly moon-cratered from acne. She's got these wide cheeks and eyes deep as cuts in rock, like if you climbed in there you'd find a cave big enough to stand in and worth exploring. She was sitting across the room at a new lunchtime A.A. meeting I was trying out. I'd gotten a steady temp job nearby (four weeks' worth of data entry at the National Association of People Irradiated in Childhood, if you can believe that) and the regularity was making me thirsty. I like the money of a steady placement but temping is bearable mostly because I get to move around. I shifted in my seat and tried to listen. Carolyn's voice was like old newspapers blowing down the street, low and rustling.

"And then I woke up one day and heard my baby crying in the other room because it was one o'clock in the afternoon and she hadn't been fed," she said, straight-backed in her metal folding chair. "There was vomit all over the floor where I'd passed out and there wasn't any food except some moldy lo mein and some sour milk that I put on the stove to heat to give to the baby because her crying was making me want to kill her. And you know I had that bottle all hot and in my hand, that bottle was ready to go in Keenona's mouth, just to shut her up, just to stop the noise in my head."

Carolyn shook her head. Her eyes were two slits in the rock and the room was quiet the way it gets when the bullshit's gone. "And I don't know. Something broke inside me. These meetings remind me who's in charge. And it sure ain't me."

Well, my leg started bouncing up and down and I had to sit on my hands to keep from cracking my knuckles like I do when I'm mad. I want to know who *is* in charge, not just that I'm not. Every day I turn on the tube and there's an-other murder or more children are starving or Vanna White is still turning cubes like she's got nothing else to do with her time and money. I'm not in charge. Tell me something I don't know.

So we got into it, Carolyn and me. I was late getting back to work that day, and the next, so we started meeting for coffee after five. I'd take the bus up Hal-sted toward Lincoln Park, hopping out on the corner before Belmont where Carolyn's shop was, handy to the neighborhood ladies. Usually I got there early and she'd have some Airedale still in suds, so I'd sit and wait in the room out front. Old magazines lay all over the end tables and one wall sported a big poster of a German shepherd sitting next to a tabby cat, presumably moments before the cat's death, with little booklets running up the side on how to keep away fleas and the importance of neutering. Carolyn is just an employee at Groom-rite but the owner is never around so she runs the place her way, with a kind of soft pizzazz like gold neon. I love to watch her operate. The ladies who come in at the end of the day purse their lips and pull long skeptical fingers through the dogs' hair while Carolyn hums softly. She touches the ladies' elbows and rubs the dogs' ears, and soon out the door they go, handled and content. In the silence afterwards, I began wanting her to notice me, too.

"Groomrite," I'd call into the back. I could hear the scroonching sound of soap on fur, the clack-clacking of dog nails and Carolyn's soothing tones. "It sounds like a place you can buy your perfect mate; washed, de-flead and possi-bly neutered."

"They ain't no perfect mate, honey," she'd say, her voice rumbling like a low-flying airplane. "Just the perfect date."

This is one of her favorite themes. Carolyn applies the one-day-at-a-time principle to everything, including sex. Personally I find this rather extreme. Nick and I have been together for almost seven years and while it's not Shangri-la, it's . . . well, Wisconsin, if you know what I mean. A familiar hop over the state line. Nick was the carpenter on a crew rebuilding the deli that had burned down near the insurance office I was working back then. I passed him nearly every day that summer, walking up from my one-roomer off Fullerton and liking what I saw under his hard hat—the bulldog nose, the bearish red beard, the butt right out of *Playgirl*. It took a while to get him to meet me for a few drinks. Actually, what it took was homework. I had to call my brother Steve, who was working con-struction by then, and ask him for a few conversation starters.

"What's that L-shaped ruler he's always fondling?" I asked.

"A framing square," he said. "It's for checking right angles."

"And how about that thing that makes all the curly shavings. I swear it looks like the wood's got pubic hair."

"Geez, Julie, when was the last time you got laid? That's a plane. I'd try not to mention pubic hairs when you talk about it." I was 28 years old then and Steve still acted like I was in dire need of an older brother's advice. Maybe that's why I *did* drop the pubic hair line on Nick. It wasn't subtle, but then Nick's not a subtle guy. The first time we slept together he made little scraping noises while his hips rocked. I'm blond and thin anyway, sort of two-by-fourish, and we laughed so hard it took us forever to come. At least, I thought that was why.

Carolyn keeps her mouth shut about Nick. She doesn't want to look like she's got an agenda, and maybe she doesn't. She does say that nothing prepared her for sober sex.

"Randall and I always got tanked before we screwed," she told me one night. We were sitting in an orange-and-white booth at Shakey's, chowing on some double-meat pizza while Wynonna Judd sang over the loudspeakers about how love can build a bridge. "Then I got sober. It was awful. He started screaming at me, screaming at Keenona. It was bad enough that I wouldn't drink with him anymore but when I stopped sleeping with him, well . . ." I reached over and stroked her hand. Nick never screamed at me. He just went silent, sitting up all night in front of the TV with the sound turned off and the picture jumping crazy on the screen.

"It'll come back," I said, hoping I was right.

"Oh, I ain't interested in going backwards," she said, a grin splitting her moon face. "It's all before me now. I don't sleep with no one I don't care to know better and who don't want to know me."

"Oh, how very mature of you," I said, making a face at her. "What ever happened to just good raw sex?"

Carolyn pulled another greasy triangle of pizza from the platter and plopped one limp end in her mouth. "Honey," she said, her words muffled by cheese and bread and all that meat. "Honesty is the hottest turn-on there is. You just got to admit what you want and show up for it. Nature will do the rest."

I hated the fact that she might be right. I thought it meant I was doomed to celibacy. As far as I was concerned, honesty was only good for people able to enforce their view of things. When I was seven I desperately wanted a banana-seat bicycle with extended handlebars. Spider bikes, we called them. I'd lie in bed at night imagining myself wheeling through the streets of my neighborhood in Gary, Indiana, expertly skirting the broken glass and rusty beer cans until I careened onto the playground of Ogden Elementary School with a triumphant squeal of tires, just like on *Starsky and Hutch*. But Dad said he wasn't working overtime just to buy some hippy-dippy bike; I could use my brother's old three-speed when I got big enough to throw my legs over the bar. So I started raking leaves for old Mrs. Cusack down the street and tipping over garbage cans for returnable soda bottles. By December I'd saved more than twenty dollars. Not enough to buy a bike but maybe enough to tell Dad what I'd done. I hoped he'd be proud and give me the rest of the money.

But Dad just looked at me over the mashed potatoes and corn when I told him. "I thought I told you to forget the bike," he said.

"But I want it," I said, looking down at my meat loaf and pushing it around with my fork. I could feel Mom's eyes on Dad and a painful pressure on my left foot. I looked to the left at Steve but he just sat there shoveling corn into his mouth.

"Your mother wants a new couch. Your brother wants a car." Dad's voice rose and he gripped his beer glass like it was the one thing between me and his fist. "I want a daughter who doesn't go behind my back and shame me with the neighbors. Raking leaves for that old witch." He sounded disgusted with me. "We all want things we can't have. That's life, I hate to tell you. Now give me the money."

I looked up from my plate and stared at him. "No," I said.

Dad's face got redder, Steve stepped harder on my foot and Mom started to slap extra potatoes on everyone's plates. "Jack, Steve, Julie, come on now." Slap, slap. "I didn't slave over a hot stove just to sit here and watch you let your food spoil."

"I said, give me the money," Dad said. "Somebody needs to learn who's in charge around here."

"No. It's mine. I want a bike." I shoved my chair from the table and ran toward the back door. Dad tried to grab my arm but I squirmed away. I stayed out for a couple of hours, halfheartedly knocking over garbage cans trying to keep my dream alive. But when I went home, Dad wouldn't look at me. He wouldn't talk to me either. Not then, not for the next two weeks. Mom's eyes grew dark with blame and when she combed my hair, she yanked at the snarls as if she didn't care that it hurt me. Even Steve turned against me. "Just give him the money, stupid," he said, grabbing his hockey skates for a game I wasn't invited to join. "He's bigger than you. Don't you get it?"

I finally pulled my cash jar out from under the rags in the basement and left it by Dad's elbow one night at dinner. He glanced at it and took another swallow of beer. "Eat up, girlie," he said. "It's poker night and I need the table."

I was only a kid so I tucked into my dinner as if it was just what I hungered for, and with every swallow all the things I wanted and all the things I didn't yet know to want pushed further down in my gut until I thought the dull feeling there meant I was full. Later, in high school, drinking made me feel full; my boyfriend Tommy Riggs did, too. We'd snitch a bottle from his dad's stash in the garage, duck under the school's bleachers at the fifty-yard line and see how far we could run before the Wild Turkey tackled us. Mr. Riggs was a foreman at the steel plant and had an in with the union, so Tommy's future was set, which meant mine was, too. At least until the day after graduation when I threw my clothes and a case of Dad's Bud into the trunk of my old Pinto and headed out I-90 for Chicago. Driving west past the grimy high-rises, I knew everyone would be shocked. But not me. To feel shock, I would have had to feel.

So far, we've had just one fight. Carolyn had finally invited me to her place, which wasn't in a great part of town. I understood her embarrassment but I couldn't seem to convince her I didn't give a rat's ass.

"Keep in mind I'm from Gary, Indiana," I said. "Armpit of the Midwest. Hairy. No deodorant. Lifted up next to your nose on the El during rush hour."

She laughed but fumbled a lot with her keys when we reached the apartment building and she wouldn't look at me as we climbed the four flights of stairs. Her face got sunny, though, when she opened the door and Keenona ran in from the back bedroom. A tall thin man with dreadlocks ambled in after her. His eyes darted between me and Carolyn. When I smiled he didn't smile back.

"Mommy, Batman beat up Joker, and Robin, he crashed through a window!" Keenona said. Carolyn bent down to hug her, stifling the rest of the story line as Keenona mumbled gleefully into her mother's chest.

"Baby, you go in there and change the channel to 32," Carolyn said. "Remember 32? That's a three and a two next to each other. Big Bird's on now."

Keenona ran back into the bedroom and in a moment I heard the sharp clicks of the TV dial.

"The streets aren't full of Big Birds. People fight," the man said, as if picking up an old argument. Carolyn turned her back to him as she hung up her coat. I licked my lips and wiggled my jaw to loosen it.

"Randall?" I said. "I'm Julie, Carolyn's friend." I was twinkling like the star of some bizarre new movie, *Miss Manners Goes to the South Side*.

"Carolyn's *friend*, huh," said Randall. He still wouldn't look at me. His eyes bore into Carolyn's back as it disappeared into the kitchen.

"Julie, you want some coffee or something?" she called.

"Uh, yeah," I said, moving toward the kitchen but Randall was a step ahead of me and I stopped to let him pass. He pulled the swinging door shut behind him. So I wandered into the back room to watch television with Keenona.

Keenona and I had just finished counting to ten with the help of the little fat hen when I heard the kitchen door pop open and someone slam their way out of the apartment. In a moment Carolyn came into the bedroom.

"Daddy had to leave but he said to give you a really big kiss," she said to Keenona. She planted a kiss on top of Keenona's head, which hadn't swerved from the screen where there was a real crisis underway. Cookie Monster had lost a cookie and couldn't find it anywhere. I got up and pulled Carolyn into the living room.

"Are you okay?" I asked, holding her hands.

"Oh, yeah," she said, even smiling a little. "Randall's okay, he just had a bad day."

"I don't care about Randall. Randall can take a flying leap."

"He's a good daddy," she said, taking back her hands.

"That makes everything all right?"

"That makes a lot all right," said Carolyn. "I'm trying to raise a child here, in case you hadn't noticed."

Well, you could have fried steak on my face, I got that hot. Here was a side of Carolyn I hadn't known existed. All of a sudden she looked like a roll-over-and-die Carolyn, not the powerful woman I'd seen handling all those dogs and people, giving me a reason to stay sober. I know, I know. No one can make you stop drinking. But sometimes a thing comes into your life that shakes you up so much, you know you've been handed a new road map and you're a fool not to follow it, never mind where it leads.

"Fine," I said. I could hear Cookie Monster in the back room throwing a temper tantrum over his lost choco-chunko-chip. "Look, maybe this wasn't such a hot idea. Maybe it would be better if we just stick to the meetings and don't know too much about each other. It's your life. I wouldn't want to interfere."

"Oh yes you would," said Carolyn, narrowing her eyes. They looked like headlights on a speeding sports car. "You just don't want to take the chance that you might not get what you want."

"What the hell are you talking about?" I said, hissing to keep my voice from reaching the back room where Cookie Monster now howled in utter sorrow.

"Forget it," said Carolyn. Abruptly she turned away. "I think the coffee's ready. Do you still want some?"

Usually I take to arguments like killer bees to cows but I didn't enjoy fighting with Carolyn and anyway, the fight itself kind of bothered me. I could tell it wasn't really about Randall or even Carolyn's reliance on him, but what it was about eluded me. I followed Carolyn into the kitchen where I let the argument slip away unresolved and misunderstood.

Things finally dawned on me one night with Nick. We'd been getting along better lately. I'd gotten a temporary placement at a book distributor that had me moving around to a different department every few days, Nick was putting in regular hours at a site not too far from where we lived, and the checks weren't bouncing. We were sitting on the couch watching a video, *E.T.,* and had just gotten to the part where the little creature reaches out one incredibly long glowing red finger to touch the boy and say good-bye before heading back into space where it belongs. I'd seen this scene a million times but I always cried. Just as I was really starting to blubber I felt this soft pressure on my shoulder.

"E.T. go home," said Nick in a scrunched-up little voice. He pressed his index finger into my shoulder, gently. "E.T. need fuck. Earth girls ugly."

I punched him lightly in the stomach. "E.T.'s ugly. And he's got nothing to fuck with."

Nick kept poking me with his finger. "Oh, yeah? And what do you think this is?" Nick reached down with his hand.

I had to admit it felt good. I kissed Nick with the first real tenderness I'd felt in a long time. We stretched out on the couch and whenever I started to get tense, I tried a few A.A. mantras: Let go and let God. Easy does it. The slogans were moronic but hey, they were working. I relaxed and felt a golden warmth spread from my belly up to my face and down to my toes. And then I realized that in my mind the hands that caressed my breasts were brown and chapped from too much soap: Carolyn's hands. Carolyn's lips traced the curve of my thighs and lightly touched the hairs that curled like wood shavings fallen to the floor of some new home. Between my legs Carolyn's round pockmarked face rose darkly like a new moon and hung there, grinning, her eyes open wide now and full of sight.

I gasped, and Nick's motions intensified. There was no stopping now. I was gone.

I stormed into Carolyn's shop the next morning. It was still early, and twittering ladies with trembling dogs filled the waiting room. Carolyn was behind the counter, signing in the dogs and leading them one by one into the back where I knew they would sit still as monks, transformed by Carolyn's touch.

"We have to talk," I hissed over the ladies' lacquered hair. Four heads turned and eight eyebrows lifted in a harmony of shock at my line-crashing. Carolyn looked at me, her face a question. "Be right there," she said.

I sat in one of the vinyl chairs, crossed my arms and wrapped one leg tightly around the other. For some reason I thought of a day back in Gary when I'd been on my way to Mrs. Cusack's, dragging the rake behind me. The metal teeth bounced along the cracked sidewalk making an awful racket and it amused me to wonder if the neighbors were annoyed. Then I passed into the shade of an old maple tree. Suddenly there was a frightful surge in the branches above me as scores of starlings poured out of the tree and into the sky in a weighty lifting rush of wing. Something of what I felt then filled me now, an electric shattering in my heart and gut and behind my eyes.

Finally Carolyn let the last lady out of the shop and eyed me as she moved toward the back room.

"I can talk but I got to keep working," said Carolyn. "A dozen to do today. Lord, some of these creatures get more baths than I do."

I stood up to follow her but my right foot had fallen asleep and I nearly fell. I hobbled into the back.

"You're limping," Carolyn said.

"Nothing gets by you, does it."

Carolyn raised an eyebrow and moved to a table where a lanky dalmatian sat panting lightly in a tub of soapy water, looking like so many reverse-colored dominoes, stacked and ready to be played. She dipped her hands in the suds and started lathering up the dog's flanks with firm, circular strokes. After a minute or two she said without looking up, "Have you had a slip?"

"God, no." I shook my tingling foot, willing it awake. "Not everything has to do with alcohol, you know." I gave a hearty laugh. "Although if there's anything tasty in one of those bottles there, now may be a good time to tell me." I laughed again, to show her I was joking.

"Come here," she said, taking her hands out of the suds and pushing the dog's tub aside. She patted the exposed tabletop. "Sit."

It didn't occur to me to resist. I limped over and hoisted my butt on the table. Carolyn took my foot in her wet hands, removed my shoe and started slapping me around the ankle and sole. Pain suffused my foot like a thousand slivers of piercing glass.

"Ow! Stop it!"

"This just moves the hurt along a little faster." She slapped harder. "You want it to stay numb?"

I grabbed Carolyn's wrists and held on. "No, but . . . Carolyn." I closed my eyes. Starlings flew through my mind and I heard Daddy say, "Now give me the money."

I pulled Carolyn's wrists up to my cheeks and held them there. Her skin felt impossibly warm and I imagined the redness of her blood moving down from her heart, each pulse carrying its essential load of oxygen and heat and whatever kind of yearning makes one heartbeat leap toward the next. There wasn't any end to the moment. Somewhere in that moment Carolyn's hands opened alongside my face until they cupped me with a sureness I had not thought to hope for. Or maybe I had. Because when she kissed me, I kissed her back. The want was there, full of itself and surprising. But rather than fill me up, the want emptied me out. I emptied into her kiss like cold water from a pail too long carried. I felt clear and clean. I felt like flight.

Nick doesn't know yet and I don't know when I'm going to tell him. What would I say, exactly? Carolyn just says, "We cross those bridges when we come to them." Seems to me like God could have set things up a little better. We should learn things all at once and get it over with. If asked, I might tell you just to cross the damn bridge and not look down. But I looked. And God knows, I'm alive.

Maureen Seaton

Suite for Violence

(Chicago)

I'm in the middle sometimes jumping around like a madwoman. I'm on the edge sometimes taking pulses. I am also sometimes the tip of another light. I went down to the Daley Center to get an Order of Protection. We stayed there, a friend and I, for eight hours, while forty people heard my story. Now all I can do is crack my fingers. God inside me like the fingers of sex. What happened, this lifting, what have I been saying to strangers?

(Counseling the Witness)

Whatever you do don't talk. It's hard enough you can't get going with the parameters of love beating on your head like a man's voice, but nothing can stop this fabrication. If I were about to murder my lover I would be nuts too. Will she kill me? Does it help to remember which she might be—murderer, murderess? I'm watching her come toward me like a murderer. She is not holding the box cutter, her words are holding the box cutter—this is how she sounds—sharp as gin. You can follow her into oblivion. Still, I will not call 911 because they use the pronoun *he* and there is no he only a woman with long soft breasts and me.

(Erie—the Flight)

Oh my God you might say and you'd be right for all around is the mask of the divine folding us wanting us. You might say something else matters and you'd be right again. Try imagining how big the body becomes when the angel passes over the blood fields, try incorporating love into your vocabulary like skulls on a back fence. Nothing as powerless as God, oh God. I fear someone who says my name again and again until the coat vanishes from the seed, until the seed bursts its tiny shelter and crawls forth. I am holy tonight listening to my own pee hit the water like hell breaking loose.

(Garrison-on-Hudson)

I keep taking photos of the same spot. The West is over there, the prairie with its needle grasses, the cottonwoods aching with sex in June. There are rattlers in these hills. The river laps around me like stereo, like footsteps. The lights go up in Rockland. I fear no sound. There is no tide and the river laps the stones. There is absolutely nothing left of us in the wind in the water. I can count on the river, the rattlers, the fading light, the tide diminished and golden and this rushed ending, this coming before I am found in all this calm by the river, the valley inside me. I am soon to grow as large as Hudson, this old life rushing toward Atlantic from a tear in the clouds.

(What She Did)

I took it like high tide, I was cave and you poured into me. The sea in your fingers inside me. The sea in your mouth that opened and drank me like the juices of apricots and figs. It's my worth, this receptivity—how I've been praised as you poured your electricity, the lava, the hot wax, as I caught your hot phlegm, the collection of all your angry tales oh Jesus. I am porcelain, and you corner me, lavish me with your lost and fevered secretions.

(West 23rd Street)

I went to the Daley Center for an Order of Protection. I heard the buzzer during *Roseanne*'s premier show and there you were sweaty and dark your life was in your face and you were gone the good gone I thought: I might die. I went to the Daley Center and the pro bono lawyer said tell me your story and my pieces flew back inside me from all around the city. They flew back in and hunkered down to see what I would say. I pointed to the bruises like old cancers, I pointed to my heart, you could hear it whirring inside my chest for recognition, I pointed to the spaces between my nerve endings where something soothed and cajoled. All my pieces waited on my shoulders to hear the benediction. I stuttered their names, I blessed them with truth.

Elsa E'der

Passion

it is a funny thing our love
I haven't touched you in months / watching moving lips
I have learned much about the continual raping of children

your words are woman, but
your eyes are six years old

for once in my life, my heart is on fire and my body is not

Untitled photograph by Luz María Gordillo

Bessy Reyna

And This Blue
Surrounding Me Again

At times, the simplest of things become even simpler. Like calling someone who lives far away, just to say "I miss you." Simple gestures, like opening a door and entering a room we have been in so many times before. Like the night I went back to her house and entered that blue room for the first time in five years. It was hot and the clothes I was wearing, long-sleeve shirt and heavy pants, made it so much worse. She opened the door, wearing a tank-top and baggy shorts. I walked in pretending not to be uncomfortable, and we sat making small talk, looking at each other and trying to guess if we really had become immune to one another. Without a word, she got up and walked away. I sat, listening to the jazz record she had been playing when I walked in. "Here, why don't you change into these clothes, you will be more comfortable," she said, handing me a pair of old shorts and a T-shirt. A simple gesture. The simple gestures of this person I once loved who was now handing me clothes, her hand touching mine when I reached for the clothes, as if nothing had happened. As if time had not been. As if the years in between never existed.

I wanted to believe it was the simple gesture of her love surfacing when she smiled. Me, wanted again, years later in this room where I now sat surveying my surroundings making an inventory of things replaced, remembering lying here on the same worn-out blue carpet, blue light, blue furniture. I never really paid attention then to how blue this room was. Even the paintings hanging on the walls are done in blues. The wallpaper used to be light blue, but now, covered with water stains, it's mostly peeling pieces of blue. The moonlight coming in from two sides makes the room look even bluer.

I want to stop all the memories flashing in front of me, aware of how this room is affecting me, merging with my mood, infecting me. Can I fight this? She probably wants me here tonight because there is no one else around. What has she done in the last five years? I found clues in her bedroom when I went to change my clothes: new faces smiling from elaborate picture frames. I found my-self smiling back at me from one of them, each frame carefully placed like those in a gallery. Did she love them?

I had thought the night I left her bedroom, five years ago, that it would be the last time I would be in that room. Did she plan for the hate? For the dryness of her sex? Lifting her body abruptly in the middle of making love, she looked amused, "You think for a moment that I enjoy sex with you? You must be kid-ding!" Her face was so full of contempt. "I am fed up with you. I have someone else now," she shouted at me. "You are just like nothing to me now," she kept saying while I was still panting from make-believe love-making that a short time back had seemed like caring. After that, every movement hurt me. Getting dressed and leaving seemed to take place in slow motion.

Earlier that day, we had gone to visit some friends for dinner, only I didn't know I was supposed to be the chef. They had bought lobsters. "We hear you are a great cook," they told me, daring me. "Sure! just give me a cookbook and I can do anything!" I never believed they would take me seriously. I had never cooked a lobster before, and this one was alive. I chose the fanciest French recipe I could find, one with cognac, hoping they wouldn't have the ingredients I needed, but they did. We were all impressed when I lit the sauce at the table. The meal was a great success, but I just couldn't eat it, not after cleaning it and let-ting all the gunk spill out into my hands. I didn't even taste it.

After dinner we sat talking to each other, the way people do when they get together, not wanting to sound too controversial or too boring. She got up from the living room, went to make a phone call and stayed away for the longest time. Who was she whispering to on the phone? I sat pretending to enjoy my after-dinner drink. "Sorry it took so long," she said casually, trying to smile, sitting next to me, touching me. I resisted her touch wondering who it was at the other end of the phone. Was I so jealous because I recognized the signs?

It was not the first time we broke up. This time it took longer for me to re-turn, that's all. We like pretending it was entirely the other's fault. Can I hate and keep on wanting? (She was right, these clothes are more comfortable.) The sim-plest gestures making the hurt come back.

It is so still outside. I turned off the light and sat in the darkest corner. She will probably notice my absence after a while and will try to talk me into returning to her bed. I can't, not tonight. Tonight I want to be part of this blue room which my mind converts into a stage set where, at the end of the play, one character moves away to another city.

I didn't hear her walk into the blue room. Next thing I know her hands were caressing me and our fingers were searching and I couldn't stop this need from developing inside of me once again as if nothing else mattered, as if I had stopped caring about anything but feeling her touch. On-again, off-again love, like changing radio stations when you don't like the music. Only it was me this time, me being changed. Does it really matter, here in this blue room? Fingers not daring to rush, to be too obvious, to get too carried away, centering on each touch, because nothing else matters but the blue warmth surrounding us and the room encouraging us to touch and to forget having left it, to forget I now have someone else who loves me, and who I am loving most of the time, except for this one moment when all this blueness surrounds me and I must find out why she left me, and why she hurt me so much and she is not going to tell me, just like before, and it does not matter because in this blue room nothing matters but her touch and the warmth around us.

She had carefully orchestrated my return, planning how to get me back. She searched for me, found me and brought me back. A message left on an answering machine, reaching out, "I had to talk to you, no one else would understand, you are the only one who understands, I have to see you." The past skillfully avoided, coming back to entice me.

She glides expertly next to me, as if she owns the space I occupy, her body surrounds me, overcomes me and I follow her rhythms losing myself for an instant and then I struggle to recapture my body as if it had been invaded. But it wasn't really; I let it happen. She was giving me something I wanted but didn't want to have, because I was used to knowing how it felt when I didn't have it and now I wish I didn't know how it feels having it again. But now I do.

I had to find out. No, didn't have to, simply wanted to.

Untitled photograph by Saskia Scheffer

Alvia Golden

Acts of Love

Sweat can be magical. When I'm suntanned that deep reddish brown I get, thanks to my Hungarian father, so my arms look strong and passionate wrapped around Becka's fair Irish body, and I'm telling her the kind of story she likes, it could be one with nuns and little girls with lace panties, or one with a big woman in a stiff uniform, any of the ones that make her start to move her ass rhythmically and lock her legs around me and improve the plot unexpectedly—then when we work up a sweat it feels so good it's supernatural. Like now, in this sweet little guest room in Kitty and Keeba's house, on a drought-yellow Cape Cod afternoon with a hint of breeze blowing across us from one window to the other, when Becka cries "Yes!" and "God, yes!" quietly, hoarsely into my ear and thrusts herself against me and sings "I love you" under her breath and moves over and under my body as easily as if we were dancers and I look down—we glisten, we're gorgeous.

From the familiar sounds, Kitty and Kee are similarly engaged in the bedroom across the hall, though when we drifted off after lunch we all swore we were "dead tired." Under cover of kissing Becka's neck, I sneak a peek at the clock on the bed table. Three-thirty. We can forget our nap, it's time for Kitty's childhood friends from Oklahoma to get here. A scant kiss 'n' caress later they're knocking on the metal frame of the screen door and singing, "Hello-oh." A melancholy "Shoot" issues from the mistress bedroom. It's Kitty. She hops past our room, banging into the wall pulling on her shoes, calls, "Coming!"

The screen door whangs, lets in squeals of delight, bags bump, car trunk thunks, Becka sighs. We kiss in passing, dressing.

By the time Becka and I put in an appearance, Kee has made hers and is back in her study—a stolid Buddha meditating amid a telecommunity of wires, lights, bells and whistles. We stand for a moment in the hall where we can see through twin arches—left into Kee's drape-darkened sanctum, right into the bright glare of the glass parlor where Kitty's fussing over her friends. They look young. Younger even than Kitty who looks twelve and a half. Maybe they've led more sheltered lives.

No question, the scandal a couple of years ago matured Kitty ahead of schedule. There was talk of indicting Kee on professor-fucking-student charges, but they were never filed. For one thing, Kitty was studying Classics and Kee was teaching in the B School, which the administration agreed "negated the power issue." For another, most of the tenured women ignored their qualms about Kee's lesbianism and fought for her. In the heat of battle, Kitty got a close-up of the academy eating its own. That'll bag anyone's eyes.

At the moment, her eyes are childishly happy. Kitty always carries on like a teenager with her hometown friends. They have different names every summer, otherwise, they're virtually interchangeable. Blonde, blue-eyed, professional, lesbian. Kitty-clones. Makes you wonder what they put in the water in Oklahoma. Whatever it is, as the song says, it's "OK!"

"Hi! I'm Jill," half of this year's couple rises respectfully to greet us, "and this is Nancy." She points to her chest, "Banker," then to her partner, "Accountant."

They are very chic. I see shorts but I hear silk. Jill is fair, in the clone tradition. Not so Nancy whose curly brown hair and bittersweet-chocolate eyes signify a later migration of less Anglo-Saxon forebears.

"We're Maggie and Becka," I point, too.

Nancy asks, "Do you work with Kee?"

"No," I admit, "I'm a writer."

"Might I have read something of yours?" Her brown eyes light.

"Not yet."

The light dims, but doesn't go out. "Do you mind if I ask what you're working on?"

"Not at all. At the moment, I'm revising a story."

The light needs more volts than that.

Jill turns to Becka, "Are you a writer, too?"

"I'm a brain surgeon." Becka hates to disappoint.

Kitty tells them, "That's Becka's joke on being a college professor," and us, "Nancy just got her first job with one of the Big Eight."

"Terrific!" Becka and I enthuse. I feel more than a little proprietary about the fact that they are well-employed. Women's Liberation, as we used to call it, strikes again.

"Thanks," Nancy smiles tightly. "We may have to make some pretty big decisions in the near future." She sounds worried.

Becka, who can sniff trouble in a vacuum, excuses herself and heads for Kee's study. I watch her merge into the companionable half-light, half-silence. I feel abandoned. I tell myself this is not an adult response. It doesn't help. Neither does Kitty's well-meant effort to redeem my reputation.

"What's happening with the novel?" she asks.

"It's making the rounds."

Silence. I hear Jill mentally filing her nails. Nancy, bless her, grabs the conversational reins and rides to my rescue.

"Kitty," she cries, "I almost forgot. You haven't heard the news." And they're off!

I'm peripheral, but stuck. I try to look abstracted, thoughtful, as I edge, I hope imperceptibly, backwards out of their force field. I wonder for the millionth time who started the myth that you don't need air-conditioning on the Cape. The afternoon sun has stifled the breeze. I'm overheating. So is Nancy.

"I know that you're never home before midnight and you're gone again by six."

Jill lets the tape run, "There'll be plenty of time to sleep when I'm fifty."

"And plenty of room in the bed."

"Will I care when I'm fifty?"

"Do you care now?"

Kitty glances my way to see if I have anything to propose in the way of damage control. Fact is, I'm torn between sympathy and outrage. On the one hand, it appears that money can't buy happiness, even for ambitious and worthy young dykes. On the other, do these young women really think that fifty is the elephant's graveyard? Are these children of our political loins suggesting we're over the hill? After we've spent our lives fighting for their place in the Big Eight?

Kitty takes matters into her own hands. "Time to get ready for dinner," she announces loudly.

The summer girls pop to attention like jolly jump-ups. Through the arches, I see Becka stand and lazily stretch. Kee's beacons go out one by one until only a few sentinel signals remain on guard. We retire to our once and future love nest to change for dinner. Becka slides into green silk. It makes her red hair blaze, and me want to stay home. I choose blue, glance in the mirror to see the color echo in my eyes. Yesss! I am dazzling, too. We are a photo op. I love us. I outline a plot in which we are daredevil pilots downed on an Amazon island. Becka says to hold the thought. Let it mature, like fine wine. Fifty my foot! We kiss good-bye and go outside to wait in the little garden of sedum and beach roses. Under the pines at the end of the drive, Jill and Nancy stand with their backs to us at the trunk of their, as they've told us, "British Green" Mercedes. They are plundering a YSL suitcase to layer fashionable bits of cloth over their basic beach outfits. They're efficient and silent.

"Remember us at that age?" Becka asks tenderly.

"Yeah," I sulk. "We couldn't afford the Cape or a designer suitcase, and there were no elderly dykes smiling benignly upon us."

"Poor baby," Becka soothes. "Want me to kiss it to make it better?"

After dinner, we stroll over to P'town's only all-women bar. We pay $5, get our hands stamped, and stand for a minute watching the strutting, stomping dancers flaunt their tanned young bodies. I'm thinking how few stomping grounds there were when I had a flaunt-worthy body, never mind that I was too scared to go to any of them. Scared I'd find out what I wanted to know.

I follow Becka and Kee heads toward the back deck that hangs, in high tide, scant inches above Boston Bay. Nancy peels off to shoot pool with three strangers. Jill is already on the dance floor, swiveling in the vicinity of Kitty.

The air on the deck is cool but thick. Keeba's black cropped hair glitters with crystal dew-beads. We order drinks from a passing waitress who's not bad-looking if you like stone diesels. For a while, we sit companionably, striking a few words here and there, not lighting anything that flares. I drift, mentally script a scenario for a cute couple who're dancing in my sight line—short-shorts, tight tees with sassy slogans, complementary orange and purple hairdos. Kee has raised her voice so Becka can hear over the crescending music.

"Always said I was trying to 'find' myself"—her grin is a marvel of self-deprecation—"maybe after all I was trying to 'lose' me."

"This was before Kitty?" Becka asks.

"For sure." Kee laughs. "Before me, too, in a manner of speaking."

"Meaning?"

"One thing's certain, the woman I was then? She wasn't this me. Being her was like having antennae out to here." Kee stretches her strong dark arms as wide apart as possible. "She'd walk into a room, within seconds she could feel it all— the pain, the desire, the easy places, the rough spots. Trouble was, fool thought she had to do something about it. Woman wanted to be held? She held her. Talked with? Talked with her. Fucked? Fucked her. Felt she had to. Like a calling." Kee drops her head and gives a short, harsh laugh, "Got so she was very popular. Very!"

"But there must have been something in it for you. Her."

"Oh sure. Feels good solving people's problems." Kee shrugs, twitches her mouth into a smile shape. "But it does get old fast."

"Then why didn't you stop?"

"I've thought about that," Kee sighs. "Close as I can get is arrogance. Truly believed I couldn't have any problems if I was solving other people's. Even when I found myself saying 'I love you' to half the Lesbian Nation, I told myself it was OK, I was doing it for 'their sake.' Doing good works."

"I was a dyke for Jesus?" Becka half-grins.

"More like a dyke **as** Jesus. High on gratitude, low on gratification. It took a while to figure out that I might be making the moves, but **they** were making the rules."

"Been there, done that," I tell her. "I thought no woman could have a problem my 'loving' wouldn't solve."

"So why did you get out of the business?" Kee asks lightly.

"Got tired of the supply-side."

Kee and I laugh, Becka doesn't. "I wonder how many like you two I've been with."

Becka's between us, Kee and I shift quickly to face her, reach out to touch her, reassure her. We look at each other across her. Kee looks ashamed but maybe I'm mistaking my face for hers. We're both about to speak when the others wander back.

"Won!" Nancy announces. Triumph becomes her.

Kitty and Jill flop down out of breath, damp. Jill barely settles before she asks me, "Maggie, what do you think about Lesbian Bed-Death Syndrome?"

" 'Lesbian Death-Bed Syndrome'?" I repeat stupidly.

"I'm not joking."

"Me neither," I protest. "Becka, you ever hear of Lesbian Death-Bed Syndrome?"

"Not 'death-bed,' Bed-Death," Jill corrects me. "It's this new thing they've discovered, about how lesbians lose interest in fucking after a while."

"Lose interest in fucking?" I ask. **"Lesbians?"**

Jill is patiently impatient, "Lesbians in **relationships.** After a while, lesbians in relationships lose interest in fucking each other."

Becka is amused, "You've got us mixed up with heterosexuals."

I'm offended, "Who's calling it a 'Syndrome'? That's like saying, 'If you can't make it in bed, don't worry. It's not your fault, it's a symptom. Maybe you aren't even the one with the disease.' "

Nancy nods emphatically. I've hit a nerve, maybe the root.

"You know"—I'm on a roll—"this could catch on. I mean, why not wife-batterer syndrome? Or child-molester syndrome?"

"Down, girl," Kee puts a hand on my shoulder.

"Mm-hmm," Becka agrees, looking at me provocatively. "What's got you all exercised?"

"Oh, come on!" I give the two of them a disgusted sigh. Surely they can see what we're really talking about here.

Kee relents. "Well, now," she says gently, "Maggie's got a point, you know."

Under the table, Becka takes my hand and does sexy things on my palm with her fingers. She's sending me a message. We've been together so long, I even understand it. It's about the afterlife.

When we met ten years ago, I had a bad case of bed-hopping burnout. Falling in love wasn't even a concept. The thought of intimacy gave me hives. Becka was beautiful then as now. Smart, interesting. When she started to look seductive, I told her the truth. The sexual excitement in a relationship lasts maybe six months. A good friendship can pleasure you forever. She said I was crazy, that sex between friends is the best, and it only gets better with time. Now, she's reminding me. Telling me not to be so quick to judge.

Fair enough, Becka. Better to remember how hard it was to ask for what I wanted. Not that I didn't ask. I'm not a boor. By the time I got to it, though, the asking was supposed to be a mere formality. If it wasn't, clearly I was not performing. Up to my audience's expectation. My advance billing. Rarely happened. I was pretty good at getting what I asked for. Never asked for what I wanted. Suppose I didn't get it?

Becka wouldn't let up. She'd press, demand. I'd lie or pretend. Lie hoping. Pretend wishing with all my heart for her to be the ranging, low-down devil of my dreams. The sly vixen in my coop who'd overpower my fears, teach me how to ask when all I'd ever known to say was, "I don't want it," or, "I don't need it." And she was. And she did. Transformed my make-believe to feeling, lies to desire.

When I started to feel exposed. Known. Decided to bolt. Start over. She helped us write a whole new script, a goddamned series for **her** to star in—resisting/succumbing in every role from the slut who can't get enough, to the virgin who's never had any. And then didn't she write one for me? One summer, based on scenes from Sade? Just thinking of them now, my body starts begging. Not that she ever hurt me. The warnings, the loving lip-licking tongue-darting salacity of the punishments she threatened. . . . Oh, how I wanted them! How she withheld them while I squirmed and begged.

. . .

Kee's talking earnestly to Nancy and Jill. "Start with the fact of the act. It's not about fucking. Men fuck. Men fuck sad. Men fuck mean, sweet, angry, gentle, vicious . . . every way but stoned and drunk when they usually can't. But when they can, men fuck."

"And women don't?" Jill's skeptical.

Kee's smile is genuinely nice. "Sure we do. Only with us, it's a lot about being women. Two women and each of you being willing to take the risk of telling."

Becka's fingers stop. "Telling?" she repeats.

Kee turns to Becka, "Your name," then back again. "Women want to know your name, want you to know mine. And once you've said your name, women want to hear your life. Do you respect yourself? What meanness was done to her? How much of your hurting has healed? How far has she come on the path she's laid out for herself? Can she heed? Can you hear? Women want to talk and hear you talk until there isn't any need to ask, because the asking's in the telling and the giving is in the listening and the woman knows you and you know her in every way—including the biblical."

There's laughter but it has its genesis in longing. Which reminds me again to feel sorry for the young of the species. For they shall inherit before they have a clue. To whit, Jill.

"I don't know," she admits, "but it sounds like you could be substituting Lesbian Bed-Death with Lesbian Talking-it-to-Death."

Nancy sighs loudly. Becka says, "Maybe, we're 'substituting' Lesbian Bed-Resuscitation." Nancy looks vindicated.

"Or," Kee adds, "if that pussy's dead enough, we may be into Lesbian Bed-Resurrection!"

This time the laughter is a release. Kitty pulls Keeba towards the dance floor. Jill follows with Nancy whose expression says dancing won't do it. Left alone, I look at Becka, who is looking at me. She is so dazzlingly clear-eyed. After a moment, I drop my gaze, lower my head. Becka takes my hand again. She puts her face against mine with her mouth at my ear.

"Don't worry," she says, "you never have to go back there again. I know you, Maggie. I know your name."

I'm laughing when I tell her, "And as for you, lady, I know your game." Then, when, just for fun, I take her hand and press it against my breast, then is when the tears fall down inside me like a rain that could make a river.

Still from *Sex Fish* by E.T. Baby Maniac

Shu Lea Cheang/ Cheryl Dunye

Vanilla Sex

from Those Fluttering Objects of Desire
a coin-operated joint installation by Shu Lea Cheang
with a segment of videostrips and text by Cheryl Dunye

So when I was in L.A., I was at this conference, and I was on this panel with these, like, white lesbians, you know, alot of them, who were talking about sexuality and their sexual practices—basically, they were, like, talking about s/m—and basically they were talking about their use of s/m and blah-blah-blah-bluh. And I found out that vanilla sex in s/m language is sex without toys . . . did you ever hear that, I never heard that . . . meaning like that regular sex without toys like what most people do or maybe some do is vanilla sex. *[Pause]* And that really kind of amazed me, because, I don't know, I was just kind of shocked at how they put it in such terms—plain vanilla—and no jimmies, no syrup. Anyway I was driving around L.A. in the car, and it dawned on me that I heard the term *vanilla sex* before—a Black woman was addressing me and my sexual practices as having vanilla sex—because I was dating alot of white women, and I felt offended then—you know—I could personalize it. I just felt like "gosh what a READ." Isn't that really interesting? Like the two different expressions in the same kinda communities; vanilla sex means two different things. It meant one thing to the Black women and something totally different to these white women . . . I don't know where to place the whole thing, you know, vanilla sex and vanilla sex—which one is really vanilla sex—I don't know . . . It just dawned on me, because it was about that time in my life when I was being called other by others. It's pretty strange.

39

"Dyke March 1994" by Morgan Gwenwald

Mi Ok Song Bruining

What It Is

Okay, I think I have it clear—
this is **not** a relationship
we're in—um, I mean
you know, we're "seeing each other"
sorta like, um, gee,
you see me and I see you
and uh, kinda like "hi and bye,"
so, well, gee, yeah, okay,
that's cool, I mean,
no expectations, no demands,
no hopes, no fears, no hassles,
no strings, no worries—
got it, yeah, I feel freer
already—okay, so, well,
I'll see ya, know what I mean?
Yeah, okay, um, see ya
whenever, wherever . . .
whatever, so, no big deal,
no problem.
Yeah, I'm glad we had this

talk to clarify that you don't
wanna go too fast and give
too much, and hey,
that's fine, that's okay,
that's cool, yeah, well, um,
good then, and we can see,
maybe, in a month or so, whether
you wanna give more and I can
see whether I wanna give more,
but hey, no pressures, right?
Yeah, okay—I'll find
my support elsewhere and you do
what you need to do
and maybe we'll be
there for each other, but hey,
I'm not asking for promises,
or hell, a **commitment,**
I mean, know what I mean?
Shit, like we're two women,
"seeing each other,"
just takin' it slow, 'cuz
you don't know what you want,
you're not ready or somthin',
and me? I'm just too serious,
too intense, but I gotta lighten up,
yeah—be so light, I might just blow
away, but hey, that's okay,
it's cool, you know? Yeah. No loss. Ha.

Cheryl Clarke

Candy calls Star to her

from Epic of Song

'Black gal!
Black gal!
Where you gone?
Git back here.
(I don't wanna face the dawn alone.)'

'Star. Star. Star.
Whatever you want.
Take my money,
my jewels, my furs.
Take it all.
Just stay with me
this one night.
That ole yella witch got me scared.
I always sees my funeral in her eyes.'

Star's resentment melted
and Candy showed her gold.

'Take that dress off
fore you come in this bed.

No sense to get it wrinkled.
Cost too much money.'

Star bristled under the order.
And under Star's emerald stare
Candy lost her bald belligerence
again
and lay back,
her head against her purple pillow.
She let her breath out soft
watching Star unbutton the dress
against her own black nakedness.

'Gal, you gon ruin yo clothes
with sweat don't you wear nothing
under em.'

'I don't sweat,'

declared Star, climbing into Candy's bed
looking square at her.
They lay together silent—
Star staring through the ceiling
to the moon,
Candy staring at Star.

'Come on, Star. Take me
in your arms.
I ain't so tough
I can lay here and
not be touched.'

Star felt a gladness shake her
to her belly and rolled toward
Candy.
Star took her in her long arms,

heard Candy's breath of desire,
saw it part her buxom lips,
the glint of gold between them.
Star, having never kissed no one
but Mama, had no choice but to press
her longing lips against Candy's.
Her tongue found Candy's.
Candy helped Star's hand find
her pot of gold and her finger
imitated the motion of her tongue.
Candy reassured her.

   'That's right, baby.'

Baby, thought Star, *now I likes the way
that sound.*
Star rubbed, pressed, and squeezed.
Candy was an overripe peach.

   'Been so long since I had a woman
   in my bed, baby.'

Candy held Star hard against her
at the waist
and their bodies moved fast against
one another's.

Star heard Candy's heart beat like
Bussy's drum.
Then her legs jerked,
her back rose from the mattress.
Star felt fear, the same fear
she felt when she saw a cow give birth.
Candy screamed,

   'Glory!'

And Mourning Star Blue, no longer afraid,
burst into laughter for the first time
since she sang in the fields.

Candy said:

> 'Go on, Star, laugh loud as you wanna.
> I'm gonna make you do it again.
> Then I'm gonna git you on the floor,
> baby. Better be ready for me.
> I'll hear yo secret high note tonight
> or you won't never sing it.'

Star repeated the lesson
then rolled off the edge of the bed
while Candy gasped.
Only the soles of her feet
and shoulders touching the floor,
Star's thighs flexed and made a
startling V.
Candy came to her,
slid on top,
her thigh planted between
Star's V.

> 'Wait, baby, hold on.
> Not yet. Let me show you.
> And then you can do it to me
> next.'

Star exhaled in short spurts
to the tickly darts of pain
in her groin.
Candy slid further down and placed
her mouth against the low part of the V,
her tongue broad-stroking Star

like she was a canvas.

'Wait, baby, wait.
One more thing.'

Candy's thumb inside her,
Star understood her rhythm.
Hard and gentle.
In. Out.

'Baby, not yet. Turn over.'

Star was puzzled but obedient.
Candy parted her own wet pussy and
pressed it against Star's tight buttocks,
and rode her.
She wound her hand around and under
Star's vibrating groin
and found her spot again.
Star was very wet now.

'Okay, baby. I wanna hear
that high note,
now!'

And Star saw the saints,
heard the angels,
and took her place among them.
She knew she was dying
and heaven was the only place
she could go.
The note shattered every glass
in Candy's railcar.

'Jesus,'

whispered Star.

> 'Candy, baby.
> Jesus don't have nothing
> to do with this here,'

said Candy.
And then bit her hard in the ass.

> 'Yes, baby.
> No cross, no crown.'

Star whirled around
rubbing her butt
and pushed Candy back
on the floor
under her and dove for her stuff
face first.
For an hour Candy let Star lick,
suck, and chew.
And as Candy drew in her breath
and made ready for her glory shout,
Star pushed away from the table.
Candy jerked up in protest, gold gleaming.
Star laughed.

> 'Yeah, Mama,
> no cross, no crown.'

Chrystos

In the Wild River
of Your Arms

where I'm carried to wet silk plunging
I lean into your strong back which doesn't give
in the sharp turns of touch
Bears me through nightmares & changing faces
lights racing a glitter of deep kisses
in darkness I didn't know was my home
until you held me & would not
let go

In the wild river of your laughter
nothing I do is crazy or too much
or can't be understood with time
No need for lies because you've no accusations
Grinning you embrace all that I am
even what I don't want of myself

In the wild river of your tongue
I travel light years away from everyone
who has lain with me claiming
some corner of my spirit as their own

read meanings into me
without my knowledge or consent
made me afraid of my own desire
ploughed me with confusion
as they called arid sand a verdant bank
tried to kill all
that surges clear in me
a wild river uncontained
without a name

In the wild river of your cunt
where I am first to shake you free & screaming wildly
I swim against the tide of brutal discarded husband
shame & rocks of regret for a woman
who would not give you this water
we drink as though the desert burns on every side
I ride you lightly as a birch bark canoe
in late spring melt
catching your wrists in a seine of desire new
& trembling as this wind
breathing between us bringing song

In the wild river of your soul
I've known you clear green & true
your hands carry no deception no bribes
My brother calls you a good old gal
& loves your laugh
I remember the child I was before
my uncle sliced her into debris
I see a long ribbon of our lives
flashing with the hope of home
I thought couldn't be

In the wild river of your eyes
I wash up new alive with colors
I open the deep pool of my tenderness

& float you down
where our toes are dancing on rocks
like crawdads waving hello with long feelers
Light as a leaf boat skimming the lights
my tongue is fishing for your pleasure
sweet water sweet grass
in the wild river
of our arms

for Denise

Photograph by Vita C. Shapiro

II

Many Houses

B o d y & S p i r i t

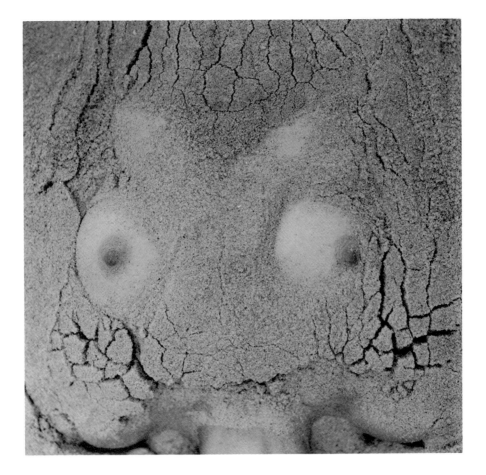

"Fire Island" by Morgan Gwenwald

"Callanish" by Elisabeth Griggs

Shay Youngblood

Estelle

from There Are Many Houses in My Tribe

When tears were rivers and mud made my mask, I ate the bark of trees. I washed naked in the river at dusk. I clothed my body in red clay and smooth white pebbles and leaves of grass and cowrie shells. I walked through the forest without direction. Branches braided into my hair, leaves became the soles of my feet. On the seventh day my eyes rested on a mystery. They stood like trees across my path. Seven women. Tall, thick, black women with wide hips and long delicate fingers. They invited me down a certain path. After many days we came to a village. There were no men there. No children or animals. Seven barren women. Seven huts formed a circle around a huge fire in that dusty place. The women offered me food and a place by the fire. At night they told stories and when it came my turn to tell a tale no sound came out. I opened my mouth to speak and in the place of words snakes spilled from my lips and slithered toward the women, wrapping around their ankles, circling their inner thighs and caressing their bellies. Seductive hissing whispers were drowned out by passionate cries as the women made the night aware of their pleasure. I watched as if from a great distance the union of snake and woman and I wept at the beauty and sensuousness of it all. Before the light of day each of the seven women had borne seven children and the next night those seven bore seven more and so on and so on, for seven days and seven nights. Beautiful girl children with gleaming white teeth and handsome boy children with proud wide noses. They grew into a tribe of two-headed people with snakes in their hair and colorful tongues that spoke many languages. The languages of trees, the languages of hearts, the languages of men and women. The face of beauty, the face of truth, the face of innocent dreams. The drums beat even their dreams.

"lovers with cane" by Tee A. Corinne

Ruth L. Schwartz

from The Kidney Transplant Chronicles

The stats are something like 95 percent patient survival, 90 percent graft survival after one year. That means there's about a 95 percent chance G will still be alive in a year, and a 90 percent chance my kidney will still be working inside her. After that the numbers go down some each year; by five years it's only about 65 percent graft survival. I don't remember what the patient survival figure is by then, but one line from the article sticks in my head: "Death with a functioning graft, particularly among diabetics, is a major cause of graft loss."

I look at my body in the mirror now, watch my reflection as my hands move down the small hills of breasts, over the mounds of ribs and stomach, through the narrowing moisture of pubic hair and back out to the expanse of thigh. The sensation in each place I touch flickers after my fingers the way the eyes, following the beam of a flashlight in a dark place, see each spot lit a fraction of a second after the beam has passed.

I know that my life is likely to continue after G's life ends. And yet she is the biggest part of my life now, she rises up through my heart like a huge sturdy immovable redwood tree, as if she's lived there hundreds of years already, as if even after her death the stump will remain there, still magnificent, making a place for all the mosses and saplings and beetles of the forest. If I don't give her my kidney she'll be on the waiting list for some indeterminate period—nine months? a year? more? She'll be on dialysis, which will keep her body alive but will not give her back to me as the woman I fell in love with, indomitable, fierce, hugely sexual; she'll live more or less as she is now, a pale shadow of herself, her movements limited, her appetites shrunken. Many people do it, but she and I are demanding; I know who she is, I know the woman who is still waiting weakened and trapped inside her damaged body, and I miss her desperately—maybe almost as desperately as she misses herself.

They say people can live fine with one kidney. That the one that remains actually grows larger, to take over the work of the other. Normal life span, they say. Barring an accident which damages that one kidney, or some freak disease- or drug-induced renal failure, I should be just fine. Avoid contact sports and Advil, radiographic contrast tests and eating too much protein—none of these proscriptions will be too difficult for me to follow.

Once I understood that I probably *could* give a kidney to G, there was no question in my mind about whether I would. My friends who have young children understand this. My own mother, who of course wishes I wouldn't do it, has a seven-year-old son by her second marriage. "Think about how you'd feel if Adam needed a kidney, and you could give it to him," I say. She understands immediately. "I'd have to."

And yet I am haunted by the fear of giving up this intact body, this effortlessly perfect health. The knowledge that I will be irrevocably altered. Will my body feel strange to me, afterward?

A friend who is an acupuncturist and herbalist says only, "It'll take months, *months* to heal. When they cut into your body, take something out . . ." Her sentences trail off, unfinished. She'll give me herbs to take before and afterward, though, to speed my recovery, to build up the chi in my bloodstream beforehand and help rechannel it afterward.

One in 1,500 kidney donors dies from the surgery itself. The medical textbooks stress that the best the donor can hope for after the surgery and the recovery period is to be "no worse off." Which, presumably, is the outlook for most of the 1,499 others. And yet these statistics, these odds, are less comforting to me than they would once have been. In my teens and twenties I *knew,* as the young do, that I was one of the lucky ones, that I would always come out on the sunny side of any risk I took. Time and the work I've done have changed me; I still tend toward optimism, but now I've talked to the people who *were* the one in a hundred, or fifteen hundred, or ten thousand. Every rare thing, good or bad, does happen to someone.

It's Saturday afternoon, and G is napping on the couch while the same two CDs play soft salsa over and over. She's got her teddy-bear blanket pulled up around her face, her bare feet sticking out; they don't get cold, though, because she's got no sensation in them. It astonishes me how soundly she sleeps. I can stand right next to her, looking down at her with so much love that I'm sure its headlamp beam will wake her, but—nothing.

After twenty-two years of diabetes, she's got every complication in the book. She's down to 20 percent kidney function, which means she's tired all the time. Cataracts have thickened over the scars from the laser treatments that kept her from going blind six years ago. She's on medication for angina, so she no longer has the pain in her arm, the gasping for breath; but she no longer walks much either, and avoids stairs and hills. The nerve damage gives her terrible leg and hand cramps, especially at night. When she gets a cold, it turns into bronchitis or pneumonia, keeps her down for months. At thirty-eight, she's got less energy than my grandmother.

For a long time I thought, *I can live without the walks on the beach, without skiing, hiking, camping.* But I wanted our lovemaking to remain sacred, untouchable. I wanted G's illness never to intrude in that one place. Of course, I didn't get my wish.

When we met, G danced naked for me, her big, ungainly body transformed by the rhythms it knew; she sang to me, serenaded me with flamenco, her gaze stripping my clothes off from across the room. That was three years ago. Mornings now, I wake up wanting her; I press my body against hers, stroke her arm, kiss her neck, hoping for some sign that she feels me, that she doesn't mind. She's grown so passive, I don't know anymore whether she wants me to stop or is waiting for me to continue. I swing my body on top of hers, trying to be gentle, noncommittal, just in case. But I can't help it; her body under mine excites me. I move my breasts against hers and my nipples take on lives of their own, begging, hardening. Then G shifts uncomfortably—her lower back aches—so I roll off, and she turns onto her side. I kiss my way down her neck and chest to her breasts, beautifully lopsided, with their huge nipples and their sagging weight. I love to burrow underneath them and kiss the slightly sour sweat that lingers there, their weight resting heavy on my face. Then I move upward, take just the tip of a nipple in my mouth.

When we were first together, G liked me to devour her breasts, to bite her nipples so hard it frightened me. But then I grew to love the red, fierce, erotic force of it; how they puckered, darkening; how her body stopped holding back and just moved the way it had to; how she crooned to me, *Tuya, tuya,* telling me she was mine. Now her breasts are tender most of the time—some hormonal shift caused by the kidney failure, or else something to do with the nerves, or maybe it's one of her medications. We don't know what it is. But her nipples are sore, and I have to approach them gradually, diffidently, to lick them soft and slow till they're not frightened anymore, till I feel her body beginning to roll beneath me with the old tide. In the middle of it, she starts coughing and can't stop. I pull myself from the bed to grab a tissue for her so she can spit out the green phlegm that builds up in her chest with every cold. She jerks her legs around like she's shooing away flies; they're cramping again.

Sometimes I've tried to make love to her standing up—her blood flows better that way—but then it's hard to part her legs enough to reach her with my tongue, so we sink back onto the bed. Desire still propelling me, I kiss her belly and the deep indentation between belly and groin—what I call *la línea del deseo,* "the line of desire"—running my tongue back and forth in its groove until we can't stand it anymore, and G pushes my head farther down. My eyes are closed, my tongue and fingers moving on their own, her thighs pulling me in until it's not me making love to her anymore, only the movements she calls out of me, both of us writhing, tumbling, and enveloping.

Later she tells me, "When I was making love to you this morning, my hand went numb, and for a minute I couldn't feel anything." Or she might say, "While you were making love to me, I was having shooting pains in my legs."

"Why didn't you say something," I protest.

"I didn't want to stop. And there was nothing you could do about it anyway."

I know both of these statements are true.

"It's just the nerve damage, that's all." She shrugs. "I just try to put it out of my mind."

It takes courage to love someone who's sick," says E, who is fifty and recovering, she hopes, from stage-three colon cancer. Ruefully she adds, "I think it would take courage for someone to love *me.*"

"It isn't courage," I tell her, my eyes unexpectedly watering, and it's only later I realize what I wanted to say:

It isn't courage, but something else, something I don't know how to name, something I too often feel I don't have. It's patience, endurance, the willingness to settle for "delayed gratification"—even when your raucous crow of an ego taunts snidely, "Delayed until *when?*" It's wanting to go out Friday night, to dance, to move, to drink and breathe in other people's smoke and heat and laughter, when you know that all your lover wants to do—or has the strength to do—is collapse. It's being so impatiently full of life and desire, feeling the little monkey who wants everything clamoring away inside you, and seeing her haloed by silence and exhaustion, her eyes cloudy with cataracts, their lids swollen with the strain. It's nights when you put her to bed and go off to read or write or masturbate or bake bread or cry, and she looks up at you with those dark, damaged, gypsy eyes and says, "I wish I could keep up with you." And you wish so, too, but that's the wrong thing to say, so you kiss her face from one side to the other, wanting to devour her, so weary of her illness, her limitations, yet loving her so absurdly much that even the Vicks VapoRub she dabs on her nose at night becomes an aphrodisiac to you because it's one of *her* smells, her bedtime scent. And, hours later, when you finally lift the covers to climb into bed beside her, it's that wordless shock you feel at your own tenderness, the hard knot in your breastbone that dissolves as you kiss her broad, sleeping back, fitting your body to hers, your life to her sleeping life.

So on Saturday night, we end up in a half-empty piano bar down by the water—about all the excitement G can handle. There's an anemic-looking, pockmarked guy hunched over the piano keys; a pale, concave, balding hippie on bass; a forty-something dyed blonde on vocals with a voice that's just too sticky-sweet. On the second song, a well-dressed older black couple start to dance, and somehow their slow, courtly steps transform the scene. The man leads, tender and elegant, and the woman molds her movements to his, the music of all their years together singing out from them until, for an instant, I glimpse compassion like a generous light cast over the room.

At the table next to us sits an oldish white man with his hair combed over as if it could hide his bare scalp. He's holding hands with a middle-aged black woman done up in so much black and glitter she looks like a movie-set witch, big hat and all. G nudges me and says the woman must be with the guy *por interés,* "for an interest," one most likely having to do with money. The man and woman are nodding and swaying, eyes closed, dreamy as clams. It's too frightening, I think: the idea of extending that glint of compassion to everyone I see, to the terrible, redeeming truth of each person's story.

Alexis DeVeaux

The Ethical Vegetarian

The kitchen stank to me. Maybe it was the smoking dismembered smell of them in the Styrofoam takeout box heaven only knows why but I clucked like a chicken as Grett sucked clean a spicy pile of buffalo wings. She looked up at me her face contorted. The lips I loved greasy with carnivorous pleasure.

That ain't funny Sahara.
You are what you eat darlin.

I tossed another stump of broccoli in my mouth for emphasis. Savored the delicate taste of sesame oil and sautéed garlic seasoning. Strictly vegetarian since college I hadn't eaten meat in ten years. It hadn't been easy to change. Over time I'd lost my taste for it though. Chicken like my momma made was hard to give up. Eating other animals was a matter of ethics to me now.

Several nights later I bolted up in bed wet with sweat. In the blink between sleep and not I struggled with shadowy worlds.

You ok? Grett mumbled.
The chicken woman took my baby.
What?

In the supermarket. I took her basket of eggs. Then she took mine. The baby was in it.

You been dreamin sugah. You don't have no babies.

But that's what chicken eggs are.

Grett sighed turning over. I drifted back to sleep restlessly.

Hovering above the sleeping characters the hand of the cartoonist drew a square box meticulously around the bedroom scene. Her freshly sharpened pencil shaded in dawn.

The smell of coffee brewing automatically awoke me early the next morning. I showered and dressed. Groggy from too little sleep. In the kitchen I poured myself a cup of the piping hot stimulant black. It burned my throat going down. I sank into one of the chairs at the table. Disgusted and out of sorts. When Grett came into the kitchen I was throwing eggs from the carton one by one into the garbage can.

Something wrong with the eggs? she asked.

No.

So why'd you throw them away?

People shouldn't breed animals just to eat their parts.

And what am I supposed to eat for breakfast?

I opened the pantry closet and took out a box of Quaker Oats. Grett looked at me like I was crazy.

You know I don't eat that shit she said. And fumed out of the kitchen back to the bedroom. Down the hall I stood in the doorway watching her. Dressed for work in a red wool sweater sheath strands of black and white African beads red and green rectangular earrings Grett was all urban Masai. At WBFM she was the only female disc jockey. Her daily talk show was number one in the city.

We'd met through mutual friends one night at Three Steps Forward. A favorite hangout of Black Brooklyn's artsy crowd. Everybody in the restaurant's bar was talking about M'Boyd Thomas's death. The well-kept secret of his AIDS. A loss to the Black dance world. Grett knew him. Laughing and crying she told us all story after story about their freshman days at Howard. There was a tough tender to her I found seductive.

·   ·   ·

Grett put on some deep-berry lipstick. Then splashed her neck with a few drops of Egyptian Musk. Checked herself out in the mirror. Watched me watching her. I blurted out something I'd overheard at the clinic.

Did you know
that embryo transfers for women
were first developed by experimenting on cows?
I really don't wanna hear it Sahara

was all she said before she snatched her coat and bag from a hook in the hallway closet. Stormed out without good-bye.

The left hand of the cartoonist poised above its storyboard. Flexed short fingers. Tired from drawing all night it swept away lint from its overused eraser. With its first finger traced the scratched-out revised dialogue above the characters' heads. The hand signed the cartoonist's code name "1619" in the lower-right-hand corner then reached for a new storyboard. Drew an outline of the brownstones jammed between stores along Nostrand Avenue.

Drew the sidewalks slippery ice traps. Stale snow frozen in dingy piles against the buildings. Gave the street a look of winter hung over not even the cold bright of blustery morning could blot out. Drew Sahara. Bundled up and bent over in a bitter wind. Maneuvering the blocks to the subway to the other side of Brooklyn. Then drew the four-story edifice which was the Franel Clinic. Nestled amid the commercial establishments on Orchard Avenue. Rows of naked trees out front of it stiff as skeletons on duty. Stopped. Started again drawing. The interior of the first floor inside. The Registration and Reception Area. Stark and sterile-looking. A streamlined counter which partially hid from view Sahara. Awash in a headful of kente-wrapped short thick dreadlocks. Frighteningly wild to the child-needy clients who stared at them. While waiting to start the process that would end in their in vitro fertilization.

Five o'clock came and I was glad to go home. But at the end of the day the streets were an obstacle course of grouchy holiday shoppers. Overburdened with bags of expensive family expectations. Suckered into the fa la lalala. Whether they could afford it or not. People carried home the biggest Christmas trees they could find. With no care for the shrinking forests. What it might feel like to be uprooted and sold. Indignant and distressed by the whole scene I walked along the outskirts of the sidewalks.

.   .   .

The hand of the cartoonist paused. Drummed an impatient rhythm on the unfinished storyboard. Doodled. Waited for the downbeat of inspiration. Slid its fingers over the pout of her mouth. The hand folded into the fingers of its mate for comfort.

The day after Christmas we went to Trazana and Roy's Kwanzaa party. The three floors of their DeKalb Avenue brownstone were packed solid as usual wall to wall. The bass blasted. Grett and I squeezed past clumps of dancers slinking to the steamy lyrics. Roy descended the spiral stairs gracefully lean. A Romare Bearden collage he was dressed in kente silk. His trim moustache tinseled with perspiration. Roy lit up when he spotted us.

Bout time yall got here.
Wouldn't miss this for nothin baby
Grett said eyeballing the crowd.

Otis died Roy said. This morning.
Oh no we both said.
Yes.
How are Carmen and the kids? I asked.
Takin it hard.
This is so fuckin unfair I said.
Grett said *and another one bites the dust* and sucked
her teeth.
He was a comet Roy said. A beautiful poet comet.

A loud crash erupted from the dining room. Trazana's scream propelled Roy through the pause of dancers. Grett gathered my hand in hers we moved toward the parlor room. And the buffet table. When she hungrily downed several devil eggs I bit my tongue. Just to keep the family peace. Pretended not to feel suddenly disgusted.

Hours later we got home danced out and giddy. Our lovemaking sweetened by the supple mauve of velvet couch our half-dressed bodies red candles burning in the living room a wee morning apartment chill the magnetic the smell of want.

Satisfied and sleepy the cartoonist cut out the lamp light on her drawing board.

I became a regular nuisance. To Grett my sermons on Black people's eating habits and good health and what if humans were bred for food were irritating.

Rude. One evening while munching some cold quiche for dinner in bed she'd begged me to please leave her food the fuck alone.

But I was out of control now. Driven to monologues on the virtues of vegetables and comparisons between the meat industry and slavery. I talked about food incessantly. Ran my mouth. Ran Grett out the bedroom to sleep on the couch.

Late one Friday night while shopping downtown Brooklyn I stopped in a Dalton's bookstore to browse. Spotted copies of *The Enchanted Broccoli Forest Cookbook*. Decided to buy one just for the hell of it. Took it home. About a week later I noticed that my taste for broccoli was now a craving. I had to have it. Day and night. Whenever Grett was late getting home from the station I experimented with broccoli recipes from the cookbook secretly. Made broccoli shakes. Fried broccoli patties. Broccoli pancakes. Broccoli soup. Broiled broccoli over stuffed steamed broccoli stalks. I was a broccoli junkie.

The cartoonist drew a box around that last frame. Of the previous night's work she particularly liked the desperate confusion executed with fine simplicity of line on the main character's face. It was the mark of an artist to do so much with so little. Was what she learned at Pratt her four years. Admired and well-liked by the faculty there she was envied by other students who found her design projects too original to copy. Already a gifted architect by her junior year she'd published her first cartoons in a neighborhood weekly City Lines. *After graduation she'd turned down a handsome offer in a Manhattan company and took a job with* The New City Restoration Project—*a group of local businesspeople who bought up abandoned houses in Brooklyn restored and sold them way below cost to deserving families. It was a job she was proud of. But it was the cartoons she could spend all weekend drawing the smell of ink and paper the sun the solitude in her Washington Avenue loft above Naomi's Beauty World and Ling's Chinese Take-out that propelled her forward. She reached for another clean board.*

But that wasn't the half of it. One morning while in the bathroom brushing my teeth I glanced at myself in the mirror. Screamed with shock. Grett ran into the bathroom.

What the hell happened to your hair?

She circled around me as the two of us bucked our eyes at the broccoli crop of dreadlocks sprouted up like a petrified forest all the fuck over my head.

"Louise Fishman" by Betsy Crowell

Canyon Sam

Conversation with a
Spiritual Friend

Memoir of an Audience with His Holiness
the Dalai Lama of Tibet

Four other westerners and I were led up a sloped road to a detached concrete building. It was a gorgeous late autumn, early winter day—blue skies sparkling and crisp at this 5200-foot elevation. We were ushered into a formal parlor with an old British feel about it: lace doilies on the backs of overstuffed chairs, magazines spread on a western-style coffee table, and the faint smell of camphor lacing the air. I was so nervous I wasn't able to read the magazine titles even though they were in English. We signed a guest ledger and filled out a visitor's form as instructed, then settled in to wait. The other westerners in my audience—none of whom I knew except Sophia, a Colombian woman—were smoothing out their white silk offering scarves and arranging small gifts in their hands. Others waited also: Tibetan artisans in handsome waistcoats bearing wood carvings and appliqué scrolls, seeking approval of their work before installing it in the new summer palace in Ladakh; pudgy Indian officials in western business suits with pomaded hair, their wives in pink and mango saris laced with gold thread, the red Hindu dot smudged between their eyebrows. No one said a word. We had plenty of time, I thought, trying to relax myself, because things rarely ran on schedule in India. Waiting was a form of yoga here, I'd discovered after three months.

I could scarcely believe that a backpacking traveler like myself, without status or title, who'd just set foot in Asia for the first time a few months ago, was really here: minutes away from meeting the spiritual leader revered and worshipped all over Tibet as the living incarnation of the Buddha himself. The man Tibetans used to spend months, even years prostrating on their hands and knees over mountain passes and across river valleys to reach. The extraordinary head of state who in the last thirty years had guided his nation through the most tumultuous period in its 2500-year history with unshakable hope, courage, and grace.

In a few minutes, the secretary rounded us up again and led us along an outside balcony a few paces, then back into the building through large double doors. He stepped up to the side of a huge grand presence in floor-length maroon robes. I looked up a moment. Oh, god, it was him! The Dalai Lama stood beaming at us in welcome. It was really him! In person! I thought we were being trundled off to another waiting room! Sophia was bowing from the waist, white scarf draped across her palms and held high above her head in offering.

Oh, my god, all my gifts were still in my bag! I jetted off to one side, swung my backpack to the floor and snatched out my offering scarf and small gifts.

The secretary called out: "*Miss Sophia Torres . . .*" as the others fell in close ranks behind me.

"*. . . from Bogota, Colombia . . .*" The secretary's voice rang with propriety as he introduced Sophia.

"*. . . South America.*"

I hoisted my caribou bag onto my shoulder again, tucked the Tibetan incense under my left thumb, the San Francisco post card under my right, and unfurled the new silk scarf. Sophia took a seat. The secretary glanced up from his cue card as His Holiness eyed me, still bumbling, with a broad, delighted grin.

Just in the nick of time, I spread the scarf across my palms and stood up. He looked six feet two—so much bigger than I expected. I took a breath and stepped toward him.

"*Miss Canyon Sam . . .*" Oh, my god, what do I do?

"*. . . from San Francisco . . .*" Bow? Slightly or deeply?

"*. . . California . . .*" Shake his hand? Isn't that too western? Too disrespectful?

"*. . . the U.S.A.*" The secretary nodded at me to acknowledge.

I usually touched my forehead to the ground three times when meeting lamas, but the others were on my heels—no time for Buddhist etiquette. What showed the proper respect? The ultimate respect? What is protocol for meeting the Buddha? I racked my mind madly for answers.

Without the slightest hint of pretense or protocol, the Dalai Lama took the scarf from me and shook my hand warmly with a remarkably strong grip. The radiant grin never left his face.

"*Mrs. Victoria Olsen . . . from Lancashire, Wales,*" the secretary continued.

I floated towards Sophia on the sofa and sat down beside her. I watched him greet the others in our party and then take a seat. His manner calmed me, and I found his physical presence striking. He was one of the largest Asians I'd seen in the East, with a large head, a big open moon face, and elegant, expressive hands. Towering physically but with uncommon lightness and ease.

The reception hall, a soothing aloe green in color, was lined with sunlit windows along two walls; at one end were hand painted, vibrantly colored scrolls of Buddhist deities and an altar with a gold statue of Sakyamuni Buddha in a glass case. The statue looked very much like the one in the Jokhang Temple in Lhasa, the most prized piece of religious statuary in Tibet. The Jokhang had been a gift to the King of Tibet centuries ago from one of his two Buddhist wives, an Indian and a Chinese, after they'd converted their husband, ruler of a warring, aggressive nation practicing animism, to Buddhism—leading in time to the conversion of the entire country. The Jokhang was the ancient, holy temple from which I used to hear the droning chants of monks resonating out like moans from the earth in the hushed hours of the dark night, when I lived with a Tibetan family in Lhasa and stomach ailments kept me from sleeping.

Six months ago I had come to China, to fulfill a life's dream to live in the birthplace of my grandparents and great-grandparents for a year. The Chinese government warmly "opened doors," inviting all overseas Chinese—including American-borns like myself—to return to visit "the motherland." I intended to teach English and improve my language skills. But after five weeks not only was I fast becoming disillusioned with my motherland—a society which could fairly be compared to Orwell's *1984*—but I visited Tibet—whose desolate landscapes of vast sky, mountain, and high desert took my breath away. And whose kind, jovial, faith-filled people healed something in me each time they hailed me across a field to join their picnic, each time a leather-faced ancient flashed me a toothy, white grin out of her dark, dusty wrinkles, each time I stood watching them prostrate for hours, wearing the temple stone shiny and smooth beneath their feet.

After two months in Tibet, I pulled myself away and forced myself to give my ancestral home another chance. Traveling through Han China again, however, only deepened my disappointment and alienation with the society and the government.

On a five-day boat ride up the Yangtze River, languishing in July humidity, I lay in my upper berth reading a book borrowed from friends. The dog-eared text, passed traveler to traveler, was entitled *In Exile From the Land of Snows* by John Avedon, and was about Tibet's modern history since the Chinese occupation. Every day as we floated further up the river, I read deeper into the book, and every day my outrage grew at what the International Commission of Jurists had deemed the worst genocide since World War II. Almost a quarter of the Tibetan population, over 1.2 million people, had died since China's takeover of Tibet in the 1950s. Ninety-nine percent—over 6,000 monasteries, the cultural equivalent of a school, a library, a church, a seminary, and sometimes even a university or medical school rolled into one small township—had been leveled. The majority of Tibetan religious art and literature had been looted or destroyed. Every imaginable and unimaginable means of torture had been leveled against the Tibetan people, as well as desecration of their spiritual beliefs. One out of every ten men had spent the 1960s inside a prison.

Buddhists with a devout reverence for all life, the Tibetans had given little attention to building a military force, and had almost no resources with which to defend themselves when the Communist army invaded. Living in peaceful isolation for hundreds of years, they had no political allies outside their country to take their part. The American C.I.A., after clandestinely training and funding Tibetan resistance fighters to oppose the Communist takeover, simply abandoned them a short time later when U.S. political agendas shifted.

In the West we knew nothing. China sealed itself off from the outside world for thirty years, asserting that its internal affairs were no one else's business. The atrocities taking place in Tibet fell behind the veil of the Himalayas.

My singular ambition became to visit Dharmsala, the capital of Tibet-in-exile in northern India. My long-laid plans for China flew out the door, like so many melon rinds my Chinese shipmates flung overboard into the wide, oceanic waters of the Yangtze, the sweetness of the fruit gone. It was here in Dharmsala that I stumbled onto the spiritual philosophy of Tibet, Tibetan Buddhism—and became introduced to the political philosophy of the Dalai Lama, who was both secular and spiritual leader of Tibet.

To a burnt-out angry radical like myself, this head of state's politics were astonishing, unheard of. Love and compassion were the moral fabric of world peace, he believed. Not love as we usually thought of it, but *sem-zangpo,* "the kind heart," an altruistic feeling for all humanity rooted in an understanding of our shared suffering. A nondiscriminating love, which seeded something called "universal responsibility"—a true sense of respect for others, friend or foe, for their rights and needs as human beings—in a way that transcended ideology, religion, sex, color, or national origin.

Sophia was introducing herself and inviting his Holiness to South America. I could sense how nervous she was, hear the small chokes in her voice, feel the delicate hairs on her arm stand on end just inches from me.

". . . a steady but growing number of Tibetan Buddhists in South America," Sophia was saying.

His Holiness listened attentively as she spoke. Yes, he agreed, he had never been to South America. He would consider her generous invitation.

The red-headed Australian and pale British woman delved into the subject of blood transfusions and donations when it was their turn to speak. They were both doctors attached to the local Tibetan hospital.

"Dozens die unnecessarily . . . People are very afraid . . . They just need to be assured it will not harm them . . ." she explained.

"A public statement from your office perhaps . . . They'll listen to you," he suggested.

The hospital was losing lives because it was unable to build up a blood bank. Tibetans feared giving blood might take their life away. In the early seventies, the Chinese took blood from them against their will to treat Chinese troops wounded in a border skirmish with India, admonishing the Tibetans that they should be glad to give blood to patriots who were building a socialist utopia for them. Scores of Tibetans died from excessive loss of blood. Many townspeople, recent refugees, remembered this. His Holiness listened carefully, and said he would take the matter into consideration.

Victoria Olsen, an owl-faced woman in her mid-fifties with a British accent invited His Holiness to visit Wales.

"Actually, I have been to England before," he replied. "A number of times . . . England, Scotland . . ."

Perturbation flickered across her face and she shifted uneasily in her seat. His Holiness looked puzzled and concerned. Spine erect, she said into the silence with quiet conviction: "But you have never been to *Wales.*"

He consulted with his secretary.

"Oh . . . mmm," he started again in English, "In-de-pen-dence move-ment. Yes?"

She wagged her chin up and down in ready agreement.

"Yes, I know," he giggled gleefully, fully grasping the situation. "Okay," he replied to her invitation. "Thank you very much."

He shifted his gaze to me and invited me to introduce myself.

"I have been traveling in China and Tibet for six months. I came to visit my roots, to travel and live in China for a year."

"Oh, overseas Chinese," he nodded. "Do you speak Chinese?"

"A little Cantonese, a little Mandarin . . ."

He asked about the situation of ethnic minority groups in China, and then whether there were many overseas Chinese traveling in the P.R.C.

"Where did you go in Tibet?"

"I stayed several weeks in Lhasa, then went east around Samye, and then west to Gyantse, Shigatse . . ." Describing the condition of the roads along these routes: rocky, corrugated, rough dirt tracks laden with potholes and avalanche danger and winding over 18,000-foot mountain passes, I jostled up and down pantomiming the horrid long-distance public bus ride. His Holiness roared in merry laughter. This guy and I were going to get along.

"I trekked to Mt. Everest base camp to visit Rongbuck Monastery, and months later I visited Amdo." Amdo was the northeast part of Tibet, his birth-place, and now part of a Chinese province.

"Did you like Tibet?" he asked with a grin.

I blinked, and my mouth hung agape. I searched his face. Nothing came out of my throat. I felt my chest squeeze and a blush of tears rise to my eyes. He waited for my answer but I couldn't get my jaw to move to say anything. I was totally caught off guard by his question. Not just the question, but *how* he asked it. So unaffectedly. With such exquisite, simple directness.

Tibet had moved me like nothing I had ever encountered in my life. And for him—the man who represented the very heart of this ancient, rich civiliza-tion, the human being so cherished as the living Buddha that tens of thousands of people spontaneously protected him with their lives the night he eluded kid-napping and escaped from Lhasa—to be asking me in perfect innocence if I liked his country flabbergasted me. The gifts Tibet had given me could not be put into words. Moments passed before I was aware that he awaited my answer, and I checked the astonished look from my face.

"I loved Tibet," I replied softly, looking squarely into his big moon face. "I liked it *very* much."

He was quiet for a long moment. His bare arms rested on the sides of his chair.

"I remember the air there was so *clean* . . . so *fresh* . . ." he said, gazing off across the room. "And the rivers were so clear . . ."

His mind seemed further and further away. I knew where it went. I knew those places. I could see the clear raging waters of the mighty Yarlong Tsangpo, its unearthly, pristine beauty; hear the lapping currents of the river on Lhasa's edge; walk again along the stretch of the Lingkor, the pilgrim's walk that skirted its riverbanks to the Norbulingka, the summer palace, the bold dust-covered hills ris-ing on the opposite shore. All so wild and untouched. My mind flew to the wide-open valleys in the high plateaus; the intensely vivid cobalt blue skies with their layer upon layer of curled clouds; I could smell the pungent, stinging scent of Hi-malayan air and see the sweep of snowy peaks stretching across the horizon.

"I wonder if this will change . . . in the years ahead?" he pondered. There was no bitterness in his voice, no fear. His mind was merely watching, as if see-ing images cross a movie screen, and he was very, very quiet.

An immense sadness washed over me. So immense I could not bear to let myself feel it fully. The land of Tibet will become an ecological and environmental catastrophe, experts believe, if China carries out its development plans there. Some of the most magnificent, unspoiled terrain in the world—indeed some call Tibet "the altar of the earth"—and one of the most peaceful, devout cultures ever to rise from human society would vanish from existence. Instead of serving as a vision for the rest of the world and an icon of hope, it was being inhaled by a powerful, ruthless neighbor. The only major pre-technological sacred civilization that had survived intact into the twentieth century would be irretrievably lost.

Today the sacred Himalayas were a secret militarized zone with hidden missile hangars carved into the mountains, and weapons poised, aimed at every strategic location in India, China's arch enemy. Nuclear manufacturing plants and nuclear waste dump sites, both were installed in Tibet by the Chinese—the unmarked dump sites causing birth deformities in the countryside to distraught, unknowing villagers. The pristine land was being pillaged of its natural resources—especially its forests—at an alarming rate, endangering the entire ecosystem of central Asia. China earned tens of millions of dollars in foreign revenue every year from marketing Tibet as a tourist attraction, most of which Tibetans never saw. But most dangerous of all, the forced relocation of millions of Han Chinese onto the Tibetan plateau threatened to overwhelm the already decimated Tibetan population, making Tibetans a minority in their own land, a fractured and displaced indigenous culture.

"What questions do you have to ask? Speak freely." His Holiness' manner was strong and commanding, but friendly.

Sophia, to my right, had saved and dreamed for almost ten years to come here from South America. Now she sat at the Dalai Lama's elbow, looking as if high voltage had zapped through her body. She asked in a small voice if it were true that when people achieved enlightenment, they were reincarnated only as men. A feminist from San Francisco, I bristled at the question, waiting with bated breath for his answer. Here was an important test.

The Dalai Lama exchanged Tibetan words with his secretary to check his understanding of the question.

"Oh no. No!" he shot back in English.

"I didn't think so," I mumbled softly under my breath. He heard this and burst out laughing—a wonderful deep robust laugh, the ringing baritone of which echoed joyfully throughout the room.

For my part, there was no dharma question save for one that I thought teachers, books, or reading transcripts of other audiences couldn't answer for me. I had to ask only that one question that I would most cherish his opinion about. The question I would ask if I had only one chance to pose a question to the carrier of the greatest scholastic and spiritual training of this highly refined philosophical tradition that predated Christianity by five hundred years.

Attachment—frustrated desire—was the source of all suffering, the Buddha taught. Once we ceased expecting, we had all things. Yet how did one renounce attachment? I was returning to the States soon, the country where one was assaulted every minute of the day through every sense organ to buy and spend, to crave and consume. The country where, a Thai friend said, she had no desire to live because "people were free to be rich, but not free to be poor."

"How is it possible," I asked aloud, "for a student of the dharma to live in the West, to practice freeing oneself of attachment . . . in a society that *cultivates* attachment? That promotes and rewards attachment?"

He nodded knowingly.

"With the Buddhist mind, you understand the *relative* nature of reality. How any, uhh . . . condition . . . can be both good and bad . . . at the same time. Not just pleasant, eh . . . unpleasant, eh . . . but good . . . when it seems bad. And bad when it feels good."

His English accent was similar to that of Indians here, yet phrases now and then carried the lilt and high squeaked inflection of the Tibetan language.

". . . so the relative nature of reality is a very, very important principle. Also altruism . . . that is . . . compassion, eh . . . patience, eh . . . tolerance . . . These qualities are *very* important.

"In the West, a person who is demanding, who is loud, is called strong. A person who is patient, who accepts circumstances, is considered weak. But actually, in Buddhism the person who can tolerate, who can accept conditions, is *stronger*. Because that person has *more* faith, *more* confidence . . . greater equilibrium . . . less fear. The person who is intolerant, who is agitated, dissatisfied, they are weaker. In their hearts they have more fear . . . more fear, eh . . . less faith."

He spoke about nonviolence, and then about pure motivation. Motivation pervaded and preceded all action, and therefore the nature of one's *motivation* determined the character, and karmic imprint of all our actions.

He talked about aligning one's actions with one's mental attitudes. "The mind . . . the action . . . the speech: all together." His thoughts were so lucid, it was as if he were doing a grand, exquisite kata exercise—the individual form in martial arts—of the mind. Without my knowing when and certainly not how, somewhere along the line the boundaries dissolved. No longer was I the novice and foreigner, the westerner hearing new concepts about life from an unfamiliar eastern tradition. No longer did I hungrily analyze his words, process them against previous knowledge, store the ideas like a forest animal squirreling acorns for the future. I realized I was not on the outside any more, but instead had tumbled into another mindstream—his mindstream—and I was on the inside.

My consciousness felt like a silver feather carried on a swollen, rushing river after a heavy winter rain. The water sparkled—shimmering like crystal, like diamonds, catching reflections from every direction. It was luminous, powerful, yet utterly light. I felt my shoulders drop, my face sigh and come to a sweet place of repose, felt my mind let go and give in to the tide. I heard the words, but without fear, without anxiety: they were of me and natural to me like the roar of the current. An utterance of its very being. One moment I had been on the outside and then seamlessly I found myself on the inside. Being there . . . marveling on being there . . . reveling in being there. But mostly . . . just being.

At one point he paused and looked out. He seemed to be searching for a word, grasping for English vocabulary to say something. The sunlight slashing in through the bank of windows lit his profile as he tilted his head up to think. "Peace," he finally said, pulling the word down from the void. "Peace," he uttered in a big deep voice. A voice rich and operatic, as if it could easily resonate through a concert hall or across a mountainside.

"Altruism gives you this peace. If you have peace of mind . . . from loving kindness . . . from not harming . . . from patience, then you can live anywhere, be any place, and you will have contentment. No upset. Peace."

He was quiet a moment and thinking. He scratched his forehead.

"Mmmm," he groaned deeply, ". . . aahyeh," he intoned concluding his answer. He looked at us again.

"More questions?" he smiled.

We spent another fifteen minutes asking questions. His mind was sharp and nimble and amazingly penetrating. He forgot nothing, always coming back to loose ends. He gave careful attention to what people said, and equal care to what he said to others. Not once, not even when people made unclear references, inappropriate requests, or when he was asked a question I knew he'd answered a dozen times before for westerners—did I detect the faintest trace of impatience or irritation. Or any sense of being rushed. Never was he less than gracious and respectful to others.

He spoke to his secretary, and the slim, gray-suited Tibetan left the room. The Dalai Lama asked for final questions.

"Can you possibly tell me . . . would you have any idea . . . what work I should take up in the States?" I ventured, launching into a subject that I had pondered for awhile about a career change. I thought perhaps he might have special insight, like some psychic ability, into which of the two courses I had in mind I should take up: counseling or medicine. I missed my psychic in San Francisco whose clear vision helped me in tough situations.

He listened carefully and considered.

"Try both things . . . and after some time . . . one year or so . . . see in which one you feel most confident."

I blinked my eyes to make sure that I heard everything, to make sure he had finished and had no more to say. He was serious; this was his answer. But this was mere common sense I was hearing.

"With the understanding of the relative nature of the mind . . . and with the altruistic attitude, eh . . . then these different studies are . . . tools, eh . . . are just different . . . *means,* you see? What is important," he concluded, "is the pure motivation . . . the 'good heart.' "

I felt like I had just washed ashore onto dry rocks. The river was dark and almost motionless. Still in damp cutoffs, I sat staring at my feet in their torn bleached tennis shoes. The sun had disappeared behind thick clouds and all was quiet. There was no rush of the current and I was alone, in my own mind again. I was back on earth, in the conventional, the mundane. There would be no easy answers, no shortcuts.

"If you still do not know . . . if it is not clear in . . . oh . . . two years," he added, perhaps sensing my disappointment, "then ask me again," he twinkled, as the secretary returned to the room.

His Holiness rose from his chair. His maroon robes, enfolded as he sat, now fell loosely down the length of his body. He adjusted the sash, tossing the end over his left shoulder and then took some softcover books from the secretary. He handed Sophia two books; then he turned to me and offered two volumes: Shantideva's *Guide to the Bodhisattva's Way of Life* and a smaller booklet, *A Human Approach to World Peace.* He continued around the circle giving everyone books.

We stood and clustered around him: offering thanks, exchanging handshakes, bidding farewell; the dharma practitioners among us clasped hands together and bowed, upon which he draped the white silk scarves over our necks that we had offered him on arrival. I saw my post card on the small pile of gifts he set aside to keep: the neat square edges framing the red towers of the Golden Gate Bridge as they arched majestically across splashing San Francisco Bay.

He suddenly broke into a few lines of Mandarin as he was saying goodbye to me. "Jijian," he said finally with his playful grin. Goodbye. I was taken aback to hear Chinese uttered from his lips—totally awed that he had taken the time to learn the language of the country that had brought such tremendous devastation to his own. I nodded.

No, I will not need to ask him anything in two years, I thought. *Sem-zangpo,* I realized watching his maroon and goldenrod robes sweep by to shake the doctors' hands—"the good heart"—underlay the calm intensity of the Tibetan people's faith I found so compelling, rebalanced them time and time again in the face of all they suffered, fed the deep reservoir of joy and wisdom they held so uniquely, and shared so freely.

As we were walking out of the room, the secretary kindly complied to take a quick snapshot of myself and His Holiness together. We stood side by side in front of the altar, in front of the richly-colored scrolls: precious images of the Avalokiteshvara, the Buddha of Compassion; Manjushri, the Buddha of Wisdom; the Creator and Destroyer; the tree of all root gurus and bodhisattvas.

When I look at this picture now, it shouldn't have come out. Others didn't. I have snapshots where the entire Honolulu airport is sharply in focus in the background, and I and my girlfriend in our swan song, our last pose before departing, are a puddle of color in the foreground. Passersby help take pictures: they center, point, and shoot. But with my simple camera when a picture of two subjects is centered, the lens focuses on the space between them, so that the two people come out blurry and instead what's behind them comes out in clear focus.

When I look at this photo months later now in the States, I see things I never saw before. There is me in my sky blue Tibetan shirt and L.L. Bean vest—all blues and grays, my cool traveling colors. His Holiness, swathed in burgandy-colored robes, with high smiling cheekbones and twinkling eyes stands next to me. He is not six feet two after all. We are both radiant, beaming. A bright light shines near my head that I never noticed before, and another light in the identical place, but in mirror image, over the close-shaven head of His Holiness, over his sash-draped shoulder.

Centered perfectly between us is the Sakyamuni Buddha on the altar behind. He wears a gold crown, the jewel-studded crown of Enlightenment. His face is feminine, masculine. His eyebrows arc serenely across a smooth forehead, his lips rest quiet and small near the bottom of his placid face.

Despite the problems I've had with this camera before . . . we are all in focus.

"Christine Burton and friend, Golden Threads Celebration 1995,"
from the documentary *Golden Threads,*
by Marian Roth/Wildlight Productions

Madelyn Arnold

One More Time, Marie

Opening the cupboard, Claire took down a can of soup, a box of crackers, and a tin of Spam. Where were the pans . . . ? Marie kept them . . . must be in the oven. She removed a skillet and saucepan and set them down on the rickety little table that served for food preparation. She found the can opener. Surprisingly, it was hanging on a nail. What to do first? No, not open a can, heat the skillet. Should she grease it? She couldn't remember. It had been too long.

Claire hauled open the refrigerator and stared at the too-many things inside: mayonnaise, milk, ketchup, sour wine, two cans of beer, bologna, cheese, wrapped things . . . (what?). Some sort of pickles. She was still perfectly capable of cooking for herself or a family (when she had been young all girls cooked) but why not wait?

She left hanging the question, *Wait for what?,* ate a cracker and drank half a beer, then lay down, suddenly sick to her gut, and was out cold.

What had happened was that they hadn't liked the movie and so had decided to have a drink, had parked in exactly the same place they always did. Their nights at the bar were infrequent. Was that incautious? People didn't know you that way. . . .

They had always stayed away from police. The times when the shop was broken into, they had always tried to avoid calling the cops, but this. They called, and the cops afterward told Claire what she herself had said, but in fact she did not remember the blows, how Marie had been—but thank God, thank God, no thanks to the goddamn SLPD—then all the questions and Marie's crying out. A heart attack. A heart. And what do the sons of bitches want to hear about but money. That's a hospital for you, like those, that piece of filthy—only without a gun!

The questions. About Claire's relationship to Marie, to that old woman in Surgery, she had snapped, "Business partner." And the ER people had written, *none.*

"None?" This to the Bright Young Man who worked in Intensive Care. This after she herself had been released from treatment. "What do they mean, *'none'* down in that looney bin? They get nothing right. I say she can't take that Lasix, her doctor says so, and I come up and if they're not about to give it to her! Said there was nothing against it on her chart. *No relationship.* Did anything else get wrote up right?"

After which the Young Man typed in *Friend* on Marie's papers for whatever. "Next of kin?"

In fact, Marie did have a next of kin, a brother in Chicago Marie hadn't seen in thirty years—a short, prognathic little thug of a man, who made you think of Mafia. Years ago he had said, stay out of his way. Which eventually had faded. He'd just got too tired to hate and gave it up; sent them a picture last Christmas of himself dressed as a silly imitation of a young buck, marrying again. The girl not quite half his age. What if he was ready to be the next of kin, decided to crowd her out, make the bad decisions? And Claire felt like hell, herself. Her face hurt.

"Next . . . ?"

"Wait, just wait, dammit!" she snarled, but he was not even mildly put out. Waited patiently, casually, helpfulness in the flesh. Of course if she didn't tell about the brother or even Leon they'd probably tell her more, but right's right, blood's thicker.

And this was the last time this could ever happen. That much she knew without being morbid, or superstitious, or boastful. St. Louis was rough—but always before they'd been lucky. Maybe they had thought by now their age would actually protect them better, but the charm had worn off; they were both too old and this was the very last time.

"Me," she snapped.

"Relationship?"

"Sister!"

"You must understand. We need a next of kin for legal matters."

How have a man in such a job? A clean job—cheat some poor girl out of a decent job. How old was he, twenty? She wouldn't explain. This was Missouri, and charity didn't mean herself and Marie.

As kin, she gave their lawyer's name and the smiling boy typed *friend* about her. *Friend.*

All that had gone on was that they hadn't liked the movie and so had decided to stop at the Karavan, had decided to have a drink. The Kar was exactly the same as it had been for years (well, with new decor), the same as back when the bar was Zenobia's and before that, the Alakazar. They had parked in exactly the same place they always did, exactly the same distance from the door (and the bouncer) and in clear sight of the bar, but statistics had caught them. Muggers, the cops had called them, but she called them filthy cocksuckers. She called them worse. Fury tore in, but its force rent only her because she was herself hurt, her nose broken and her face bruised, which was why the packed ice, and her padded wrist actually was broken. But Marie . . . Marie, Marie.

As if Claire herself didn't look like hell. Dried blood all over her face, swollen blue-black—white bandages across her nose like a bandit, the adhesive pulling loose on both sides. Except where blood glued it to her skull, her hair stood straight up. Hadn't there been a time when a hospital cleaned you up? Or maybe that was only in the movies.

She ran water into the basin and, finding the sound intensely comforting, wetted a towel and began to gently, carefully, pat the bloody night off her face. No, she had told the police, she had not seen them clearly, but not one of them had been black, or not very black at least, and she would have scratched the memory out of herself. If somebody in the bar hadn't screamed to high God—

Look at that hair. Thin and coarse like a Brillo pad, always had been thin; well, now it wasn't thin but sparse, and one day from behind her Marie had said, *I tell you what, honey. The day you turn sixty-five we're going to chop off all of that fringe and I'm going to get you a real nice Elvis wig. You always did look cute in a DA.*

In spite or maybe because of her appearance, the intensive-care young man bent the rules and, only for a minute, she was inside. Which restriction might have been pronounced even for family.

Walking into the room Claire had most been aware of a gentle sort of *shh-click, whiiii,* from a dozen sites, in random order around the room. In front of, behind curtains. With difficulty, she recognized Marie against the far wall, and frowning to clear her eyesight she could not be rid of the sense that Marie had a trunk like an elephant. Marie liked the zoo, she would think that was pretty funny. Wait till she heard—

Someone kept trying to ask Claire what she was doing. She was breathing.

12:30 P.M., THURSDAY

Claire found herself on her feet, answering the heavy banging down the hall, aware that it was now broad day—shambling to the door in an undershirt over a sundress, leaving her glasses on the back of the commode and her teeth in a jar by the bed; Claire did not realize that she was in fact awake and the knocking door would likely have somebody on the other side. She was never the one to answer. As she opened the door full out to let in the light from the hallway, she heard rather than saw the dumpy person in front of her, heard that little "oh!" delivered for nearly all occasions around Claire, knew it was her sister's girl, Janine, who blew hot and cold on saving Claire's soul. As if it helped, she usually brought her kids.

Miss Kitty Kat must have thought she brought them too, skitting past Claire's huaraches in a Great Escape. Without her glasses Claire lurched into the hall after all that she was capable of seeing, which was a black streak against a red rug.

"I'll get her, Aunt Claire," sighed Janine, and down the hall there was a squeal as her little girl spied the nice kitty and grabbed, unfortunately with real good aim.

Claire carried in the spitting Miss Kitty and dumpy, patient Janine carried in the screaming child, raked across both hands.

"I'll stick her in the back," yawned Claire, continuing down the hall. She meant Miss Kitty. "You stay with your ma," she said firmly to the boys, who, abashed, hung back a full second. About this point she realized how her own face looked, that they were horrified.

Once in the bedroom, Claire kissed the cat on the ear, squeezed her and bowled her under the bed, from which she glared as the now shoeless boys tore in and out from the hallway, sliding on Marie's waxed wood floor in stocking feet. Claire was now awake to the way she looked. No use looking jakier than your fate. Bending over the Jacobean nightstand, she fished her teeth out of their jar, and making horrible faces, thrust them into her jaws—jerked them out— shoved them in—to the horrified delight of her grandnephews.

And having done the right things as soon as she could find the tea, she demanded, "To what do I owe the honor, anyway?"

Janny wouldn't drink her tea; it was what she gestured with. "It's about last night." She sighed.

"What?" snapped Claire. "What do you mean, what do you know about it?"

"Dear. Well. The eleven o'clock news? Right after the Cardinals . . . I'm so sorry about—"

"What goddamn news? What in hell are you—"

"Please . . ."

Janny meant, of course, the little angels—two of whom had collared some of Marie's figurines, of which several hundred were arranged upon frail maple corner-brace shelves. Seeing Claire's face, Janny made the kids put down a shepherdess and several slightly sticky lambs.

"About the mugging," she resumed, forgetting to sigh. "Channel Six said this strongarm ring that preys on . . . I called the hospital and they told me you were out. I didn't know if you needed anything. Maybe I could cook you a meal."

Claire was blowing smoke out her ears, furious.

"Hmm," sighed Janny. "I wanted you to see that you can call on your family to—"

"My family! There's cabs, they're cheaper, and there's takeout Chinese, too. Family! I don't need any help from you. I've been lower than Satan's spit to my family for forty years—" Her blood pressure. She slowed herself. *"Family* told me in 1945 to get blanked and they won't get a goddamn out of me. If you think I'm giving up and giving you the store, you got one other think coming, you hear? I've left the kids a little something and there's *nothing* for your ma and *nothing* for you and George, and you tell your ma that. It won't work, and we don't need help—" The words hooked in her throat.

Up, Marie. For God's sweet sake, get up—

3:45 P.M., THURSDAY

By the shouting, she knew it was Leon downstairs. That boy could not ask nor answer a question in a reasonable tone of voice, not once in the last forty years. It came to her that she had not been down in the shop all day, and that buyers were coming around to look at some new estate stuff. *Estate.* And for some of the auction stuff, she had a warehouse full, and here came Marie's idiot nephew. Marie, diplomatic Marie, Marie took care of the talk part. . . .

Claire shook off the robe and the Mother Hubbard and slid on some slacks and a blouse. It was almost four, but she stopped and again called the hospital—no change, no anything. She made to leave, still wearing the huaraches.

Instead of walking down the front stairs, onto the street, and hauling herself in the front doors of Marclar Antiques—as she customarily did for the simple reason that her baby-elephant entrance gave Pat and Louey the time to snap to and look intelligent—she climbed out the kitchen window onto the fire escape and stepped down onto the office window ledge, practically onto the old black Standard. She squeezed her bulk in the big window, over the ledge and onto the floor, and in the next second or so Felix, one of the movers, the part-timer, stuck his head in under the curtain and stayed to stare, bug-eyed. Not at her entrance. For a moment she entertained the notion that they were all doing something illegal or expensive out in the showroom. Then Claire remembered her face.

"What are you gawking at?" she croaked; not her usual bark.

"Hell, Claire—what the hell? You okay? You have an accident? You call the cop—"

"Say," she snapped, "you doing the news?"

She did not have to look in another mirror. But with the way her clerk and the movers kept looking at her, she finally, huffily, moved into the lavatory she and Marie had declared was for women, and surveyed the taped nose, bruised eye (it wasn't going to shut, she thought) the small bruise on the point of her chin—that shouldn't have happened. She hadn't been that easy to deck, not ever. Time was—drake's-tail, jacket, scar next to her eye (from barbed wire when she was about six)—nobody screwed with this one. Assholes at the station, ugly mugs on the street. It helps to be *ugly*. But hurts your feelings sometimes . . .

The last time anybody'd cold-cocked her was her brother, in '45; their only real argument. He had brought Marie home a few times from the Wayne Avenue USO, but she'd kept coming out to the pantry. The giggles . . . That was a fight. Before that, everybody knew Claire as just ugly, unmarriageable. . . . In 1965 he had died of cancer. No, it was later.

There was a time, back then, when you tried to explain yourself.

Actually she was never much of a fighter, she was just ugly. Nothing to be done with *this* face. But that nose. She had always hated that dough-lump German nose. Wouldn't it just be great if it healed distinguished? Marie would say—

Get up, honey. Marie . . .

Claire headed out of the small room dizzy, but straightened when she saw they were all staring at her. Mournful to make her crazy. Louey, Pat, Felix . . . the bookkeeper, Alice—behind her that ape, Leon. Hell, couldn't he learn to smile? Or get himself glasses? Not a bad businessman in his own right; owned a hardware store up north. Reasonable type, but what did he know about auctions? About styles? And what was he messing with that estate junk for?

"Well, what do you want?" This to Leon.

"Wanted to know, do you want that shellac. Got a half drum. That and I was in the area—" He was looking around; crates in the middle were opened. "Aunt Marie go out?"

The veins swelled froglike in her throat, in her temples. "Don't play dumb with me! You could have had the decency to wait. She ain't dead yet!"

His jaw dropped.

"I don't believe that innocent act! Not for one moment do I believe that in-nocent act! Wait—damn you, wait! You're the heir all right, but wait!"

Oh, he would inherit. They had never been able to work around the *unsound mind;* if they had anything, a will would go to court and the family would win; survivorship had seemed too far away. And you couldn't borrow money in both names—not until you already had a *business* partnership. Besides, it was Claire and her blood pressure scheduled to ship out first; and the place hadn't been sup-posed to do that well. Because they had bought into the building and fixed it up; then bought out the store, and before their handling it had always lost money. That part of the block would be a tax writeoff, but they worked too hard. First Marie had quit her job and filled in—her mom and dad had been in the furni-ture business. Marie knew all the styles, the fix-ups, the polish—then Claire had quit the railroad—did minor repairs, putty and shoe polish, built the inventory. They had so well absorbed their losses that the insurance two years in a row ac-tually *dropped.* Marie knew markets. . . .

But auctions: Those were Claire's. Shoving through, hat over brow—she loved her effect on the thick-headed farmers. Gab and grab—*no*body elbowed Claire out. She got just about anything she had ever set her hat for.

Maybe Leon *didn't* know, and she should say. Maybe Leon really didn't know. It was his right. And he would inherit half; maybe she should say—

No.

He can have the place, but her grief . . . No, the *hell* he could have this place!

5:30 P.M., THURSDAY

They had parked in exactly the same place they always did. Though the place had changed, Lord. The Mafia used to keep it safe. Making it legal, now *nothing* was safe. The bars were different. It used to be, at the bar you dropped your out-side mental clothes and were easy in yourself. This was your home. Now bars were just a place you went when you needed to remember you were garbage. Lower-class. (Equals butch and femme—equals old.) Their old bar at the same place had had a pink neon parrot and a sign that said, *We made an agreement. The bank don't give drag shows and this bar don't cash checks.* Now these new bars with the cute ways, the ferns and loud music so you couldn't talk but you didn't need to try to. Nobody to listen, couldn't find even half the friends you had known all your life, and the men and women were strictly separated. And the ages too. Bartenders didn't see you even if they knew you had good money, not if you're no spring chicken. Better to be a pretty, young deadbeat. But it always had been better to be pretty and young. She herself had been privy-plain, while Marie—

We were so hot, then. Oh, it was bad of course, but back then they were actually afraid of us, stayed out of our places. Queers had their sections; dangerous for us down certain streets—but me and that haircut. Bull dagger, bull dyke, butch, *Lesb*ian . . . *Gray* Panther.

She smiled her most horrible smile at the mirror, giving up on her hair, and stepped out into the muted lighting of the unit, where the first thing she noticed was the shhhhh-click!-ing around her.

"Ms. Kohler?"

He was either from deeper south, or women's lib had made him hypocritical.

"How's she doing?" Claire mumbled. Her mouth swollen, the cheap teeth hurt her.

"No change," said a brisk nurse.

Said the Young Man, "Well, she might have been briefly conscious. It's hard to say with—"

Claire froze. "She said something?"

"She isn't able to say anything. She has a tracheal tube," corrected the nurse. "What she was probably doing was an involuntary—"

"You mean she *tried to* say something—did—"

"We were clearing the trach and Dr. Findalito said it looked a little like she was moving her eyes. That was about . . . half an hour . . . Please understand that this is not the same thing as her being conscious, of course, but there were some indications. We haven't been checking any electrical functions but cardiac—"

"Take it out. Take that tube out of her—"

Objections.

"For a minute. Just for a minute so I can ask her about—" What. What do you say. "Business. She's my— We own a store. I've got to ask her about some business—" Ask her Leon's cut. Something.

"It's not a matter of simply removing the tube." They spoke slowly, evenly. Teachers of the not-too-bright. "She cannot talk or move. She has had medicine that completely relaxes her muscles. When a patient has been intubated, the curare—"

"That's poison." She had read this in a Perry Mason novel. "Curare, that's, that's a suffocating—"

"Without relaxed breathing muscles, she might waste the strength she does have fighting the respirator. Mrs. Kohler—"

"Ain't she doing bad enough already, and now you go and *poison* her?"

"It is only given because—"

"She can't talk with it. She can't talk. Is she going to live? Is she going to get better? Is she going to get to say anything first?"

Silence.

"Take it out, then! Maybe she wants to talk!"

"Ah, with permission of the next of kin—"

"That's me! I give permission. I— That woman has just spent the last forty-two years of her life with me, nobody but *me* in the same bank account, in the same damn bed. If there's anything she's got to say, it's to me! *Nobody, no* kin is as close, nobody in this world—take it out!"

"Well, you see," they said politely.

Which meant, Nothing. They probably understood, but what of it.

7:00 P.M., THURSDAY

She couldn't stay long.

She had guessed finally that you could visit only one at a time, so the very first relative visiting would displace her. That would be Leon. He'd get off work, go to supper, drive down to the middle of St. Louis. Down to displace her.

Wake up.

By now everybody would know what had happened; they'd be rushing forward with sentimental claims, grasping fingers.

Claire had spent the last hour and a half shaking violently through her thoroughly imperfect memory, trying to think what were the last words she had heard Marie say. About the movie? Neither of them had liked it. . . .

Head ringing with how dangerous you are. Marie was the girl in the dark piqué and Claire with her brother's massive old Dictator with the muffler that fell off in the middle of the night out in front of Marie's. So much for elopement. How dangerous they were. (And there had been others before and over the years, and for both of them, but they never except once discussed it. Claire had cried that time, cried all night. That wasn't like her.) When it had all come out, Marie had lost her ticket-selling job downtown—which was just as well. Too many rumors. When everybody'd found out, Claire was banned from her mother's house, her little sisters looking through the fence. Didn't look back. She had disciplined herself to think how she was lucky to keep her job with the railroad, growing a fine crop of ulcers wondering when it would all fall in. What attention she and Marie had commanded, for nothing much. Never thought dangerous now. Now dykes and queers gave sucker lines on sitcoms. Only one way to command much attention now.

At the store, as she was leaving, she had heard Leon asking what shape the books were in.

In and out with that elephant thing, Claire was breathing with her. Shhhh . . . click! Shhhh . . . click! —*Open your eyes. Open your eyes and show me who I am. Say my name. Only one more time.*

Still from *Nitrate Kisses* by Barbara Hammer

Pat Califia

from Slipping

A gay man tells me that he thinks lesbians have AIDS envy. It makes him impatient when women talk about safer sex because it isn't really a problem for us. We are, he thinks, just trying to jump on the bandwagon.

I am in Cynthia's kitchen. I have to swallow some aspirin. I take a glass full of water off the table. "That's mine," she says, warning me. "I just drank out of it."

"I know. I don't care."

This is our ritual. When we eat sushi, I dip my tekka maki in her sauce. I steal slices of ginger off her plate. "Don't worry," I tell her, "I don't have a cold. You won't catch anything."

She is my friend. Once she was my lover. She has AIDS. I will not let her drift beyond the world of human touch.

I read about the first lesbian case of AIDS in December of 1986. The letter in the *Journal of the American Medical Association* was curt and all the more frightening because it contained so little information. The *Village Voice* ran an article that included a few more personal details. One of the women was dead already. She'd been an intravenous-drug user, had sex with men. The implication was that she was a junkie and a whore. Her lover had ARC. She had not used drugs. She had sex (with condoms) with one bisexual man after getting involved with her female lover. So nobody called her an innocent victim. The two women, the *Village Voice* said coyly, had had "traumatic sex" that caused bleeding.

I wondered who those women were. How did they meet? Were they black, Latino, white, Asian, Native American? How long had they loved each other? Did they love each other? Who was taking care of the survivor? Did her family know? What the hell was "traumatic sex," anyway? It sounded suspiciously like something a doctor would say about my sex life. Did either of them own a leather jacket?

On bad days, I don't think safe-sex education is working. I think a few gay men are using condoms, but most of them have just quit fucking. It's probably harder to get AIDS from sucking cock, but by now we've had so much bad news that I can't convince myself that it's safe.

Lesbians still don't believe that AIDS has anything to do with them. The best-educated dykes will grudgingly concede that the disease might be able to pass from one *woman* to another, but not from one *real lesbian* to another. We already knew that real lesbians don't have sex with men, for fun or for money. But because of AIDS, the pool of women-loving women, pussy-eating, cunt-fucking women who also qualify as "real lesbians" has grown even smaller. Real lesbians don't shoot drugs, share needles, or play sex games that expose them to somebody else's blood. We're all in twelve-step programs, but none of us are junkies. Real lesbians don't sleep with straight women or bisexual women. Real lesbians don't have heterosexual histories.

If a woman has AIDS, she must not be a real lesbian. She's not our problem. We can keep ourselves safe if we don't touch her.

It reminds me of the way good girls never talked to the girls who were easy in high school. As if it were a contagious condition. Girls who got pregnant just dropped out, even if they got married. As if they carried some deadly disease.

I remember the conversations I had with my gay male friends early on, when this disease was still being called "gay pneumonia." All of them wanted very much to believe that only the fist-fuckers were going to get sick.

In 1987, Dr. Margaret Fischl at the University of Miami reported that 119 women with AIDS survived for an average of 6.6 months after diagnosis, compared with an average of 12 to 14 months for men with AIDS. She said, "AIDS in women may be a different disease." In 1992, the Centers for Disease Control still refuse to make official a new definition of AIDS that would include the pelvic and vaginal infections that are unique to HIV-infected women as criteria for an AIDS diagnosis.

Lesbians know why gay men get AIDS. It's a natural consequence of male selfishness and dirtiness and violence. A hard cock has no conscience. Men just want to be able to stick their hard dicks any place they feel like it. They have no sense of responsibility toward their partners—or themselves. They can't think past an orgasm to its consequences.

Every dyke knows that semen is dirty and vaginas are clean. Menstrual blood can't be equated with the blood in a dirty syringe or scum in a queer boy's butt. If we are at risk—if this clean community of young, attractive, feminist women has been contaminated by a foul male disease—it's because I and women like me have encouraged other dykes to imitate men. We've encouraged promiscuity, S/M, bisexuality, drug use, working in the sex industry.

Of course, all this stuff was happening before, but those goddamned leather dykes have insisted on talking about it, and once you label something, you have to admit it's going on. You have to admit that lesbians are not exempt from giving each other chlamydia, herpes, trichomoniasis, hepatitis, even AIDS. You have to talk about the sweaty, messy stuff that lesbian solidarity is based upon—the sound of bellies slapping together in the dark, the taste another woman leaves under your tongue, scrubbing shit out from under your fingernails, the mean way women sometimes have of saying no just because you really do want them, taking her tampon out with your teeth, wondering if buying a sex toy will save your marriage or make her finally leave you, thinking about somebody else while she makes you come, wondering how much longer it's going to take to make her come, getting wet just because she looked at you.

The essential ingredients of lust are awkward and embarrassing, and they remain the same whether you are into leather, vanilla, cherry, chocolate, or some other flavor of lesbian sex. There is no such thing as a sexual encounter in which you don't have to deal with power as well as germs. It's interesting that the girls who are into exchanging power are the ones who are the least likely to be exchanging viruses. If she has handcuffs on her belt, chances are she has some gloves in her pocket. Prophylactic paraphernalia has become a new signifier for S/M. In the larger lesbian community, if you ask somebody how she feels about safer sex, chances are good she also expects you to ask if you can tie her up. Women who refuse to talk to S/M dykes don't seem to want to talk to each other about AIDS. They would rather pretend it is somebody else's problem. No wonder they don't want leather dykes at the Michigan Womyn's Music Festival. But, like New York City, vanilla dykes are quickly running out of places to put the trash.

A year after Cynthia's death, the mixed-gender S/M organization that she founded, the Society of Janus, asked its membership to vote on whether they should require safe sex at their parties. After bitter debate, the majority voted not to "force" members to have safer sex at Janus events because AIDS isn't an issue for heterosexuals.

A gay male friend who sees the latex stash by my bed tells me sadly, "Gee, I was really hoping that you girls were still carrying on without having to worry about bagging it. I guess I thought if the party was over for us, somebody was still having a good time." I try to tell him I'm still having a good time, but he doesn't want to hear it. The details about what I do with my pussy or anybody else's pussy make him queasy.

When I start telling friends that my new lover has a chronic, debilitating disease of unknown origin, which her doctor will eventually label chronic fatigue immune dysfunction syndrome, many of them advise me to leave her. "Think what a negative impact it will have on the rest of your life," they say. The same friends would be absolutely scathing if two men broke up because one of them could not deal with his boyfriend's AIDS diagnosis.

There are days when my lover is in so much pain and so disoriented that she can't get out of bed and go to the bathroom by herself. We have a running joke about waiting for our Shanti volunteer and our free bag of groceries. But soon we realize that most of our gay male friends have dropped us. I think it's because we are no longer on the list of potential caretakers. The joke isn't funny anymore.

I have become progressively more angry about gay men's ignorance about women's sexuality, bodies, and health issues. I have started talking about the fact that breast cancer is an epidemic. People think I am a crazy separatist. And of course that's the very worst thing you can be—a woman who puts other women first. But I am tired of taking care of men who have no idea what I do to get off, what my other passions might be, why reproductive rights are important, or what I do when I am not picking up their laundry, giving them medicine, or cleaning up their puke.

I have stopped going to AIDS benefits unless the money is earmarked to provide services to women. I even tell one of my gay male friends that if he gets AIDS now, he has no excuse, and I am not going to take care of him. I can't tell if I'm just depressed and burned-out, or if I really mean it.

Suppose it's true that sexual transmission of HIV from one woman to another is practically nonexistent. Suppose it's true that every lesbian who is HIV-positive got the virus because she had unprotected sex with men or shared needles. What should these women do now—stop having sex? Who thinks it would be safe to put her hand inside one of these women without a glove? Would you put your tongue on her? Would you do it if she was having her period?

Would it help her, do you think, to be told that she is part of a community that has historically behaved in a very faddish manner? Do you think she needs to know that a dental dam really fits into a lot of people's shame about their sexuality? Would her girlfriend be comforted by the information that dental dams have never been tested for efficacy? Do you think at that point that either of them really gives a damn how this disease entered their lives?

Queer Nation girls would hit the streets if the government started rounding up HIV-infected men and shipping them to quarantine camps. But how many of us are doing anything about the invisible quarantine that exists around the bodies of bisexual and lesbian women who have AIDS?

Maybe the handful of dykes who have AIDS are like the handful of men who had PCP in the seventies. Maybe they represent the tip of the iceberg, and ten years from now we will be sorry we didn't anticipate a deluge of lesbian AIDS cases. Maybe not. Maybe there will always be only a few women who have AIDS who want to have sex with and love other women.

There isn't enough money to go around to fight this disease. So is it okay if a dozen women a year die in isolation, and possibly infect others because they don't know any better? How about two dozen? Two hundred? A few thousand? What's an acceptable cutoff point before we divert resources to prevent this tragedy? What's the bottom line? Does it make a difference if these women don't speak English as their first language? If they are not white? What if they don't call themselves lesbians? Do they have to be in recovery? What if they have children? Maybe they want to have more children. Maybe they used to be hustlers. Maybe they still turn tricks.

It's confusing. It would be so much simpler to think about these issues if women would just be consistent, have simple identities, and stop behaving in complex ways that are affected by their culture and their need to survive. What we need is a little more monogamy and purity and all the other virtues of the white middle class. Including the money. Most of all, we could use the money.

Audre Lorde

from Zami: A New Spelling of My Name

Maybe it was her direct manner. Maybe it was the openness with which she appraised me as she motioned me towards the chair. Maybe it was the pants, or the informed freedom and authority with which she moved. But from the moment I walked into her house, I knew Eudora was gay, and that was an unexpected and welcome surprise. It made me feel much more at home and relaxed, even though I was still feeling sore and guilty from my fiasco with Bea, but it was refreshing to know I wasn't alone.

"I've been drinking for a week," she said, "and I'm still a little hung-over, so you'll have to excuse the mess."

I didn't know what to say.

Eudora wanted to know what I was doing in Mexico, young, Black, and with an eye for the ladies, as she put it. That was the second surprise. We shared a good laugh over the elusive cues for mutual recognition among lesbians. Eudora was the first woman I'd met who spoke about herself as a lesbian rather than as "gay," which was a word she hated. Eudora said it was a north american east-coast term that didn't mean anything to her, and what's more most of the lesbians she had known were anything but gay.

When I went to the market that afternoon, I brought back milk and eggs and fruit for her. I invited her to dinner, but she wasn't feeling much like eating, she said, so I fixed my dinner and brought it over and ate with her. Eudora was an insomniac, and we sat talking late late into the night.

She was the most fascinating woman I had ever met.

Born in Texas forty-eight years before, Eudora was the youngest child in an oil-worker's family. She had seven older brothers. Polio as a child had kept her in bed for three years, "so I had a lot of catchin' up to do, and I never knew when to stop."

In 1925, she became the first woman to attend the University of Texas, integrating it by camping out on the university grounds for four years in a tent with her rifle and a dog. Her brothers had studied there, and she was determined to also. "They said they didn't have living accommodations for women," Eudora said, "and I couldn't afford a place in town."

She'd worked in news all her life, both print and radio, and had followed her lover, Franz, to Chicago, where they both worked for the same paper. "She and I were quite a team, all right. Had a lot of high times together, did a lot of foolishness, believed a lot of things.

"Then Franz married a foreign correspondent in Istanbul," Eudora continued, drily, "and I lost my job over a byline on the Scottsboro case." She worked for a while in Texas for a Mexican paper, then moved into Mexico City for them.

When she and Karen, who owned La Señora, were lovers, they had started a bookstore together in Cuernavaca in the more liberal forties. For a while it was a rallying place for disaffected americans. This was how she knew Frieda.

"It was where people came to find out what was really going on in the states. Everybody passed through." She paused. "But it got to be a little too radical for Karen's tastes," Eudora said carefully. "The dress shop suits her better. But that's a whole other mess, and she still owes me money."

"What happened to the bookstore?" I asked, not wanting to pry, but fascinated by her story.

"Oh, lots of things, in very short order. I've always been a hard drinker, and she never liked that. Then when I had to speak my mind in the column about the whole Sobell business, and the newspaper started getting itchy, Karen thought I was going to lose that job. I didn't, but my immigration status was changed, which meant I could still work in Mexico, but after all these years I could no longer own property. That's the one way of getting uppity americans to keep their mouths shut. Don't rock big brother's boat, and we'll let you stay. That was right up Karen's alley. She bought me out and opened the dress shop."

"Is that why you broke up?"

Eudora laughed. "That sounds like New York talk." She was silent for a minute, busying herself with the overflowing ashtray.

"Actually, no," she said finally. "I had an operation, and it was pretty rough for both of us. Radical surgery, for cancer. I lost a breast." Eudora's head was bent over the ashtray, hair falling forward, and I could not see her face. I reached out and touched her hand.

"I'm so sorry," I said.

"Yeah, so am I," she said, matter-of-factly, placing the polished ashtray carefully back on the table beside her bed. She looked up, smiled, and pushed the hair back from her face with the heels of her hands. "There's never enough time to begin with, and still so damn much I want to do."

"How are you feeling now, Eudora?" I remembered my nights on the female surgery floor at Beth David. "Did you have radiation?"

"Yes I did. It's almost two years since the last one, and I'm fine now. The scars are hard to take, though. Not dashing or romantic. I don't much like to look at them myself." She got up, took down her guitar from the wall, and started to tune it. "What folksongs are they teaching you in that fine new university up the mountain?"

Eudora had translated a number of texts on the history and ethnology of Mexico, one of which was a textbook assigned for my history class. She was witty and funny and sharp and insightful, and knew a lot about an enormous number of things. She had written poetry when she was younger, and Walt Whitman was her favorite poet. She showed me some clippings of articles she had written for a memorial-documentary of Whitman. One sentence in particular caught my eye.

I met a man who'd spent his life in thinking, and could understand me
     no matter what I said. And I followed him to Harleigh in the snow.

The next week was Easter holidays, and I spent part of each afternoon or evening at Eudora's house, reading poetry, learning to play the guitar, talking. I told her about Ginger, and about Bea, and she talked about her and Franz's life together. We even had a game of dirty-word Scrabble, and although I warned her I was a declared champion, Eudora won, thereby increasing my vocabulary no end. She showed me the column she was finishing about the Olmec stone heads, and we talked about the research she was planning to do on African and Asian influences in Mexican art. Her eyes twinkled and her long graceful hands flashed as she talked, and by midweek, when we were not together, I could feel the curves of her cheekbone under my lips as I gave her a quick goodbye kiss. I thought about making love to her, and ruined a whole pot of curry in my confusion. This was not what I had come to Mexico to do.

There was an air about Eudora when she moved that was both delicate and sturdy, fragile and tough, like the snapdragon she resembled when she stood up, flung back her head, and brushed her hair back with the palms of her hands. I was besotted.

Eudora often made fun of what she called my prudishness, and there was nothing she wouldn't talk about. But there was a reserve about her own person, a force-field around her that I did not know how to pass, a sadness surrounding her that I could not breach. And besides, a woman of her years and experience—how presumptuous of me!

We sat talking in her house later and later, over endless cups of coffee, half my mind on our conversation and half of it hunting for some opening, some graceful, safe way of getting closer to this woman whose smell made my earlobes burn. Who, despite her openness about everything else, turned away from me when she changed her shirt.

On Thursday night we rehung some of her bark paintings from Tehuantepec. The overhead fan hummed faintly; there was a little pool of sweat sitting in one wing of her collarbone. I almost reached over to kiss it.

"Goddammit!" Eudora had narrowly missed her finger with the hammer.

"You're very beautiful," I said suddenly, embarrassed at my own daring. There was a moment of silence as Eudora put down her hammer.

"So are you, Chica," she said, quietly, "more beautiful than you know." Her eyes held mine for a minute so I could not turn away.

No one had ever said that to me before.

It was after 2:00 A.M. when I left Eudora's house, walking across the grass to my place in the clear moonlight. Once inside I could not sleep. I tried to read. Visions of Eudora's dear one-sided grin kept coming between me and the page. I wanted to be with her, to be close to her, laughing.

I sat on the edge of my bed, wanting to put my arms around Eudora, to let the tenderness and love I felt burn away the sad casing around her and speak to her need through the touch of my hands and my mouth and my body that defined my own.

"It's getting late," she had said. "You look tired. Do you want to stretch out?" She gestured to the bed beside her. I came out of my chair like a shot.

"Oh, no, that's all right," I stammered. All I could think of was that I had not had a bath since morning. "I—I need to take a shower, anyway."

Eudora had already picked up a book. "Goodnight, Chica," she said without looking up.

I jumped up from the edge of my bed and put a light under the waterheater. I was going back.

.   .   .

"What is it, Chica? I thought you were going to bed." Eudora was reclining exactly as I had left her an hour before, propped up on a pillow against the wall, the half-filled ashtray next to her hand and books littering the rest of the three-quarter studio bed. A bright towel hung around her neck against the loose, short-sleeved beige nightshirt.

My hair was still damp from the shower, and my bare feet itched from the dew-wet grass between our houses. I was suddenly aware that it was 3:30 in the morning.

"Would you like some more coffee?" I offered.

She regarded me at length, unsmiling, almost wearily.

"Is that what you came back for, more coffee?"

All through waiting for the *calendador* to heat, all through showering and washing my hair and brushing my teeth, until that very moment, I had thought of nothing but wanting to hold Eudora in my arms, so much that I didn't care that I was also terrified. Somehow, if I could manage to get myself back up those steps in the moonlight, and if Eudora was not already asleep, then I would have done my utmost. That would be my piece of the bargain, and then what I wanted would somehow magically fall into my lap.

Eudora's grey head moved against the bright serape-covered wall behind her, still regarding me as I stood over her. Her eyes wrinkled and she slowly smiled her lopsided smile, and I could feel the warm night air between us collapse as if to draw us together.

I knew then that she had been hoping I would return. Out of wisdom or fear, Eudora waited for me to speak.

Night after night we had talked until dawn in this room about language and poetry and love and the good conduct of living. Yet we were strangers. As I stood there looking at Eudora, the impossible became easier, almost simple. Desire gave me courage, where it had once made me speechless. With almost no thought I heard myself saying,

"I want to sleep with you."

Eudora straightened slowly, pushed the books from her bed with a sweep of her arm, and held out her hand to me.

"Come."

I sat down on the edge of the bed, facing her, our thighs touching. Our eyes were on a level now, looking deeply into each other. I could feel my heart pounding in my ears, and the high steady sound of the crickets.

"Do you know what you're saying?" Eudora asked softly, searching my face. I could smell her like the sharp breath of wildflowers.

"I know," I said, not understanding her question. Did she think I was a child?

"I don't know if I can," she said, still softly, touching the sunken place on her nightshirt where her left breast should have been. "And you don't mind this?"

I had wondered so often how it would feel under my hands, my lips, this different part of her. Mind? I felt my love spread like a shower of light surrounding me and this woman before me. I reached over and touched Eudora's face with my hands.

"Are you sure?" Her eyes were still on my face.

"Yes, Eudora." My breath caught in my throat as if I'd been running. "I'm very sure." If I did not put my mouth upon hers and inhale the spicy smell of her breath my lungs would burst.

As I spoke the words, I felt them touch and give life to a new reality within me, some half-known self come of age, moving out to meet her.

I stood, and in two quick movements slid out of my dress and underclothes. I held my hand down to Eudora. Delight. Anticipation. A slow smile mirroring my own softened her face. Eudora reached over and passed the back of her hand along my thigh. Goose-flesh followed in the path of her fingers.

"How beautiful and brown you are."

She rose slowly. I unbuttoned her shirt and she shrugged it off her shoulders till it lay heaped at our feet. In the circle of lamplight I looked from her round firm breast with its rosy nipple erect to her scarred chest. The pale keloids of radiation burn lay in the hollow under her shoulder and arm down across her ribs. I raised my eyes and found hers again, speaking a tenderness my mouth had no words yet for. She took my hand and placed it there, squarely, lightly, upon her chest. Our hands fell. I bent and kissed her softly upon the scar where our hands had rested. I felt her heart strong and fast against my lips. We fell back together upon her bed. My lungs expanded and my breath deepened with the touch of her warm dry skin. My mouth finally against hers, quick-breathed, fragrant, searching, her hand entwined in my hair. My body took charge from her flesh. Shifting slightly, Eudora reached past my head toward the lamp above us. I caught her wrist. Her bones felt like velvet and quicksilver between my tingling fingers.

"No," I whispered against the hollow of her ear. "In the light."

"Ruth Ellis, Golden Threads Celebration 1995,"
from the documentary *Golden Threads,*
by Marian Roth/Wildlight Productions

Melanie Kaye/Kantrowitz

Grogging

from Meditations on Choice: New York, 1994

if i could stop here. if it hadn't happened. it's purim, ramadan. last night erev purim a continent apart we each went to shul to hear how a jewish woman saved her people from massacre.

each of us at the queer shul: cbst, shaar zahav. at cbst sharon the rabbi wore shorts, the crowd was wild and raucous, many in costume, in drag. in the row behind me three women all in black leotards with pink netting around the waist, and a pink net puff in their hair waved pink puff wands. they sat with their children and i couldn't tell which child was whose. when it came to the part where the king orders vashti to dance naked, and she refuses *absolutely,* read the text, we all clapped and hurrahed and one of the pink-net women shouted *absolutely, absolutely, vashti refuses absolutely* and shook her wand. i loved her fierceness. and when vashti is exiled, when esther replaces her—a scab—i wanted you there with me

then came a break for the children's costume contest. i am sick of scores and judgment—but the winners were, like the non-winners, adorable: a tiny girl cow, who the announcer knew and called by name, *our chana the cow.* the second winner was a boy knight, he came from the row of pink-net women and when his victory was announced (and he, like the cow, won a fine wooden grogger) the whole row of pink net women and children cheered wildly and shouted his name, *rafi, rafi.* they weren't afraid to be so out there, the women, cheering for their boy. he beamed and flashed his tinfoil sword, not afraid to be caught feeling pride and pleasure, and i thought, that child is loved.

then i went to the bima to read the part where esther denounces haman to the king. i could pronounce everything and i got to say, *IT IS HAMAN!* and everyone grogged and grogged. i laughed and right at that moment i had a hot flash, and i just breathed because what else could i do and it passed and i sat down, while the story takes haman to the high gallows, the grogging a bit muted, some of us troubled by bloodlust.

last night a continent apart we each heard in shul how a jewish woman saved her people from massacre. this morning the news. hebron. the tomb of abraham. to massacre muslims kneeling to pray—is that a jewish thing to do? nachuma, i wish we were stronger. i imagine someone enters the shul, mine or yours, spitting bullets. the soldiers stand by or shoot too.

today a continent apart four o'clock finds us each at the israeli consulate to say with our bodies, a jew did this not in our name. their foreheads were touching the floor, in prayer. the blood. goldstein a doctor. one funeral home refused to prepare his body. in his eulogy the rabbi said, *one million arabs are not worth one jewish fingernail.* i want to carve the words out of his heart, his jewish heart i would give anything to disown. *the chosen chosen chosen.* if sarah and hagar had cheered for each other's children. we are all worth exactly the same, priceless.

January 1994

Joan Larkin

To Spirit

. . . God of breathing,
I pray that my mother will make her breakfast and really eat it,
that she will wash herself and walk to the kitchen without falling,
that my brother will shut up about the nursing home,
that she will dress herself in mint and pink polyester,
pay her rent,
take heart medicine,
sleep through the night,
read a book again.

That her friend Sandy will bring soup,
that Mary Hoyt will sit with her,
Marian shop for her,
Meals On Wheels feed her.
That nightmare will not harrow her,
no man frighten her,
my brother not bully her, bully her,

God, do not abandon us in our age
or worse, let condescending children control us.

For choice is the life spirit in her
even as she becomes a child.

And as work is taken from us,
and as home is taken from us,
and as sex is taken from us,
and as the body is taken from us,
and writing is taken
and the mind lightens
and we are divested even of sense—
let Self remain—
and choose—
Spirit, all praise to You—
choose, even on the last day.

"Great Sand Dune" by Margaret Randall

III

Drinking the Rain

Friendship

"Maua Flowers and Bruni Vega" by Morgan Gwenwald

Carol O'Donnell

The Telephone Call

It takes some people a while to figure out they're being ignored. Not me. I can feel another mind ho-humming right away. A girl I haven't seen in two years, somebody from high school, calls me up and asks me to name the three people I admire most. What kind of question is that? Folks who leave Wee-haukin Valley think the rest of us here are stuck, dinosaurs in a coal mine. They think 'cause they talk about sex on the phone that they're having more of it, that theirs is hotter. It doesn't matter if they flock to worse or better jobs. They al-ways come back with booklists and expensive chocolates. And explain to me please, why we are "fifteen years behind the rest of the world" because we call tomato pizza "reds" and cheese pizza "whites"? They want us to take them to rattlesnake roundups and deer hunts, and then they wonder how we can stand to have neighbors named Moose, Petey, and Junior.

"Tell me about New York," I ask Cory, and she laughs, wondering how any-one could be so childish. And like all those New Yorkers—cousins, the doctors where I work, the hospital's visitors—she starts breaking up the city into so many little pieces, Upper this, Lower that, easts and wests of everything. They make New York confetti, and then they throw it at you. Not me. I close my eyes and set up the whole valley on a game board. The mountains are still and steady when people aren't. I touch a different tree every day—stop my car, rub the bark, play rough with the roots. I can hop roads, skim woods, dangle from railroad bridges if I want to. The Valley runs off my screen in Jr. Pac-Man scenes, ready forever to be fished from the edge.

Who has time for admiring three people MOST? I admire people who can make a story out of anything, out of a squirrel with a pork chop bone, out of vacuuming a hall runner. I admire the person who invented the magnet on top of the can opener, and nurses who wink at you before they take your blood. I admire the people that everyone admires: Sylvester Stallone and Madonna, the Pope, the Kennedys, especially Caroline and John-John. And my parents. Yeah, they're cute.

"No Shannon, not movie stars. I mean real heroes like Gandhi and Harriet Tubman."

I refuse to answer because everybody knows the Pope is not a movie star, and for some reason, Cory thinks she's the needle and I'm the thread. If Cory were really interested, she'd ask what it's like to help raise Mary's daughter, Sherri, or not be able to make a patient smile.

I mean, I like Cory. We went to school together, we're both gay, but that's another thing . . . being gay is all she wants to talk about. She's got a whole grocery list of people we know, and she asks about every damn one like she's having them for dinner. She knows I don't see anybody anymore, what with livin' with Mare who's super-jealous. I get darts and daggers thrown at me the entire time I'm on the phone the way it is. Mare starts narrowin' her eyes at me until even little Sherri's a xerox of her mother, and everyone's looking at me from behind venetian blinds. Mary finally stomps into the bathroom, pointing to the clock like Vanna on *Wheel of Fortune,* purposely trying to make my Hummel figures fall over.

I whisper to Cory, so she'll realize I'm not just a heifer on a hill, "I got my eye on a few chicks at the hospital."

"CHICKS?" she asks real loud, so it's a good thing Mare isn't in the room. "Is that the word you think of when you see a woman you like?"

When I see a woman I like, I don't think words. I hear cymbals; I see an arm slip out of a sleeve. Chicks is just what I say. When I spot a good-looking woman, I start imagining her. Pets, passions, the thought that makes her saddest. A teacup collection? Does she bake lasagna, play the accordion; maybe she's the sporty type who fishes at Lake Wallenpaupack. Anything's better than all the TV Mare and I watch. Mary doesn't like going out because she says you can't really be yourself anywhere anyway, and the bars are full of butch mashers who want to come between couples. She always closes her eyes when she says this and won't open them until I agree.

Not having friends right now is sort of like not having clean clothes. You just have to make do until the big day. After all, your friends are your furniture and your lover is your house. Mare and I do everything together: we work the same hospital, she takes aerobics while I'm in the weight room, we go to the playground with Sherri almost every evening and hang on the monkey bars. I cook pasta, she does meat. Gay women in the Valley spend so much time looking for Miss Right that you have to get used to your friends being breezes, going, going, gone.

Once I was in Keefer's Army and Navy, just about to finger the flannels when I saw this woman peer out from behind the down jacket rack. She knew that I was, and I knew that she was. The look on her face could've cleared a racetrack. I mean HUNGRY, I mean so desperate that she forgot why she was there. Everywhere I went she followed: Joe Nardone's Gallery of Sound, the pizza place, Boscove's, card shops, until I couldn't stand it anymore and left.

I don't ever want to be that lonely. I want to be able to look a woman right in the eye and appreciate her for the moment. I'd like to tell Cory this, and how, when I set up my game board of the Valley, I'm always making sudden turns and reverses, hoping to bump into everything at once: the porch, the rockers, friends, a lover. Cory does this to me every two years—calls, stirs up so much that I swear I'm pregnant in my head. Nothing changes. The nights get a little friendlier out on the porch, and I tell Mare to turn down the TV so I can hear the glider moan and little Sherri talking to her unicorn. I might try to explain this to Cory except she already hung up, telling me I'm more sexist than her father.

"Christopher Street, NYC, 1988" by Kathryn Kirk

M.C. Randall

C.I.W.

I can write about this place only from the outside, yet even so, it will seem more "inside" than many people have ever been. C.I.W.—California Institute for Women—is surrounded by steel fencing, topped with rolls of sharp, shiny wire. The first time I visited, I was frightened. Sometimes I still am.

The long, low buildings are set in an open field. There is a sense of winter here, even in summer heat, a winter of stubble and dried weeds, not beautiful snow and peaceful silences.

Inside the glass doors, a small, square table, with forms and a pen. The name of the person you're visiting. Among the mundane is heartbreak. The card asks our relationship; I write "friend," and wish we could do things friends normally do—go to the movies, go shopping, take a walk. I sign my name on the line marked "signature" and drop the small white sheet into a box with others like it. I sit on an uncomfortable, hard, orange plastic chair and watch the children across from me on a green sofa. They wriggle and poke each other, as if compelled by the furniture to increase their own, and each other's, discomfort. Their grandmother, ignoring them, leafs through a magazine.

My name is called. I go to the counter, take off my shoes and earrings and bracelet and place them all in a wooden box. My change purse, see-through plastic, special for the occasion, goes into the box too. After relinquishing my driver's license, I step through the metal detector. The detector doesn't buzz—I've done this before.

They return my shoes, and let me outside. I stand in a small pen, electric gates on both sides, six-foot metal fencing all around. There is a tall tower and a small figure—a man—at the top. Buzz! The gate opens. I go inside and walk down a path planted with roses.

Beyond the roses, grass, and The Fence. In the center, several low buildings. I am glad it is sunny. The guards get nervous and snappish in the fog—in limited visibility, escape attempts increase. Last winter, a woman threw her coat over the fence, a fabric barrier between the bright wire and her legs. She managed to scale up and got stuck halfway over. The guards found her there and laughed. Told her she'd better get down and hope she landed on the right side. Otherwise, they'd shoot her.

The institution places a lot of emphasis on separation, on coldness, on what they view (no doubt) as "individual responsibility." The inmates often respond by moving to protect each other in any way they can. My friend Norma—"Norm"—is a lifer, an old-timer, an elder. Her "kids"—younger women—turn to her for advice on how to survive, stay out of trouble. Sometimes trouble comes knocking—like the woman who died in her cell last year, due to inadequate medical attention. That required response. The women went on strike, demanding better medical care.

Strike? It is a news flash to most outsiders that prisoners work. For instance, a guard can take his car to the auto mechanics class and get it repaired for the price of parts. Labor is eighty-five cents an hour.

Today Norm comes through the door wearing blue jeans, moving fast. White T-shirt against dark skin. Dancing eyes. Short hair with gray in the waves. She hugs me. We're allowed to touch only twice—when I arrive, when I leave.

She got a letter from someone in Germany. Can't read the letter, which is in German, but recognizes her name. She is pleased to get mail from so far away. All prisoners know this—the more visible you are on the outside, the safer on the inside.

She's angry with a new inmate, who has become famous for killing the man who molested her child, and who is now fighting to survive cancer. I am startled—it seems like the new woman's had a hard time, deserves sympathy. Norm explains:

"She's demanding 'special privileges' around her cancer—special diet, more time with the doctor. There are other sick women in here. Several with AIDS, who get almost no medical care. Her—the TV shows love her. But when she's interviewed, she never mentions anyone but herself."

Norm sits, not across the table, but right next to me, and as I twist sideways to see her, I wonder why. Then I notice the two women behind her, leaning into each other, not quite touching. Between them longing so fierce, it shimmers. Beneath the table, their legs are intertwined, a sight blocked by Norm's body. One—in prison blues—glances at Norm, who smiles.

Donna Allegra

The Birthday Presence

When Odette sashayed over to our table, the snow had salted her eyebrows and the dissolving flakes glistened on her skin. She swept off her cape in a large seamless movement that cast snowflakes swirling around the immediate vicinity, sprinkling us all, and causing the fire in the grate behind our table to sniffle. The cloche hat which covered her head, the scalp shorn sleek as a waxed seal, remained in place.

She strode directly to where Leslie sat and fixed Leslie's attention by singing, "Heavy birdy doo doo, heavy birdy doo doo. Heavy birdie dear Lezzie, heavy birdy doo doo." Odette then handed Leslie a paper-wrapped bouquet saying, "The flowers were all frozen, so I brought you carrots instead," and indeed, under the dark green tendrils, Odette handed over bright orange stalks.

Odette then sat in a chair at the edge of the table, quite pleased with herself. She hummed the tune of Stevie Wonder's version of the birthday song. At this point, all the straight couples, trios and quartets in the restaurant openly stared at us. Our table sat seven women ranging from late twenties through forty, with me in the middle distance.

With Odette's arrival, Leslie now had to make her fourth round of introductions: her lover, Janice; Diane and Barbara, in their glowing twenties; Elizabeth, single and seductive, bracing the far end of the age bracket; and me.

Odette already knew Elizabeth, Janice, and of course, Leslie. Odette likely would have been as surprised as I was that we had a common friend in the birthday girl, but apparently, I didn't hold a place in her memory. I knew, or rather, recognized, Odette from dance class.

She'd always stand front and center during the warm-up as if to dare the teacher's attention to fall, like lightning, upon her for corrections. When it came time to learn the choreography, Odette would position herself to stand directly behind Kaya or Rafaella or whoever was conducting the intermediate jazz class I occasionally had the nerve to take. I always wondered, often with longing, sometimes with distaste, how Odette had the gumption to learn and make her mistakes at the front of the room before God and everyone. But then, even her errors had style.

At our table in The Natural Way Restaurant, as in dance classes, Odette seemed to relish being in the company of others with whom she could engage. I was already making excuses in my mind in order to leave early, probably right after I finished my entree. All these women were smarter, more attractive and wittier than I. And where was the waitress anyway?

Elizabeth, as regal as her royal name, said in her clipped British accent, "So Leslie, when is your girlfriend due to arrive and bless us with her presence?"

I felt confused and wondered why Elizabeth was blind to Janice's hand caressing Leslie's back? That was a girlfriend's palm resting at Leslie's waist, a girlfriend's fingers playing on Leslie's thigh, all indications of loverhood. Though such open displays of affection left me feeling embarrassed at best, I could sometimes peep upon others' intimacy to fuel my own fantasies.

Barbara, as perplexed as I was by Elizabeth's "girlfriend" remark, spoke up. "Janice is right here," and Elizabeth, as if waiting for that very cue, mimed surprise. Then she spoke her punch line, "Oh, I thought she was blonde. I do hope I didn't blow it, did I?"

Odette immediately chimed in, "Dag, Leslie, I told you to brief everyone about the other woman beforehand."

"Well, I thought you all knew, except Janice, of course," Leslie replied. To Janice she said, "Sweetie, there's a little something I've been meaning to tell you. Maybe we can have a chat later tonight." Janice chuckled and wagged her finger at Elizabeth, as if to chide, "Bad dog."

Barbara laughed then as well, pink amusement creeping into her face. I'd have blushed my embarrassment if I could, for not picking up on the joke, but fortunately, the chagrin heating my face wasn't so obvious as Barbara's new-grown rose.

A waitress finally came to take our orders, and Odette asked only for tea. Unlike the rest of the company present, she left the rich black squares of bread to rest in their wicker basket, poorly defended by the gingham cloth topping.

Odette hadn't said anything about the dance classes we had in common at Jazz Town Studios and thus confirmed my certainty that she did not recognize me at all. Probably because she was so stuck on herself in the mirror throughout class that she could hardly notice who else might be in attendance. Well, I wasn't going to say anything to feed that already overstuffed ego and add to her conceit. Diane bit off a crust of bread and remarked, "Odette, Claudia is a dancer too."

Odette looked at me from her elegant hooded eyes and said, "I thought I recognized you from class. You take Kaya Thursday nights and Rafaella on Tuesdays, sometimes, right? I nodded, in the hope to shut her up, rather than encourage her. "You have good form, why are you so timid with the movements?" she flung at me, as if she were a prosecuting attorney and I a criminal defendant. I felt both flattered and shamed. So she had noticed me in class, but now I wished she'd be quiet about it. I thought she had eyes only for the good dancers, like herself.

She complained to everyone at our table, "This woman has excellent placement and an elephant's memory for steps and she won't take up any space in the dance studio. If I could get the dance sequence as well as Claudia does from the back of the room, I wouldn't have to ride the teacher's behind so closely. Do you know how hard it is for me to be on the alert about her stopping short and finding me rammed up her ass?" Barbara, clearly tickled, looked to Diane to share her delight in how Odette took the stage.

To me Odette said, "Have I embarrassed you enough or should I tell them about the excellent figure of a woman that you insist on hiding under baggy sweatpants and layers of T-shirt?" Again she spoke as if aggrieved. She sighed to the others about me, "Ah, life just isn't fair." Finally she languished to silence.

By now I couldn't hold back or adequately disguise the pleasure I felt that Odette not only had marked me in dance class, but had my number down to the decimals. The fire behind the grate gave off a cackling sound.

The waitress returned with our entrees, relieving me from the hot seat. Everyone's interest now turned to her meal and everyone else's food. Odette took upon herself the task of filling all our water glasses as we ate. She managed to remain unobtrusive with her presence. Still, I was all too aware of how she sat quietly, occasionally sipping from her teacup.

I quickly finished my Buddha's Delight platter of steamed vegetables and brown rice and then felt at a loss for what to do as the others continued eating. Even Barbara seemed to possess more poise than I had, though heaven spare me from having to go through my twenties again. Odette smiled my way for a moment, and continued her mild rocking to the music filtering through the room, a kind of New Age answer to Muzak.

I wondered what Odette was thinking. Chastened that I'd read her entirely wrong, while she knew my act in dance class down to a tee and still smiled my way, I felt petty. Clearly more heart than ego pumped through the soul of her. I was good for getting up on my high horse, but now I tired of riding that pony. The saddle of criticism just left me bruised and sore.

What also softened me towards Odette was that she expressed admiration for me. It takes a moment to smooth my ruffled feathers, but I can turn around with a change of heart. Surely there is pardon for sinners, mercy for the wicked?

When it appeared that everyone was at least close to finished eating, Odette proclaimed to the table at large, "I'd say it's about time for a gathering of the presents." Clearly she was someone used to taking command of a situation. She didn't give orders, but people naturally obeyed someone as sure of herself as Odette.

I obediently dislodged my birthday card and cassette tape from the large pocket in my coat and passed it over to Leslie. I hoped she would not read the card aloud. I'd written "Many happy returns to a friend who asks only for my presence."

Odette opened the portfolio she'd placed on an empty chair when she'd come in, and pulled out a cylinder of scrolled papyrus. Elizabeth, Janice, Diane and Barbara put their gifts on the table and Leslie laughed or exclaimed over each one.

Elizabeth had given her Audre Lorde's *Sister Outsider.* Janice handed over a hand-knitted red sweater from which fell satin hearts and flowers when Leslie unfurled the bulky fabric. Diane and Barbara had gotten Leslie a gift certificate to Eve's Garden and a packet of several issues of *On Our Backs.* I'd made a cassette recording of my favorite sacred music—Gregorian chants, gospel choirs, and a cappella selections. Odette's scroll unfolded to reveal a careful handprinting of "The Song of Solomon." She'd also included incense in the flavors of the scents mentioned in that Bible book: frankincense, myrrh, spinkenard, calamus.

I let loose an "ummm" of approval over the time and effort that Odette must have put into the task. She heard me and shrugged her dance-sculpted shoulders. "It kept me out of trouble between classes."

Leslie seemed genuinely pleased with everyone's gift. I wanted to cheer for us all. These were good friends and I was proud to number among them. Yet, why was I ever resistant to take part in social gatherings?

With the meal over, as was the unwrapping of the presents, Barbara and Diane engaged in a conversation with Elizabeth, who held court at her end of the table. Elizabeth too is a graceful woman and held enormous allure, but I didn't want her to know I felt this, lest she laugh at or toy with me.

After the waitress left us with coffee refills, Janice and Leslie started to pass glances between each other like kittens in a litter who had been wrestling with each other and scolded to behave. The reprimand didn't hold for long; they were starting to sneak cuddles, clearly wanting to play.

Now was clearly the time for me to go. I'm usually the third leg around a couple or fifth wheel in a group. I've learned to leave early before I feel too lonely in the crowd as the odd woman out.

I started calculating: since Diane and Barbara lived in Park Slope, as did Leslie and Janice, they'd all likely go in Elizabeth's car. Odette seemed like someone who could gather her cape around herself and have it turn into a magic carpet that would whisk her home. More likely, she'd hail a cab and a dozen taxis would screech to a halt at her feet.

I thought it clever how I ferreted out her address. On a day when Odette had arrived to dance class just ahead of me on line, I took note of the last name she gave to William who sat at the reception desk taking class cards. Her last class had been stamped, so she needed to buy a new card for a series of ten classes. I casually looked at the check she handed William and saw the spelling of her name: Odette Cousins.

Once I returned home, I checked the phone book and found an address on East 5th Street. Like me, she lived close to the dance studio. We were neighbors, barely half a mile away from each other.

I was ready for the walk across town from this West Village restaurant to my East Village walk-up. I turned to say as much to Leslie and saw her lean into Janice's shoulder to whisper. Leslie was flirting with her lover, using her breasts as bait. She was quite proud of those breasts and played them often to good effect. I certainly found them more than just a little distracting at times. There'd be no breaking into their conversation now.

I shifted my gaze to Janice's hair, falling like a stream from a faucet, across her back. When I turned to look away, I found Odette regarding me with interest. She said, "You caught me staring. I hate to be rude, but I also don't want to give up the view."

I couldn't think of anything to say and again the waitress acted as an angel of mercy by arriving with the check, which Odette immediately took charge of. "Okay, five thousand dollars divided six ways. Birthday woman is not included on this deal," she declared.

Leslie said, "Well, I'm glad to see you haven't lost any of your bullying ways, hon."

"It's called assertiveness, Les," Elizabeth said. "Take charge of your life, and everyone else's as well."

To my surprise, I was enjoying the company and repartee. I was no longer so ready to leave and go home alone.

Despite what Elizabeth had said and in contrast to my first impressions, it had become clear to me that Odette didn't need to be in the spotlight all the time. I'd been wrong to assume she'd use people to highlight her performance on center stage. I'd seen her sit quietly at the table with her tea, alive to the surroundings, interested in others, and I was now more intrigued by her than self-consciously uncomfortable with myself. People who can be still in a crowd compel my attention far more than cymbals clashing.

I now felt giddy with an inspiration towards Odette, so tipsy, in fact, you'd think my water had been turned to wine. Fast on the heels of the feeling, an idea, pure gift, settled on me.

The water glass seemed as expendable an item as any. When I was certain no one watched closely, I tipped mine over. "Oh," I said with a gasp of surprise. The rivulet pooled by my plate, then seeped into the tablecloth.

I was right in my second estimation of Odette. It took her only a second to come to my end of the table with her cloth napkin to sop the puddle I easily could have contained. She held no criticism in her manner for my apparent carelessness.

"Ah, thanks," I said.

"No major damage," she replied.

"Who else do you take class with?" Now that I had her at my beck and call, I planned to keep her here for a while.

"Kaya is my mainstay for jazz and Lonnie is my ballet master. I go to Joffrey sometimes and let him stretch me within an inch of my life."

"I haven't been a ballet girl for a while now. What times does he teach?" I asked.

"Oh, we should make a date to do that class together sometime."

"Yes, that'd be good," I said of the brilliant idea I had been leading her to propose for us.

Leslie entered the conversation. "Well, now that the dancers have connected, it's all over for the rest of us mere mortals ever getting on board the discussion."

As if in response to my unspoken question or maybe to the edge apparent in her voice, Leslie said to me, "You know Claudia, when Odette and I lived together, the only way I could get any nuptial attention out of her was to pencil myself around her dance class schedule."

"A girl's got to know her priorities and keep them in order," Odette responded.

"I had hopes of being further up on the list, but that was in our past life," Leslie put in quickly, backing off from what was still a sore spot between them. "Oh anyway, everyone, I decided that I'll just have to let Odette duke out dance class with someone else." Leslie finished raising her water glass in toast to Odette.

I could see this was an old argument for them, a familiar merry-go-round covering the same territory, but breaking no new ground. Odette had declined to take up the gauntlet and Leslie let it lay there with a laugh.

I could easily understand Odette's side in this. The way I'd voiced the dilemma in the weekly group-therapy meeting, where Leslie and I had met, was to say, "How can I have a girlfriend and still go to class?" Or else I'd console myself in a private conversation with Leslie by saying, "Besides, who wants a girlfriend when I can dance?" We both knew this was a smoke screen I raised to keep people from getting too close, and anyone within talking distance was too close for my taste.

Odette sighed and her eyes held Leslie's. The look that passed between them contained understanding, regret, clemency. Now I remembered when Leslie had requested, then demanded, my presence at this birthday fete. I'd teased with her, "It's a good thing this party is not on a night I have dance class or else I couldn't make it and you'd be out of luck." Her response held an odd vibe, like I'd dropped a stone down a hole without a bottom. After a moment, she finally said lightly, "Yes, we'd both be out of luck then."

Diane and Barbara were making motions to gather their possessions and ready themselves to leave. Elizabeth also seemed like she would welcome a cue to exit.

Janice said, "Well girlies, what say you we call this a night? I'd figured on putting the birthday girl to bed early, but it's a little late for that now."

My watch read 9:30. I was starting to feel tuckered and torn myself. We gathered our belongings, divided up the check, not allowing Leslie to pay for anything.

Outside the restaurant, the snow fell softly, like the flakes in those glass globes. All seven of us stood outside on the powdered street, readying to do the last movement of the social dance by saying our "good nights."

Janice discovered she had left her umbrella in the restaurant and went back inside to get it. The snow started to fall like rapid tears, moist and melting instantly. This was the moment when winter could be beautiful in New York, before traffic plowed the white element under, leaving slush and grime in its wake. I looked upwards, my face open to the giving sky.

Odette put a secreting arm around Leslie and I overheard Odette say, ". . . I couldn't have chosen a better woman for you." The silence between them spoke volumes. I watched them reflected in a glass door and wished I could enter that warmth and snuggle between the two of them.

Leslie finally made a reply, sphinx-like, "Well, I'm working on one for you," and Odette looked quizzically and asked, "You don't mean . . ."

I couldn't see or hear Leslie's response because Janice burst out the glass door, triumphant, bringing a fan of warm air and food smells from the restaurant. "Got it," she happily announced.

The wind that had been tempered and tame exhaled a gust that caught Odette's cloche hat in the updraft. The black felt cap rolled awkwardly across the sidewalk, like a winter-wrapped grade-schooler, pushed relentlessly by the wind, and was swallowed into a sewage drain at the end of the block.

Odette's shaven head gleamed in the cold. She had caramel-colored skin with red and gold tones; a freshly-cut mahogany, I finally decided, and now it was exposed to the bite of the wind.

Without stopping to think or restrain myself, I unraveled the African fabric from around my neck and went over to Odette. "Here," I said, and I began to make a minor production out of wrapping the cloth around Odette's naked scalp. I took my time, savoring the scent that rose from her—a hint of frankincense, vanilla and something maddening that I couldn't place, but would gladly bury myself in.

I could have finished tying the head wrap a lot sooner, but that wasn't my intention. I didn't even need to concentrate on getting the elaborate tie correct. What filled my mind was a thought of one of my favorite transition steps in dance, pas de bourrée. In one of its more common variations, you took a step to the back, one to the side, and then to the front. The step didn't necessarily take you anywhere, but a pas de bourrée let you reposition yourself for a change in direction.

"There," I finally pronounced. "That gelee," I motioned her to move as I pretended a critical inspection of my handiwork, "looks far better on you than it ever did on me, so please do me the favor of keeping it."

The head wrap did look good. Everyone had gathered around to watch. I was so used to wearing African fabrics that I forgot their effect on others. And I did have a remarkable talent for tying cloth into head wraps. I am not a very assertive person in conversation. I lack Leslie's flair, Elizabeth's class and Odette's flamboyant high style, but I have my ways to get my fair share of attention. And just so she wouldn't forget me, I put another tuck in the wrap I'd fitted to her scalp.

We all stood around Odette to oooh and ahhh from different angles. For once she seemed a bit flustered from the attention, poor baby. Something other than the cold weather had planted shining apples in Odette's cheeks. I took sly pleasure in how Leslie poured the compliments on, tormenting Odette even more. I hadn't anticipated what a role model Leslie had become for me, but I could see it in my new behavior. I'd have to study her ways more closely.

"This is such a gorgeous design; I couldn't take it from you," Odette protested, sincerely touched.

"Well, you'll have to get used to owning it. It'll grow on you—kind of like a haircut," I teased, and that last clause made her smile.

"Well . . ." she allowed. "Thanks. I don't know how I'll repay you. It's precious fabric."

Leslie put in, "It's a gift, sweetie. Just say 'thank you' and then shut up."

"Or pass it on to the next woman," Elizabeth suggested. I truly enjoyed how Odette looked—her face held the startle of a horseback rider about to be thrown from her pony.

My previous calculations as to the rides home had been accurate. Elizabeth dangled her keys around the circle of Brooklyn girls to indicate that she would be driving them. Odette and I were the Manhattan residents and both on the east side of town.

"Are you within walking or cab-hailing distance?" I asked, as if I didn't know, but wanting to check her preference.

"The latter, but given racial politics in this town, it usually ends up as the former that takes me back to East 5th Street," Odette said with a mockery she knew I'd understand.

Leslie, who'd been occupied with wrapping her sweater more tightly under her coat, said, "Claudia, you and Odette must share a cab cross town. This weather is so treacherous. I'd worry myself sick if I didn't see you safely into a taxi."

"Why don't we start walking?" Odette invited, despite Leslie's suggestion. "We can talk shop about dance. The weather isn't that bad, Leslie," she coaxed.

Leslie made as if to protest, but surrendered before we could take her seriously. We all gave hugs and kisses good-bye. Leslie had requested my presence for this birthday fete, but I felt I was going home with a gift to unwrap.

After we waved Elizabeth's car off, I said, "Let's go," and with a little pas de bourrée, Odette fell in step beside me.

"Mari, I'm Sorry" by Zoe Leonard

Chea Villanueva

from Girlfriends

JUNE 9, 1986

Dear Wilnona,

You better sit down before you reads this and I knows you ain't gonna believe it, but Miz Pearly say she ain't gonna do it no more! I couldn't believe it, either, but after she done told me what all happened to her, Lord have mercy, I don't think I want to, either! Now I knows why you stay in that little apartment by yourself and not sleep with nobody for two years. After what happened to poor Miz Pearly I don't blame you one bit.

Anyways, like I tol' you in the last letter, Pearly had this big date comin' up with this oriental gal. Now I could never understand what she see in them hussies, but you know Pearly always was a little touched in the head (and after her and Miss Nadine broke up she just been a little more outta hand).

Well, Friday evenin' came and Pearly went and got herself a new suit *and new shoes*. (I knew this one was important 'cause she didn't bother to wear them high-top sneakers like she always do.) And finally she rush on over to the barbershop to get her hair cut and all slicked back.

Well, by the time Pearly got home, Miss Nadine was there. Now you know somethin' was up 'cause ole Nadine ain't been home in a long time (and I hear tell that was part a the reason they got a divorce). But Nadine sure been jealous lately.

Miz Pearly's new girlfriend been callin' her up just 'bout every night, and
Miss Nadine was havin' a fit! But Pearly didn't pay her no mind and right away
starts gettin' ready for this big date. While Pearly was takin' her bath, Nadine was
answerin' the phone and lookin' through all the stuff that Pearly bought. Girl, she
even found the present that Miss Pearly was gonna take to Miss Ju-Lee (that Miz
Pearly new girlfriend name). I never found out what it was, but you know Pearly
buys her women nice things. She used to buy Miss Nadine all kinds a gold chains
and earrings, diamond rings, fancy clothes, and *all* the right stuff. But you know,
Nadine never did care for the stuff. (Never deserved any of it, either!)

Girl, if I wasn't hooked up with ole Bessie I'd go for Miz Pearly myself. Ha!
(And I hears she real good in bed, too).

Well, by the time Pearly got done scrubbin', cuttin' her nails, brushed her
teeth with Ultra Bright, and combed her hair till you could see yourself in the
shine, Miss Nadine was really mad. When Pearly walk outta the bathroom Nadine was sittin' there like some big ole nasty spider. That's when she tell Pearly
that her girlfriend call and that she (Nadine) don't want her to go anyplace that
night. Poor Miz Pearly. It was already eight o'clock and she only had a hour to
get ready to meet this gal. And anyway, Miss Nadine had no right to do that to
her, 'cause they been broken up all this time and all of a sudden she wanna be
with Pearly.

But Pearly stayed and the two of them start to argue. Girl, the whole block
could hear *all* their carryins on! Nine o'clock came and went and they still be
screamin' and cussin'. Miz Pearly was callin' Miss Nadine a bitch and a dick
lover. Miss Nadine was callin' Miz Pearly a bulldagger and a motherfucker. And
the two of them be callin' each other a whole lotta nasty things! Girl, you know
I had the glass to the wall! I thought Pearly was gonna let loose and hit her this
time 'cause you know Miss Nadine really deserved it. But just when it was gettin' good, Nadine's family showed up at the door and the two of them shut up.
Do you know they came all the way from South America just to see ole Nadine? Well, you know Pearly. She always been polite to them people and her and
Miss Nadine were just the picture of the loving couple. Anyways, when Nadine
see her sister they start talkin' real good 'bout how was everything in the old
country, and Pearly see her chance to get away. She went right back into the
bathroom and started runnin' the shower water. I guess she worked up some
kinda sweat fightin' with Miss Nadine. By the time Pearly got done (again), Nadine went to the store and Pearly was rushin' to get her suit on. And then the
phone rang! It was Miz Pearly new girlfriend and she was cussin' up a storm,
'cause it was a quarter to eleven and Pearly ain't even left the house yet. (That

Miss Ju-Lee musta been wantin' Miz Pearly somethin' fierce, 'cause she been waitin' all that time.) Anyways, Pearly tried to explain what was goin' on, but Ju-Lee never did hear it 'cause she hung up before Pearly could say she'd be there in fifteen minutes. And Pearly so upset she almost tripped runnin' in them new shoes and forgot all 'bout the package she was gonna take to Ju-Lee.

Lucky for Miz Pearly that she caught a cab right away. She got there by eleven o'clock and was so happy that she give the driver a extra tip for gettin' her there so fast. Girl, them New York City drivers always good in a emergency!

Anyways, Miz Pearly went inside the bar (where she was meetin' Ju-Lee) and found her drunk and carryin' on like trash with these two white butches. And that Miss Ju-Lee just ignored Pearly like she was some kinda bum.

Well, the three of them start to dance and Ju-Lee starts to rubbin' herself all up in this white girl's face and just lovin' it! Poor Pearly just stood there watchin' the whole thing till Ju-Lee and the white girls went downstairs to the bathroom. They never did come back up, so Miz Pearly went to see what was goin' on. Anyways, there was Miss Ju-Lee standin' in the bathroom with her dress all pushed up around her neck and lettin' these two butches kiss all over her and justa feelin' her titties all over the place. Well, Miz Pearly started yellin' for Miss Ju-Lee till one a the white gals was ready to fight with her. And then that hussy Ju-Lee slap Pearly across the face and tell her she don't want nothin' to do with her ever again. Girl, I wish I coulda been a fly on the wall that night! Anyways, that Pearly can be so stupid sometimes. She went on up the stairs like nothin' happen, and come on home. And that was the end of Miz Pearly's big date.

But Lord have mercy! Wilnona, that's not all of it! The next day she never did hear from Ju-Lee and on Sunday she didn't hear from her, either, so she decided to go back to the club. I don't know if it was to look for Ju-Lee or what, but Pearly went outta the house that night lookin' wild.

Anyways, the way I heard it, Miz Pearly met these Koreans there and one of the gals took a liken to Pearly and they decides to go have some wild sex. Well, they ended up in some sleazy hotel by Washington Square, and when Miz Pearly get all her clothes off, the bitch pulls this big rubber dick outta a bag and wants to do it to Pearly! Well, you know Miz Pearly ain't havin' none a that and she throwed it out the window! Wilnona, I sure wish I coulda been there to see this big white dick come sailin' across the street! I bet some faggot justa snatched it up for himself. Well, after that it got a little rough 'cause then the gal get some handcuffs and a whip outta the bag and wanna do more stuff to Pearly. Poor Pearly damn near scared to death 'cause you know she ain't havin' none a that stuff, either and they starts to fightin'. I know you don't believe this, Wilnona, but it's the Lord's honest truth. I saw Pearly when she got home. She had hick-eys all over her neck and was all bruised from the bitch punchin' on her. Came home justa all shook up, but in one piece. (And I heard she had to jump outta the window with half her clothes on, too.)

Anyways, because of the Koreans, South Americans, and everybody else, Miz Pearly has had enough of women. Been typin' away on her typewriter till all hours a the night she ain't got time for anything. *Not even for a little pussy.*

Pearly say she don't do it no more, and ain't about to for a long time. Well, if Pearly don't, Mae *might,* and if I can convince her maybe she'll just pay me a visit sometime. Sure would be nice . . . Maybe you could use a little a Miz Pearly's lovin' yourself. Been too long since you had any and if you keep wearin' them socks and sweatpants with the crotch sewed up to bed you ain't never gonna get any. 'Cause Ci-Ci sure ain't gonna put up with that for too much longer. Ha!

Well, sis, write back soon. Give my love to Miss-Mae.

Love, your *horny* sister,
Mae-Mae

"June as the champ, West Oak Lane, Philadelphia, 1962,"
from *The Watermelon Woman: The Fae Richards Photo Archive*, 1995,
by Dunye/Leonard

Note: The archive of photographs was shot as a collaborative project by
Cheryl Dunye (filmmaker) and Zoe Leonard (photographer) for the film *The
Watermelon Woman*. Because the character, Fae "The Watermelon Woman"
Richards, is fictional, her photographic past was created by staging private
and public events from her illustrious life.

"Her Truck" by Margaret Randall

Hawk Madrone

Vigil

FRIDAY, JUNE 2, 1995

The sun skips from cloud to cloud, turning the manzanita leaves outside Tangren's living room window from gray to bright yellow-green, to gray again. The climate inside this house is similar, as Tangren moves through these days of grief, and hope, and hopelessness, of responsibility and blessing. One week ago her mother fell, injured her spinal cord, is paralyzed from her neck down. The doctors say now that there is no hope for recovery anywhere near approximating the life Jessie wishes for herself. Tangren, her three brothers, and father, have been vigiling in the intensive care unit at the hospital for seven days, struggling with decisions, with fear and despair. Now they must all decide if the machines keeping Jessie alive, keeping her breathing, keeping her lungs from filling with fluid, should be removed. Tangren asked Jessie if she wanted the family to make that decision, and Jessie's nod has given them permission to do what they believe is the truth for them, a truth these women and men have discussed many times together over the years. They have all promised each other many times not to keep any of them lingering before death by the use of "life-preserving" machines. And they have all made out living wills to declare this strong intent. So tomorrow, after Tangren's daughter has joined them from Portland, they will go forward, and the doctors say Jessie should die within a few hours.

My dog Muphin and I have been here since Monday, coming as soon as I could after getting a message from Tangren on Sunday, via a mutual friend at Writers'

Group, asking me to be with her. I took care of the essentials at home before I left: got all my house plants watered, the hens' food hopper and water trough filled, and wrote out instructions for my land partner. She'd have to take over the daily tending of the cats and hens, watering my many flower beds, as well as the work I had planned to do in our large all-season vegetable garden, work that would now fall to her shoulders in addition to her own chores and projects in our forty-acre isolated home. I packed enough kibble for Muphin for a week, staples for myself, and to share with Tangren, threw a variety of clothes into a duffel, boxed some paper and pens, a book, my journal, and set out for the two-hour drive by midmorning.

Here in Tangren's house that nestles on an Ashland hill, I feed Joe, her big black cat (bigger than Muphin's fourteen pounds), water the flower boxes on her small deck, take out the trash, clean the kitchen, make sure there is food prepared, answer the phone a lot, this last a stark contrast to my country life where there are no phones, not even a neighbor for three miles. Here the phone rings a few times each daytime hour and I bring callers up to date with the information Tangren gives me, gently break the news about Jessie to people who did not already know, connect people with each other. A lot of the time I am just hanging out, keeping my time open to be with Tangren whenever she is home from the hospital for good food and rest, and needs a listener. I give her my thoughts and try to ask helpful questions as she works her way through this moral and emotional dilemma, hold her while she cries, and just generally be here in whatever ways are helpful, including trying to be invisible when it's clear she needs some solitude.

And, yes, this is a stretch for me. Ashland is a lovely town, but it is a town, and some moments I feel pared down to too little of my reclusive country-living self. But this house sits above the town, with its back to it, in fact, and the canyon in front, the roar of Lithia Creek far below, snow-covered Mt. Ashland visible to the south, the paths I can drive to for long walks amidst beauty, Muphin's constant company . . . all comfort me, ground me, remind me of who I am.

I am honored that Tangren asked me to come, glad to be useful, glad to use my skills. A couple of days ago, when she was thanking me again for coming, she said there was no one else she'd want to accompany her right now. I was a little surprised at that for I think of Tangren as having lots of women friends, including ex-lovers, nearby. While we have been knowing each other for close to a decade, our friendship has not included the intimacies of family or relationship crises, though I have given her time as a co-counselor a couple of times. I've been a guest in her home maybe a dozen times in these years, sometimes making a weekend of it when Writers' Group meets for a Sunday here. At those times I have luxuriated in the comforts of this town house, and given myself a break from being so busy with the work at home, laid abed way past my usual hour. I read and wrote to my heart's content, and enjoyed Tangren, who appreciates and reflects my instinct for solitude interspersed with stimulating conversation. We share space easily, are comfortable with each other's habits, preferences, and proclivities, without any romantic entanglement. Maybe it's just this combination of connection and detachment that makes for the perfection of my companionship now when what is needed is my availability as well as my self-sufficiency.

I don't know how much longer I will be here—what day it will finally be easy enough for me to leave, for Tangren to be essentially on her own. There are other Lesbian friends who leave phone messages that they will be glad to nurture her if she calls on them. I shall certainly be here through tomorrow, when this story takes a dramatic leap and the hurdle of death and loss is cleared. Then there will be the ritual with the body, and the funeral. Perhaps once the death is done Tangren will feel free of much of the anguish of this week, and her usual solitude in her home will be more appealing than my company, however grateful she has been for my presence here.

My role here is so much behind the scene of the drama. I will never even see Jessie except as I remember her: proudly showing me the details of the magnificent house on the hill just above Tangren's house, the house Jessie planned and executed with her husband for their old age, the last of the many houses for which she was the contractor in her lifetime. She got to live in this dream house only a few months. I would like to smile to her face, to accompany her for a moment on this journey. But that is not for me, and I focus my caring on her daughter, my friend.

There are lessons for me in all this. The lesson of knowing that life can be stood on its head at any moment, that all expectations about the future can be erased in a flash. The lesson that service requires the suspension of ego, as well as the certainty of self-love, self-nurturance: if I am not well taken care of, I cannot be the caretaker I want to be, that my friend deserves. In this scene I am my own caretaker, so I take my vitamins and eat well, and get good sleep, and reach out for company that feeds me, like dinner out with Mab and Joan on Tuesday, a long sisterly phone call with Sarah Wednesday evening which sharpened my knowing of my own family, a long walk with Mab and frequent check-ins with her, and a walk with Tangren to a pond where I delighted in the birds.

Tangren came home this morning after another night at the hospital at her mother's side, getting but little rest stretched out awkwardly on a couple of chairs. A brother came by early to take up the watch, so Tangren could bring her exhaustion home. After a few hours' sleep, she came back downstairs and sat heavily on her low footstool in the living room. I moved to the floor in front of her, held her hand, attended her with my steady gaze as she talked about the ordeal of the night. Her words soon gave way to tears, tears that increased to full-flowing currents of her sadness for her mom, at the pathos of a vigorous and enthusiastic life cut shorter than Jessie had anticipated. Tangren leaned her head onto my shoulder and let her eyes and nose weep without restraint, without embarrassment, letting me midwife the deep release that left her feeling lighter.

After a long soothing shower, some food, and a sweet loving session with Joe, who has been missing Tangren's affection these last days, she asked for solitude on her deck where she meditated and sang and grieved alone. When I first heard her moaning, I wondered if I should ask if she wanted me after all, but thought better of that. She was doing what she needed to, and being alone with this loss is a truth only she can comfort sometimes. She came in later looking radiant, spoke of how thankful she feels that she and her family are having this time together, that they are helping each other through this passage so beautifully. "We are doing the right thing" she said, with a new confidence.

SATURDAY, JUNE 3, 1995

Muphin and I returned to the pond that Tangren took us to for a brisk walk on Wednesday, or was it Tuesday? Anyway, I parked along the highway, near an entrance path that was closer to the pond. It was hot and neither Muphin nor I really wanted a long walk. I wanted to go back to the pond, this time with camera and binoculars, and Muphin and I gave ourselves a more leisurely pace. I stopped to photograph a wild rose, and other colorful wildflowers, and site a few birds with the binoculars: red-wing blackbirds, swifts, robins. When I reached the pond there was a man sitting on the bench near where I had thought to stop, so Muphin and I continued on the path to another access. We were both glad to find a place that had just enough shade at the water's edge and Muphin waded belly-deep on her short little legs into the cooling water. I settled into watching a few birds, too far away to see colors or markings, then discovered that the sun-warmed shallows was busy with a school, nay a university, of minnows. I doubt they'll show up in the photograph I made of a few contesting for possession of a pale, drowned worm. There was a story there: a worm, its clitellum developed and ready for giving birth to an egg, somehow is engulfed by the water, its own moist body overwhelmed by a liquid shroud. It suffocates and dies, soon bleached by its grave and the sun, becomes food for fish hatchlings. Nearby, there are larger fishlets, and, out in the depths of the pond, I see full-grown adults jump for insects that fly close to the surface. I suspect more than a few of the worm-eating minnows will also become food for bigger fish. And a sign along the path announces the future uses for this pond and wetland in the process of reclamation, including fishing. Life gives way to life, gives way to life, gives way to life.

The man had left the bench by the time we started back, so Muphin and I went down to the water's edge where we had sat with Tangren. With my binoculars I could see what those two blackbirds were protecting from the intrusive kingfisher the other day: held by a tangle of grass and roots growing on the side of the small island in the middle of the pond, at the edge that stood about six feet above the water, was a nest. The less iridescent-black of the pair, the female I presume, was standing akimbo on the top of the woven twigs with her wings spread against the heat and intense light of the sun, her head nodding in staccato conversation with her young whom I spied when the mom suddenly flew off from the nest. I could see at least two distinct heads, with big open mouths, bobbing up into the empty space. The other parent perched nearby on a branch of a cottonwood sapling, his blue-black feathers gleaming, his eyes darting about in keen watchfulness. The mother returned with food pinched in her beak, and proceeded to stuff the gullets of the babies, while the male went off, presumably in search of the next course. He soon returned with his bounty and joined the family on the nest. The mother adjusted herself for a better purchase on the edge while her mate fed the young, then she made herself into an umbrella again when the male returned to his branch.

I remembered to breathe deeper again after I had been intensely focused on this scene for several minutes, and with my breathing came moisture to my eyes. I have never before been privileged to such intimate witness of a family on their nest, to see infant birds in their beginning of life. As Jessie lay dying, with Tangren as a loving witness, a balance came in the form of bald heads with big gaping mouths, reaching for sustenance and life. I watched the birds as they continued to shelter and feed their young, then gathered up my things, and Muphin and I headed back to the car and the vigil I was keeping at Tangren's side.

SUNDAY, JUNE 4, 1995

Tangren called early this morning, still at the hospital though she assumed she would be coming home last evening. Yesterday, at around two P.M. the life-support systems for Jessie were stopped, all except the water apparently. The family had been told it would only be a couple hours before Jessie would die. Tangren seemed at peace when she left here yesterday afternoon, ready for this next and final step, grateful for these days she has had with Jessie, with her family. But she was in tears when she called, needing to be held by at least my voice as she cried deeply. Jessie does not die. Her body holds on to life, her vital signs strong. So the waiting is a long, slow crawling, a dying that has its days instead of hours, a process in the opposite direction of the baby birds as they fledge.

Sandra called from California, feeling her own grief as Tangren, her former lover, and still dear friend, loses her mother. I was able to tell her what I have learned of Jessie, and Tangren, today, as well as comfort her a little in her own sense of loss of Jessie. Toward the end of our conversation she asked how I am doing, and it was good to talk of that for a little. I am doing all right really, though I have my moments of loneliness, of missing my isolated home, my work on the land. I do not give myself permission to be away from the house now, because I want to be here for Tangren, though I know she does not want me to deny myself. I will stay close in, be nurtured by this sweet little house and the birds and the views and Muphin's unconditional love.

After Sandra's call, I phoned Sarah, left a message on her machine that I am still here and would enjoy a call if that would be good for her. Not urgent. She did call later, around noon my time. Oh, how sweet to have this sister with whom I can talk so candidly, who can talk to me about the goings-on in her life, calling to me a sense of my own life larger than this house, this story, this family, and who loves me so dearly. She is there for me in such a solid unquavering way.

Tangren came home early in the afternoon, exhausted, needing sleep. Her mother was still alive, though seemed not to be suffering. Tangren thought to sleep as long as she needed, then would go back to the hospital. After a few hours, a call came from, I assume, one of her brothers. He asked me to awaken Tangren and tell her "Jessie is gone." I went quietly up the stairs to where Tangren lay asleep, though she responded immediately to my gentle rousing, and gently spoken message. Though this news had been anticipated, waited for with some agony during the long night, it was nonetheless a blow that I could see on Tangren's face as she grabbed my offered hand and held on. Perhaps half a minute passed in silence before Tangren said, "Come lie beside me" as she abruptly released my hand and pushed the bedcovers back. Then I, who at fifty-six have never lain in intimate caress with any woman other than whoever was my lover, gladly stretched myself belly-to-belly along Tangren's body, wrapped one leg over hers, one arm under her neck, the other around her shoulders, enveloped her exploding sobs with my softness. Her head lay on my breast and I tenderly stroked her hair, murmured little encouragements for her wailing.

A shower, a renewing of spirit, and she was off again for a last scene at the hospital.

Hours later: a phone call. I recognize the ex-husband's voice by now, which is good because he no longer identifies himself, just barks some question or another. This time it was "Has Jean (as he calls her) gotten home all right?" Out of the blue. But, no, she hadn't walked in yet, though maybe I just heard her car. That seemed to satisfy him and he was gone, like he had performed some duty. But Tangren did not appear and because of his bolt, I got worried. Then waiting for Tangren was an anxious pulling on her to get home safely, which she soon did, having stopped to pick up some special coffee on the way.

So Tangren walks in the door. Her mother has died, this part of the story is finished. As she puts her things down she looks at me and says slowly, ponderously: "It sure is a rite of passage when your mother dies." Pause. Her eyes look childlike and yet impish. "I feel more *grown*-up." The combination of innocence and imp set me laughing, and laughing, until I am wide open with uncontrollable laughter, Tangren right with me. Both our vigils have reached their climax and the denouement flips us momentarily from sadness to hilarity. Our laughter ebbs as she comes around behind my chair, sits on the adjacent couch and leans to me; reaches around my shoulders to place her hands on mine on my chest, lays her head on my shoulder, and we breathe together, slow and deep, slow and deep.

Tomorrow, Muphin and I will go home.

"Barbara Deming, Kady Van Deurs and Jill Johnston, 1973—Writers and Activists"
by Diana Davies

Alix Kates Shulman

from Drinking the Rain

The postcard from Margaret Flood gave no arrival date, but it wouldn't be a day too soon. Since I sent her a map and a ferry schedule I'd been watching for her. I need her help with my divorce.

Seeing a small figure moving slowly across the beach, I rush to the edge of the deck. Before I can see her face I recognize the long silver hair, the flowing red garment, the shopping bag in each hand. (A great adapter, Margaret always travels light, supplementing from local thrift shops.) I wave my arms and hoot, then take the steps two at a time and sprint across the sand. I lift her small body off the ground and twirl her—first human touch in months. After I set her down she continues to twirl like a dervish, her arms spread to the sky. "Here I am," she announces in a high melodious voice.

Though I sometimes jokingly refer to Margaret as my guru, we've seen each other seldom over the years, and only in the city; she's never before been to Maine. Now we're both suddenly struck by the utter implausibility of either of us, much less both of us together, winding up on this remote northern beach; and before we've even reached the cabin we're already shrieking our joy and laughing like mad. Two mad ladies in tennis shoes.

"My-oh-my-oh-my," exclaims Margaret quaintly, taking in every large and tiny thing. I trail behind her through the cabin, looking through her eyes. "Holy moly!" she says, picking up a large bleached spiral shell.

"Moon shell," I report, and tell her how it can be found only when the new moon or full moon pulls the tide far enough back from shore, and how delicious are pounded moon-shell steaks. We stop in front of the three shelves I've hung on the wall outside the storeroom, their animal, vegetable, mineral contents arranged shelf by shelf. "What's this?" she asks like a child. "What's this?"

One would never guess, seeing this pixie woman examining a feather, that her true vocation is gadfly and general provocateur whose free, sometimes shocking behavior and ideas, however sweetly expressed, can goad her adversaries to sputtering rage. "It doesn't surprise me when they explode," she explains. "If someone's really sleeping soundly, you know how it feels to be woken up." To me, she's simply the most interesting person I know, daringly rolling an idea along the thin edge between outrageous and enlightening, like a child skipping alongside a hoop, hitting it with a stick. She has six children and ten grandchildren, plus two lovers her children's age, whose doings endlessly intrigue me.

I settle Margaret in the corner room that was always the children's, placing her shopping bags on one of the two iron cots. She lifts a bottle and a book out of her bag to offer me. Chardonnay and the *Tao Te Ching*—the second copy of the *Tao* she's given me. Is she losing her memory as well as her teeth? A pang of protection crosses a wave of pure love—the same love I felt the moment I met her. She plops down on a cot and lifts a curtain to peer out the window to the sea. I back quietly out of the room to leave her all the space she needs.

"Ready for the grand tour?" I ask, tossing Margaret some zoris and a pair of old jeans that I find in the trunk. We set off clockwise around the nubble to pick our dinner. At the bottom of the stairs we stop to sample beach peas—as sweet as garden peas, only half the size. In the cove I point out sand hoppers, brine shrimp, hermit crabs that live in any old empty shell, wandering from house to house—just like Margaret who, lacking a permanent address, might be regarded as homeless but for her large extended family constantly vying for her healing visits. A specialist in crisis intervention, besides counseling her friends and family, she has nursed earthquake victims in Guatemala, marched with the Madres in Nicaragua, lectured in free schools and prisons on several continents, ministered to the dying and the newborn.

We scramble up the jagged rock outcroppings at the tip of the nubble over to the ocean side, and on down to my waving seaweed gardens. Then we detour to the Bathtub, a deep semi-enclosed hollow in the rocks where heavy stones trapped in the pit tumble in the roiling surf.

As Margaret sorts through stones, I study her aging body to see what's coming next for me. Her small breasts sag gracefully, her smooth legs are brown and firm. As she tips her face toward the sun it's as if time has forgotten her.

Like mine, Margaret's second act began at fifty. One day, when the last of her children was grown, she packed a bag and, leaving everything behind, including house, pool, and philandering husband, hitchhiked down to Mexico with no resources but what came to her through serendipity. There she took a new name, studied midwifery, and joined a birthing community just in time to deliver her first grandchild. That was more than a dozen years ago. I met her soon after, on one of her brief New York visits, when we found ourselves side by side standing in a line to peer through a plastic speculum at a volunteer's cervix—a piece of every woman's anatomy that many of us were seeing for the first time. It felt challenging and risky, like prospecting for gold. That meeting had been organized to learn "menstrual extraction," a new technique for early abortion that women could perform on one another in defiance of the legal and medical professions' proclaimed monopoly of our bodies. Margaret radiated such radical free spirit, such electricity, that I fell directly in love. That I was a hard-nosed East Coast activist, she an antic hippie mystic (eventual veteran of mystic schools in Scotland, England, Iran, and India) made no difference at all. I took her home from the meeting and kept her with me for a night and a day, until she had to leave the city. We never even bothered to sleep.

Finally we arrive at my exhibition mussel bed just after the tide has turned. The pool is clear and still, filled with perfect specimens. Margaret digs in. We take two dozen blues and a dozen of their predators, the small green crabs that are never far away. I show her how to spot a crab beneath the rockweed and grab it from behind without getting pinched, grasping the widest points of its carapace between thumb and forefinger.

When we've reached our quota we pick our way back to dry land, balancing on slippery rocks, seeking those covered with barnacles for better traction. I show her the erosion that's gradually toppling this bit of nubble into the sea. "In a hundred years this may all be gone," I lament.

Margaret chuckles: "So will you."

Crossing the nubble's neck to Singing Sand Beach, I introduce her to the salad bar. We pick orach and lamb's-quarters, yellow dock and charlock, sea rocket and the delicate red fruit of the strawberry goosefoot. When our buckets are full, we top the tour with a skidding riff of singing sand.

We sit on canvas chairs on the front deck—I in the shade of the overhang, she facing the sun—and settle down to talk. After months of near silence, broken only by Saturday-morning phone calls and occasional exchanges with an islander, I want to gorge on conversation. Not chitchat, for which the purity of silence has only made me more unfit, but the intimate life-and-death talk we always have.

Having exchanged no more than a few letters and phone calls (though much telepathy) between our rare visits, we've barely begun to tell our stories or explore each other's lives. Though we share passions, desires, and doubts, we are constantly startled by how differently we approach and express them. Until now, at least, we've been yin/yang soul mates: she mystical, I political; she unifying, I analyzing; she spiritual, I historical; she sociable, I solitary; she the Buddha's advocate, I the devil's. Now I want to reconcile our differences, learn her ways.

I fill tall glasses with an infusion I've made from the astringent red cluster flowers of staghorn sumac, sweetened with honey—a kind of mock pink lemonade. Then I raise my glass and offer a libation to my beloved.

She sniffs, tastes, swallows, smiles—and as we sip the potion the conversation levitates, carrying us out of ourselves into a world of leaps and loops, puzzles and conundrums. My new discoveries, so fragile and hard to name, gain substance through Margaret's understanding, which often yields a perfect parable. Her mind, tuned to essential questions, sees connections so clearly that she can reach all the way around the most distant digression and draw it like a shy child into the center of the conversation, making it fit right in, rendering even the most casual offhand remark pertinent, consequential, apropos. If in my excitement I sometimes, apologizing, interrupt her, she graciously reminds me that it's impossible to interrupt her, since everything we say is connected. And indeed, that's the pleasure of this conversation—the way it stretches and expands till it explodes in revelation.

All afternoon we soar, leaving our separate egos below on the deck, growing greater than the sum of our parts until the last stray picnicker has left the beach, the last few boats have set sail from the cove, and suddenly it's dinnertime. So soon! Margaret stretches her back, shakes out her legs, pushes back her silver hair, and slapping her hands together like cymbals says, "Since this discussion is endless, we might as well end it here."

After half a lifetime of cooking several meals a day for a family of eight, Margaret cozies right up in my kitchen. I can see that she too considers cooking an outlet for creative expression—like music or dance. Work and worship are one to her. Since she left her husband's house she has earned her keep variously as a cook, vender, salesclerk, housepainter, floor scrubber, teacher, adviser, companion, comforter—to the battered, the homeless, the elderly. When her Social Security check fails to last the month, or whenever her help is needed, she takes another job.

We assemble our ingredients, take up our instruments—our knives, mixing bowls, measures—and begin. We slice green apples from my tree, scrub mussels and crabs, extract periwinkles from their shells. Margaret mixes dough and rolls out the pie shell; I measure the rice and season the mussel broth with juniper, bayberry, Irish moss, and a dash of wine. Then we build our salad, sampling each wild thing as we add it to the big wooden bowl. Finally we set the table on the front deck facing the empty beach. Margaret pours the wine, I bring out the steaming paella, dense with mussels and periwinkles, dotted with red crabs and tiny peas. Our gorgeous salad shines in the wooden bowl. When we're finally settled, Margaret takes my hands in hers and looks me intently in the eyes. From our steaming plates rise invisible vapors, wafting delicious aromas to our nostrils, and I feel like a birthday child wishing on candles. We wish. Then we click our glasses, pick up our forks, and fall to.

Margaret eats without a trace of squeamishness, concentrating on each new ingredient as if it were one of her children needing a dose of undivided attention. Not even her missing teeth prevent her chewing up the little crabs, legs and all.

The sun disappears behind the ridge, and twilight arrives, turning the sky the color of ripe berries. For a while we savor the light. But soon we are again deep in our conversation, exploring the paradoxes that rule the nubble like perverse commandments: *yield and overcome, bend and be straight, empty and be full,* as the *Tao* says. A cricket joins in, one of the lamps hums a low hum, but what I want to hear is Margaret. Our talk is as nourishing as food, as satisfying as sleep. I can't seem to get enough of it.

Evidently, neither can she, for even after we finally go to bed we continue our exchange, laughing and shouting through the night across the partitions that separate the rooms.

The next morning over breakfast on the shady back deck we're at it again. And each subsequent morning. Our breakfast talk is often sober, touching my divorce. Who needs a lawyer with Margaret to explain how "divorce is simply the continuation of marriage by other means." Having had six children to console when her marriage ended, she comforts me as I weep over my two, whose sadness and anger leak through the wires when I phone them on Saturdays.

When the dishes are done we take vows of silence. Margaret heads for the rocks, leaving me alone with my notebooks and books until lunchtime or low tide, whichever comes first. We forage for an hour at low tide, maybe lunch on the beach. Then she disappears again (to where, I never know) until, haloed in backlight from the setting sun, she climbs the stairs to resume our culinary experiments and our conversation. On other days, if it seems right, after lunch we toss our resolutions into the air and catch whatever comes floating down—a clam dig, a swim, a berry expedition, sand sculpting, a walk to the dump. Because, what the hell, we're both over fifty, alone, and free.

Against Silence

F a m i l y

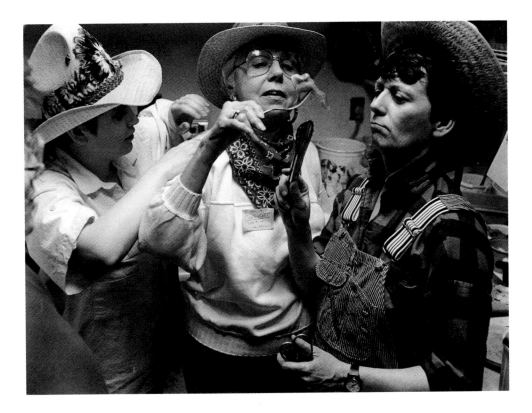

"Tasters" by Margaret Randall

Lisa Kron

My Brother's Getting Married . . .

from 2.5 Minute Ride, a performance piece

My brother is getting married. In Peggy's family when someone is getting married, her parents say, "Oh, isn't it exciting? They're so in love." In my family, when someone gets married my parents say, "Well, I hope they know what they're doing. They seem to be crazy about each other." I don't understand a single thing about my brother. He is a very nice boy and I can't seem to have a conversation with him. He talks really, really loud. He gets his hair cut at Sears. He lived in the third floor of my parents' house until a few years ago when my mother asked him to go live in the attic of my dead grandmother's house. Peg and I spent a month living in the house the summer after my grandmother died, seven years ago, to help my mom organize an estate sale. The house was packed, floor to ceiling, with things. There was a whole room full of Avon she bought because she felt sorry for the Avon lady. We figured after a while, the Avon lady had dropped all her other customers and was sending her son to college solely on the proceeds of my grandmother's standing order of "Tender Reckonings" hand cream. We tried to sell as much as we could but there was just too much and there was the added problem of my mother's attitude. When someone would ask for a lower price my mother would snatch it out of their hands and say, "I know exactly how much my mother paid for this and if you don't want it for that price, I'll keep it myself." So now, six years later, the house is still full of stuff although it has all been organized on the first floor on steel shelving along with the large collection of gay male pornography left by my grandmother's brother who also

151

lived in the house. He was a horribly twisted and bitter old closet case who never had a cheerful or generous word to say to anyone. He lived to drive my grandmother crazy and in the years when I was growing up, he accomplished this by mowing her lawn every day. His two most often used phrases were, "My god in heaven," and "99 percent of the people"—as in the sentence, "My god in heaven, 99 percent of the people who go to that breakfast bar at the Big Boy just shovel the food into their mouths. They just shovel it in!" The month we stayed in Lansing to help out we lived in the house with him. He refused to learn Peg's name, referring to her only as "that girl." But one day my friend Dale came. A tall gorgeous gay boy in cut-off shorts. And all of a sudden I saw a different Uncle Robert. "Well, hello young man. Would you join me later tonight and watch my video copy of *Irma La Douce?*" Anyway, now my uncle is dead and my brother lives in the house so that my mother can keep it insured. Peg says that David better never get in trouble with the law because he lives like a serial killer. "I mean look at the facts" she says. "He lives in the attic of his dead grandmother's house filled with gay male pornography because his mother makes him."

My brother met his fiancée on the computer. He wanted to meet a Jewish girl and he lives in Lansing, Michigan, so he signed on line and went right to the Jewish singles room where he got down to the business of finding a wife. He had a several-month thing with one girl but she backed out a week before they were actually supposed to meet. And so after that, he would talk to a girl a few times and if it seemed interesting he would get in his van and drive out to meet her. Every girl seemed really great to him. I tried to grasp his standards. They seemed to me to be something like, "Well, she doesn't have body odor. I think I'll marry her." Finally he met the right girl. Shoshi from Brooklyn. They asked us to be bridesmaids. "Yes, we'd love to!" we said on the phone when they called to tell us they were engaged. It seemed like such a funny joke. A few days later we realized we had agreed to be bridesmaids. I, in particular, realized I had agreed to wear a matching outfit with my girlfriend. This seemed to me to be a special kind of nightmare. Wearing a matching outfit with someone three inches taller and forty pounds thinner. Oh no. I called Shoshi and told her how terribly honored we were but we just couldn't be bridesmaids but we would be happy to sing. I don't know why I told her that. I think I wanted them to know we accept them even though they're straight. I wanted to write a funny song for the reception. Peggy was horrified. "What kind of a funny song?" she said. "David, we thought you were a neuter / until you met a girl on the computer?" Then they wanted us to sing a Hebrew song in the ceremony. Then they told us we couldn't sing because their rabbi is orthodox and he told them that orthodox men cannot be in the presence of a singing woman. They said they hoped we weren't offended by that. "Hey," I said, "it's your wedding and we want whatever you want." I'm trying to take my mother's advice. She says, "I'm just going to go to the wedding and pretend I'm watching a *National Geographic* special on TV." But I have a horrible vision. I see myself at their wedding wearing a men's suit and chomping a big cigar and I think that every time the rabbi walks by I will compulsively sing, "There's no business like show business!"

So we went to this wedding.

I didn't even buy new panty hose. I just put on an old dress from the back of the closet and Peggy dug something up and off we went to the Seaview Jewish Center in Carnarsie.

Shoshi had asked us to come early to help her get dressed. Because we're in the theater and so we know something about costumes. The Seaview Jewish Center sports a wonderful design out of a 1972 James Bond movie with mirror sculptures on the wall and little fountains in the corners with colored lights which dance and shimmer when you plug the brown cord into the eye-level wall socket just to the left. The floors are peel and stick parquet and the rooms are separated with big motorized accordion partitions which run on tracks in the floor. You know the kind of partitions—the kind that, it was always rumored, had crushed a child to death in gym class.

Peg and I went into the Bride's Room, as instructed, and there was Shoshi surrounded by women dressed in pastel lace dresses having her makeup done by an orthodox woman with one of those weird turban-y scarf-y hats covering her hair. "Everyone, I want you to meet my two new sisters," said Shoshi. And the makeup lady said, "Really? Wow. You two don't look like sisters at all!" And we said, "No, we're not sisters. We're (sigh) um . . . we're . . ." And then came that moment, that moment of trying to think of the word that no one has invented yet, the word that will describe a long-term lesbian relationship. Girlfriend? No. It's too insubstantial. Lover. No, too oogily. Spouse might have been good, but I got afraid that it was too strong. I had a frightening vision that if I said spouse, these women's heads would explode and leave a tattered charcoal-y ball sitting on their necks. And so I said, "We're partners." And they went, "Oh . . . oh . . ."—And I could see them thinking, "Partners in what?"

It reminded me of the time Peg and I had gone to visit her sister, Rosie, and her sister's family in Virginia. We had gone camping on the way there. Peg got impatient with me during the trip because the whole time we were in the South I kept repeating over and over, "Those two girls were kissing so I had to kill 'em." We had a wonderful time with Rosie and her twin girls. They were about five at the time. We went to King's Dominion and we spent the afternoon in the water park. At one point Peg and Rosie had gone off to ride on a big water slide while I played with the girls in a little pool. We were having a wonderful time when a woman approached me and said, "Is that Anna and Mary?" "Yes," I said. She told me she was their Sunday school teacher and she went over to talk with them. They had a little chat and the girls were stiff and polite the way little kids are talking to adults out of context and at the end of the conversation the lady gestured to me and said, "Is that your aunt?" And the girls said, "No." And the lady said, "Oh, well then, who is she?" And the girls said, "We don't know."

My mother had planned for the day after the wedding what she called a "post mortem," which was, basically, a get-together in which all the members of our family would gather for the purpose of making fun of the wedding. I made a note of the encounter with the makeup lady to share. I started mentally practicing how I would tell the story and I prepared myself to translate many such awkward encounters into goofy stories for the family to enjoy.

But an unexpected thing happened at my brother's wedding. I became enchanted. We all became enchanted by this wedding. When all the lights came on I had never seen any place as beautiful as the Seaview Jewish Center in Canarsie. And when the band began to play I danced and my cousins danced and Peg twirled around my aunt in her wheelchair. And during the dinner Peg got everyone at our table whipped up into a frenzy yelling, "Table 12 rules the wedding." And everyone got so excited. And this guy who I grew up with turned to me and said, "Peg is incredible." And I said, "Yes, well, she's got that Irish-Catholic camp counselor thing going." And he said, "Well it really works. I mean for just a second I found myself thinking, 'I think table 12 is the best.' "

And during the service, when my parents walked my brother in and stood with him under the Chuppa, I cried. You know, many months ago I was in San Francisco doing a show and on my night off I went to see the movie *Little Women*. It was a big theater and there were only about thirty people there and they were all women. And they were all sitting separately, scattered about in this huge theater. And when Beth dies, all the women in the theater were crying but it wasn't the usual quiet sniffing you hear sometimes in a theater. These women were racked with sobs. All around me I could hear noises like [makes loud sobbing noises].

And that's how I was crying at my brother's wedding.

It had never dawned on me in a million years that I would feel anything other than a big judgey reaction to the whole thing. But, when I saw my father all I could see was the soul in this little old man who lost his mother and father and country and culture and it's all gone forever and this was the closest he was ever going to come to it again and it didn't feel like enough and it felt like too much for me and so I cried and then I made everyone sitting around me take an oath that they hadn't seen me doing it because I can't be going around crying at weddings.

Photograph by Vita C. Shapiro

Beth Brant

Swimming Upstream

Anna May spent the first night in a motel off Highway 8. She arrived about ten, exhausted from her long drive—through farmland, bright autumn leaves, the glimpse of blue lake. She saw none of this, only the gray highway stretching out before her. She stopped when the motel sign appeared, feeling the need for rest, it didn't matter where.

She took a shower, lay in bed, and fell asleep, the dream beginning again almost immediately. Her son—drowning in the water, his skinny arms flailing the waves, his mouth opening to scream with no sound coming forth. She, Anna May, moving in slow motion into the waves, her hands grabbing for the boy but feeling only water run through her fingers. She grabbed frantically, but nothing held to her hands. She dove and opened her eyes under water and saw nothing. He was gone. Her hands connected with sand, with seaweed, but not her son. He was gone. Simon was gone.

Anna May woke. The dream was not a nightmare anymore. It had become a companion to her, a friend, almost a lover—reaching for her as she slept, making pictures of her son, keeping him alive while recording his death. In the first days after Simon left her, the dream made her wake screaming, sobbing, arms hitting at the air, legs kicking the sheets, becoming tangled in the material. Her bed was a straightjacket, pinning her down, holding her until the dream ended. She would fight the dream then. Now, she welcomed it.

During the day she had other memories of Simon. His birth, his first pair of shoes, his first steps, his first word—*Mama*—his first book, his first day of school. His firsts were also his lasts, so she invented a future for him during her waking hours: his first skating lessons, his first hockey game, his first reading aloud from a book, his first . . . But she couldn't invent beyond that. His six-year-old face and body wouldn't change in her mind. She couldn't invent what she couldn't imagine.

She hadn't been there when Simon drowned. Simon had been given to her ex-husband by the courts. She was judged unfit. Because she lived with a woman. Because a woman, Catherine, slept beside her. Because she had a history of alcoholism. The history was old. Anna May had stopped drinking when she became pregnant with Simon and she had stayed dry all those years. She couldn't imagine what alcohol tasted like after Simon was born. He was so lovely, so new. Her desire for a drink evaporated every time Simon took hold of her finger, or nursed from her breast, or opened his mouth in a toothless smile. She had marveled at his being—this gift that had emerged from her own body. This beautiful being who had formed himself inside her, had come with speed through the birth canal to welcome life outside her. His face red with anticipation, his black hair sticking straight up as if electric with hope, his little fists grabbing, his pink mouth finding her nipple and holding on for dear life. She had no need for alcohol. There was Simon.

Simon was taken away from them. But they saw him on weekends, Tony delivering him on a Friday night, Catherine discreetly finding someplace else to be when Tony's car drove up. They still saw Simon, grateful for the two days out of the week they could play with him, they could delight in him, they could pretend with him. They still saw Simon, until the call came that changed all that. The call from Tony saying that Simon had drowned when he fell out of the boat as they were fishing. Tony sobbing, "I'm sorry. I didn't mean for this to happen. I tried to save him. I'm sorry. Please, Anna, please forgive me. Oh God, Anna. I'm sorry. I'm sorry."

So Anna May dreamed of those final moments of a six-year-old life. And it stunned her that she wasn't there to see him die when she had been there to see him come into life.

Anna May stayed dry, but she found herself glancing into cupboards at odd times. Looking for something. Looking for something to drink. She thought of ways to buy wine and hide it so she could take a drink when she needed it. But there was Catherine. Catherine would know, and Catherine's face, already so lined and tired and old, would become more so. Anna May saw her own face in the mirror. Her black hair had streaks of gray and white she hadn't noticed before. Her forehead had deep lines carved into the flesh, and her eyes, her eyes that had cried so many tears, were a faded and washed-out blue. Her mouth was wrinkled, the lips parched and chapped. She and Catherine, aged and ghostlike figures walking through a dead house.

Anna May thought about the bottle of wine. It took on large proportions in her mind. A bottle of wine, just one, that she could drink from and never empty. A bottle of wine, the sweet, red kind that would take away the dryness, the withered insides of her. She went to meetings but never spoke, only saying her name and "I'll pass tonight." Catherine wanted to talk, but Anna May had nothing to say to this woman she loved. She thought about the bottle of wine: the bottle, the red liquid inside, the sweet taste gathering in her mouth, moving down her throat, hitting her bloodstream, warming her inside, killing the deadness.

She arranged time off work and told Catherine she was going away for a few days. She needed to think, to be alone. Catherine watched her face, the framing of the words out of her mouth, her exhausted eyes. Catherine said, "I understand."

"Will you be alright?" Anna May asked her.

"Yes, I'll be fine. I'll see friends. We haven't spent time with them in so long, they are concerned about us. I'll be waiting for you. I love you so much."

Anna May got in the car and drove up 401, up 19, over to 8 and the motel, the shower, the dream.

Anna May smoked her cigarettes and drank coffee until daylight. She made her plans to buy the bottle of wine. After that, she had no plans, other than the first drink and how it would taste and feel.

She found a meeting in Goderich and sat there, ashamed and angered with herself to sit in a meeting and listen to the stories and plan her backslide. She thought of speaking, of talking about Simon, about the bottle of wine, but she knew someone would stop her or say something that would make her stop. Anna May did not want to be stopped. She wanted to drink and drink and drink until it was all over. *My name is Anna May and I'll just pass.*

Later, she hung around for coffee, feeling like an infiltrator, a spy. A woman took hold of her arm and said, "Let's go out and talk. I know what you're planning. Don't do it. Let's talk."

Anna May shrugged off the woman's hand and left. She drove to a liquor outlet. Vins et Spiriteaux. *Don't do it.* She found the wine, one bottle, that was all she'd buy. *Don't do it.* One bottle, that was all. She paid and left the store, the familiar curve of the bottle wrapped in brown paper. *Don't do it.* Only one bottle. It wouldn't hurt. She laughed at the excuses bubbling up in her mouth like wine. Just one. She smoked a cigarette in the parking lot, wondering where to go, where to stop and turn the cap that would release the red, sweet smell before the taste would overpower her and she wouldn't have to wonder anymore.

She drove north on 21, heading for the Bruce Peninsula, Lake Huron on her left, passing the little resort towns, the cottages by the lake. She stopped for a hamburger and, without thinking, got her thermos filled with coffee. This made her laugh, the bottle sitting next to her, almost a living thing. She drank the coffee driving north, with her father—not Simon, not Catherine—drifting in her thoughts. Charles, her mother had called him. Everyone else called him Charley. Good old Charley. Good-time Charley. Injun Charley. Charles was a hard worker, working at almost anything. He worked hard, he drank hard. He tried to be a father, a husband, but the work and the drink turned his attempts to nothing. Anna May's mother never complained, never left him. She cooked and kept house and raised the children and always called him Charles. When Anna May grew up, she taunted her mother with the fact that *her Charles* was a drunk. Why didn't she care more about her kids than her drunken husband? Didn't her mother know how ashamed they were to have such a father, to hear people talk about him, to laugh at him, to laugh at them—the half-breeds of good-old-good-time-Injun Charlie?

Anna May laughed again, the sound ugly inside the car. Her father was long dead and, she supposed, forgiven by her. He had been a handsome man back then, her mother a skinny, pale girl, an orphan girl, something unheard of by her father. How that must have appealed to the romantic that he was. Anna May didn't know how her mother felt about the life she'd had with Charles. Her mother never talked about those things. Her mother, who sobbed and moaned at Simon's death as she never had at her husband's. Anna May couldn't remember her father ever being mean. He just went away when he drank. Not like his daughter who'd fight anything in her way when she was drunk. The bottle bounced beside her as she drove.

Anna May drove and her eyes began to see the colors of the trees. They looked like they were on fire, the reds and oranges competing with the yellows and golds. She smoked her cigarettes, drank from the thermos, and remembered this was her favorite season. She and Catherine would be cleaning the garden, harvesting the beets, turnips, and cabbage. They would be digging up the gladioli and letting them dry before packing the bulbs away. They would be planting more tulips. Catherine could never get enough tulips. It was because they had met in the spring, Catherine always said. "We met in the spring, and the tulips were blooming in that little park. You looked so beautiful against the tulips, Simon on your lap. I knew I loved you." Last autumn Simon had been five and had raked leaves and dug holes for the tulip bulbs. Catherine had made cocoa and cinnamon toast, and Simon had declared that he liked cinnamon toast better than pie.

Anna May tasted the tears on her lips. She licked the wet salt, imagining it was sweet wine on her tongue. "It's my fault," she said out loud. She thought of all the things she should have done to prevent Simon's leaving. She should have placated Tony; she should have lived alone; she should have pretended to be straight; she should have never become an alcoholic; she should have never loved; she should have never been born. Let go! she cried somewhere inside her. "Let go!" she cried aloud. Isn't that what she learned? But how could she let go of Simon and the hate she held for Tony and herself? How could she let go of that? If she let go, she'd have to forgive—the forgiveness Tony begged of her now that Simon was gone.

Even Catherine, even the woman she loved, asked her to forgive Tony. "It could have happened when he was with us," Catherine cried at her. "Forgive him, then you can forgive yourself." But Catherine didn't know what it was to feel the baby inside her, to feel him pushing his way out of her, to feel his mouth on her breast, to feel the sharp pain in her womb every time his name was spoken. Forgiveness was for people who could afford it. Anna May was poverty-struck.

The highway turned into a road, the trees crowding in on both sides of her, the flames of the trees almost blinding her. She was entering the Bruce Peninsula a sign informed her. She pulled off the road, consulting her map. Yes, she would drive to the very tip of the peninsula and it would be there she'd open the bottle and drink her way to whatever she imagined was waiting for her. The bottle rested beside her, and she touched the brown paper, feeling soothed, feeling a hunger in her stomach.

She saw another sign: Sauble Falls. Anna May thought this would be a good place to stop, to drink the last of her coffee, to smoke another cigarette. She pulled over onto the gravel lot. There was a small path leading down to the rocks. Another sign: Absolutely No Fishing. Watch Your Step. Rocks Are Slippery. She could hear the water before she saw it.

She stepped out of the covering of trees and onto the rock shelf. The falls were narrow, spilling out in various layers of rock. She could see the beginnings of Lake Huron below her. She could see movement in the water coming away from the lake and moving toward the rocks and the falls. Fish tails flashing and catching light from the sun. Hundreds of fish tails moving upstream. She walked across a flat slab of rock and there, beneath her in the shallow water, saw salmon slowly moving their bodies, their gills expanding and closing as they rested. She looked up to another rock slab and saw a dozen fish congregating at the bottom of a water spill—waiting. Her mind barely grasped the fact that the fish were migrating, swimming upstream, when a salmon leapt and hurled itself over the rushing water above. Anna May stepped up to a different ledge and watched the salmon's companions waiting their turn to jump the flowing water and reach the next plateau.

She looked down toward the mouth of the lake. There were others, like her, standing and silently watching the struggle of the fish. No one spoke, as if to speak would be blasphemous in the presence of this. She looked again into the water, the fish crowding each resting place before resuming the leaps and the jumps. Here and there on the rocks, dead fish, a testimony to the long and desperate struggle that had taken place. They lay, eyes glazed, sides open and bleeding, food for the gulls that hovered over Anna May's head.

Another salmon jumped, its flesh torn and gaping, its body spinning until it made it over the fall. Another one, the dorsal fin torn, leapt and was washed back by the power of the water. Anna May watched the fish rest, its open mouth like another wound. The fish was large, the dark body undulating in the water. She saw it begin a movement of tail. Churning the water, it shot into the air, twisting its body, shaking and spinning. She saw the underbelly, pale yellow and bleeding from the battering against the rocks, the water. He made it! Anna May wanted to clap, to shout with elation at the sheer power of such a thing happening before her.

She looked around again. The other people were gone. She was alone with the fish, the only sound besides the water was her breath against the air. She walked further upstream, her sneaker getting wet from the splashing of the salmon. She didn't feel the wet, she only waited and watched for the salmon to move. She had no idea of time, of how long she stood waiting for the movement, waiting for the jumps, the leaps, the flight. Anna May watched for Torn Fin, wanting to see him move against the current in his phenomenal swim of faith.

Anna May reached a small dam, the last barrier before the calm water and blessed rest. She sat on a rock, her heart beating fast, the adrenalin pouring through her at each leap and twist of the salmon. There he was, Torn Fin, his final jump before him. She watched, then closed her eyes, almost ashamed to be a spectator at this act, this primal movement to the place of all beginning. He had to get there, to push his bleeding body forward, believing in his magic to get him there. Believing, believing he would get there. No thoughts of death, of food, of rest. No thoughts but the great urging and wanting to get there, get *there*.

Anna May opened her eyes and saw him, another jump before being pushed back. She held her hands together, her body willing Torn Fin to move, to push, to jump, to fly! Her body rocked forward and back, her heart madly beating inside her chest. She rocked, she shouted, "Make it, damn it, make it!" Torn Fin waited at the dam. Anna May rocked and held her hands tight, her fingers twisting together, nails scratching her palms. She rocked. She whispered, "Simon. Simon." She rocked and whispered the name of her son into the water, "Simon. Simon." Like a chant. *Simon. Simon. Simon.* Into the water, as if the very name of her son was magic and could move the salmon to his final place. She rocked. She chanted. *Simon. Simon.* Anna May rocked and put her hands in the water, wanting to lift the fish over the dam and to life. As the thought flickered through her brain, Torn Fin slapped his tail against the water and jumped. He battled with the current. He twisted and arced into the air, his great mouth gaping and gasping, his wounds standing out in relief against his body, his fin discolored and shredded. With a push, a great push, he turned a complete circle and made it over the dam.

"*Simon!*" Torn Fin slapped his tail one last time and was gone, the dark body swimming home. She thought . . . she thought she saw her son's face, his black hair streaming behind him, a look of joy transfixed on his little face before the image disappeared.

Anna May stood on the rock shelf, hands limp at her sides, watching the water, watching the salmon, watching. She watched as the sun fell behind the lake and night came closer to her. Then she walked up the path and back to her car. She looked at the bottle sitting next to her, the brown paper rustling as she put the car in gear. She drove south, stopping at a telephone booth.

She could still hear the water in her ears.

Dorothy Allison

from Two or Three Things
I Know for Sure

Not until I was thirty-four did my sister Anne and I sit down together to talk about our lives. She came out on the porch, put a six-pack on my lap, and gave me a wary careful grin.

"All right," Anne said. "You drink half the six-pack and then we'll talk."

"I can't drink," I said.

"I know." She grinned at me.

I frowned. Then, very deliberately, I pulled one of the cans free from the plastic loop, popped it open, and drank deeply. The beer wasn't as cold as it should have been, but the taste was sweet and familiar.

"Not bad," I complimented Anne.

"Yeah, I gave up on those fifty-nine-cent bargains. These days I spend three dollars or I don't buy."

"I'm impressed."

"Oh, don't start. You've never been impressed with anything I've done or said or thought of doing. You were so stuck up you never noticed me at all."

"I noticed." I looked at her, remembering her at thirteen—the first time she had accused me of being weird, making fun of me for not wearing makeup or even knowing what kind of clothes I should have been begging Mama to buy me. "You don't do nothing but read, do you?" Her words put her in the hated camp of my stepfather, who was always snatching books out of my hands and running me out of the house.

165

"We didn't like each other much," Anne said.

"We didn't know each other."

"Yeah? Well, Mama always thought you peed rose water."

"But you were beautiful. Hell, you didn't even have to pee, you were so pretty. People probably offered to pee for you."

"Oh, they offered to do something, right enough." She gave me a bitter smile.

"You made me feel so ugly."

"You made me feel so stupid."

I couldn't make a joke out of that. Instead, I tried to get her to look at me. I reached over and put my hand on her arm.

When we were girls, my little sister Anne had light shiny hair, fine skin, and guileless eyes. She was a girl whose walk at twelve made men stop to watch her pass, a woman at thirteen who made grown men murderous and teenage boys sweaty with hunger. My mother watched her with the fear of a woman who had been a beautiful girl. I watched her with painful jealousy. Why was she so pretty when I was so plain? When strangers in the grocery store smiled at her and complimented Mama on "that lovely child," I glared and turned away. I wanted to be what my little sister was. I wanted all the things that appeared to be possible for her.

It took me years to learn the truth behind that lie. It took my sister two decades to tell me what it was really like being beautiful, about the hatred that trailed over her skin like honey melting on warm bread.

My beautiful sister had been dogged by contempt just like her less beautiful sisters—more, for she dared to be different yet again, to hope when she was supposed to have given up hope, to dream when she was not the one they saved dreams for. Her days were full of boys sneaking over to pinch her breasts and whisper threats into her ears, of girls who warned her away from their brothers, of thin-lipped adults who lost no opportunity to tell her she really didn't know how to dress.

"You think you pretty, girl? Ha! You an't nothing but another piece of dirt masquerading as better."

"You think you something? What you thinking, you silly bitch?"

I think she was beautiful. I think she still is.

My little sister learned the worth of beauty. She dropped out of high school and fell in love with a boy who got a bunch of his friends to swear that the baby she was carrying could just as easily have been theirs as his. By eighteen she was no longer beautiful, she was ashamed: staying up nights with her bastard son, living in my stepfather's house, a dispatcher for a rug company, unable to afford her own place, desperate to give her life to the first man who would treat her gently.

"Sex ruined that girl," I heard a neighbor tell my mama. "Shoulda kept her legs closed, shoulda known what would happen to her."

"You weren't stupid," I said, my hand on Anne's arm, my words just slightly slurred.

"Uh-huh. Well, you weren't ugly."

We popped open more cans and sat back in our chairs. She talked about her babies. I told her about my lovers. She cursed the men who had hurt her. I told her terrible stories about all the mean women who had lured me into their beds when it wasn't me they really wanted. She told me she had always hated the sight of her husband's cock. I told her that sometimes, all these years later, I still wake up crying, not sure what I have dreamed about, but remembering something bad and crying like a child in great pain. She got a funny look on her face.

"I made sure you were the one," she said. "The one who had to take him his glasses of tea, anything at all he wanted. And I hated myself for it. I knew every time, when you didn't come right back—I knew he was keeping you in there, next to him, where you didn't want to be any more than I did."

She looked at me, then away. "But I never really knew what he was doing," she whispered. "I thought you were so strong. Not like me. I knew I wasn't strong at all. I thought you were like Mama, that you could handle him. I thought you could handle anything. Every time he'd grab hold of me and hang on too long, he'd make me feel so bad and frightened and unable to imagine what he wanted, but afraid, so afraid. I didn't think you felt like that. I didn't think it was the same for you."

We were quiet for a while, and then my sister leaned over and pressed her forehead to my cheek.

"It wasn't fair, was it?" she whispered.

"None of it was," I whispered back, and put my arms around her.

"Goddamn!" she cursed. "Goddamn!" And started to cry. Just that fast, I was crying with her.

"But Mama really loved you, you know," Anne said.

"But you were beautiful."

She put her hands up to her cheeks, to the fine webs of wrinkles under her eyes, the bruised shadows beneath the lines. The skin of her upper arms hung loose and pale. Her makeup ended in a ragged line at her neck, and below it, the skin was puckered, freckled, and sallow.

I put my hand on her head, on the full blond mane that had been her glory when she was twelve. Now she was thirty-two, and the black roots showing at her scalp were sprinkled with gray. I pulled her to me, hugged her, and kissed her neck. Slowly we quieted our crying, holding on to each other. Past my sister's shoulder, I saw her girl coming toward us, a chubby dark child with nervous eyes.

"Mama. Mama, y'all all right?"

My sister turned to her daughter. For a moment I thought she was going to start crying again, but instead she sighed. "Baby," she called, and she put her hands out to touch those little-girl porcelain cheeks. "Oh baby, you know how your mama gets."

"You know how your mama gets." The words echoed in me. If I closed my eyes, I could see again the yellow kitchens of our childhood, where Mama hung her flowered curtains every time we moved, as if they were not cotton but spirit. It was as if every move were another chance to begin again, to claim some safe and clean space for herself and her girls. Every time, we watched her, thinking this time maybe it would be different. And when different did not come, when, every time, the same nightmarish scenes unfolded—shouting and crying and Mama sitting hopelessly at her kitchen table—she spoke those words.

"Oh, girls, you know how your mama gets."

I clenched my hands on my thighs, seeing my niece's mouth go hard. She clamped her teeth as I remembered clamping mine, looked away as I would have done, not wanting to see two tired, half-drunk women looking back at her with her own features. I shook my head once and caught her glance, the wise and sullen look of a not quite adolescent girl who knew too much.

"Pretty girl," I said. "Don't look so hard."

Her mouth softened slightly. She liked being told she was pretty. At eleven so had I. I waved her to my hip, and when she came, I pushed her hair back off her face, using the gestures my mama had used on me. "Oh, you're going to be something special," I told her. Something special.

"My baby's so pretty," Anne said. "Look at her. My baby's just the most beautiful thing in the whole wide world." She grinned, and shook her head. "Just like her mama, huh?" Her voice was only a little bitter, only a little cruel. Just like her mama.

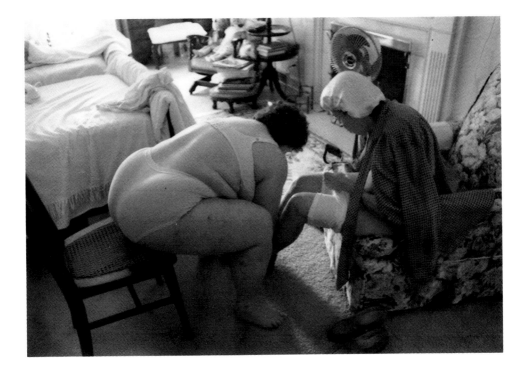

"wrestling pantyhose" by Lisa Morphew

Kleya Forté-Escamilla

Journal 1974–75

Note: In 1974, I made a decision as a single lesbian to have a child. The following journal excerpt describes a planned pregnancy.

November 6, 1975

Tomorrow is the anniversary of our first real meeting and conversation. I've been thinking a lot about everything I've lost, and what I suddenly see is what I have—exactly these memories of one full year of our life together. Have any feelings ever been as unclouded as those I felt for Gabriela? And yet they are somehow the most difficult thing to write about.

It was on my mind to talk to her the night of Abe's birthday party. I had to know. My period was two weeks late. I saw her wearing a long black dress and a Levi jacket, her full curly black hair and her face shining out of it moving towards the door with that quick long stride and then I wasn't going to reach out, not yet, and Sue said isn't that Gabriela and then we were together to get through the door and I said, Gabriela! Later I saw the black armpit hair curling against white skin, and that beautiful sleeveless black dress, the two incongruous but natural like a woman of the Mediterranean too full of life for this environment.

I wish I could paint her simply, white skin, black dress and hair, dash of red mouth caught in midturn in an otherwise indistinct room. . . . When I told her I might be pregnant, she kept saying that's wonderful, over and over again, her response so warm I felt my smile would burst out of my skin, that I had to contain it—don't say too much or I'd show too much, indeed Sue saying when I walked back you look like you've just found your long-lost friend, jealously. Yes, the feeling . . . of recovering a friend from that strange wheel of time and existence; that things had lain fallow for so long but seeds had been dropped by need and desire and left to grow in unfocused love—and Gabriela came out, appeared, a rose of wonderment. She was like the rose, radiating heat from within.

I had to leave her and I couldn't wait to get back to her. She asked if I could put her up for the night and I said yes, there was an extra bed in the living room. Me in my room downstairs and Sue in her room, but yes there was room, because she would then take my urine sample back with her in the morning. I couldn't say I slept.

She came by for my urine early in the morning, and I gave her a full jar of it wrapped up tight in a paper sack. And I went down to the car and she got in and I was desperate not to let her go without showing her somehow the wordless . . . so I reached through the window and hugged her and she laughed and hugged me back and we hugged each other. A quick strong motion like so many of hers and she drove away in her white Toyota over the hump in the street in the center of Penngrove and out of sight.

I didn't expect to hear from her until late afternoon, so I went out and I got back and Jean called downstairs to say I had a message from Gabriela to please call her immediately at General Hospital, so I dialed the number at General and asked for Dr. Gabriela Romano and she said, wait a minute, I'll connect you with her office and did and Gabriela said hello, gladly, and she said congratulations, you're pregnant. And I said just a minute and started to cry to Jean, Jean I'm pregnant. I was shaking inside and outside and Gabriela said goodbye.

I got sicker and sicker and then it was Saturday and time to go to Gabriela's clinic in Chinatown and I called Billie to drive me to the city. I couldn't eat and was so weak I could hardly walk—intense yang symptoms—I kept breaking out in a sweat and when we got there Billie parked down the block by the veggie restaurant and went in and got me a cup of carrot juice and some yeast powder and I drank it sitting in the car and I said I could walk up the block then, and we found the clinic upstairs. . . . I'm lying on the table my knees in the air and Gabriela comes out of me, pulls off her rubber gloves . . . she draws blood for the tests . . . and then says come here as I'm walking away. I'm wearing my long brown coat, I'm freezing all the time, and she holds me for the first time, and I bite her through her turtleneck. We just keep holding each other and the ladies of the clinic just go on about their business around us. I feel the heat rising in me from far away from another land, the heat of caring and passion that I had put aside. I haven't been able to eat for weeks, the baby the only spot of strength in me . . . and now I can eat again. . . .

Gabriela and I in her apartment in San Francisco: for a moment I wish, how I wish I wasn't with child. Because I wanted with her the kind of life you can have with someone when you're really in love and there are no children—total centeredness on the beloved. I had suddenly found her and I was pregnant. Two incontrovertible facts. The timing was so incredible.

Now, sitting together in her apartment, I'm confused, not knowing who I want to be, but I can't find words, only dimensions of feeling more intense than any I have ever known, and she says I want a family too. And I love her so. Her hands on my neck. Her carefulness. And I know that my life is irradicably changed. It has all come to this Flower. One night we make love and the triangle is complete: me, our child, and Gabriela. We are together as one unit, come together through all the forces of our desire. It is an accomplished fact.

JANUARY 25, 1974

Last night we felt the baby move for the first time. Gabriela felt it first, her head on my stomach, her hands spanning my waist. Excited, placing my hands beside hers, feel it? Blip blip . . . ? The baby's the size of a little fish right now. . . . We're huddled beneath down sleeping bags, wearing thermal underwear, the only heat from the fireplace. She shows me how to recognize that tiniest of movements, a flick impossible to even feel from the inside. And then suddenly she sits up, she's almost crying, saying, promise me, promise me no matter what happens you'll never take this baby away from me! Promise me, I love this little baby so much. What I felt was surprise—the thought already inconceivable. I've accepted her relationship to my baby as naturally as my own. It's strange but that's how it is. I don't know how I can love her more. . . .

JULY 2, 1975

The doctor said I'll start labor within twenty-four hours; the baby's head is already down and in position . . . he's not supposed to come for two weeks and nothing was ready so we went crazy today, looking all over for a diaper changer and a dresser. Gabriela found one and painted it white, and we put stickers on it, an owlie and grasshopper, and now we're exhausted but ready.

July 4, 1975

We went up to Jamie's place for Fourth of July and lit sparklers and I ran down the road with Gabriela running beside me, trying to start labor, but nothing. I'm waddling around with a bowling ball between my legs: I can't sit down and I can't stay still so I pace endlessly. It's driving Gabriela crazy. I can't stand it anymore, she says, and I'm suffused with terror that she'll leave.

July 18, 1975

Baby boy born yesterday July 17, 8:15 A.M.

July 18, 1975, entry continued:

Five A.M. I got up to pee; to my surprise, Gabriela follows me into the bathroom. I feel water running down my leg and look down, befuddled. Did you pee? she asks. No. Your water broke. You're in labor, she states. The pains start. Gabriela on the phone. I look through the window. It's Jamie roaring up to the steps, the station wagon turned around. She opens the back, there's a mattress there. Too late, too late I tell her, then Gabriela, she's in transition. I'm glad, but scared too. I'd wanted to have the baby at home, but gave in to Gabriela's caution and now there's no choice. All I can do is pant. Gabriela runs around washing out the pot that has brown rice in it from dinner, because there's nothing to boil water in. The doctor's out of town this weekend. She calls a midwife. And then it seems everybody's here. Somehow I'm surprised to see Abe sitting on the floor, wrapped in his poncho, eyes so big. I can't look in the mirror, too confusing between what I'm doing, feeling and the image. Just want to look in Jamie's eyes, holding me like an anchor, Gabriela and the midwife at the other end. Too fast, no time to get ready, just have to go with it. It's like the force of the whole universe moving beyond the mind beyond the body, moving through me the biggest letting go I've ever done. Not even aware when the baby leaves my body I hear a short cry then this being on my stomach my baby my baby I'm trying to pull him to me and someone, Gabriela I think, says the cord's too short. It seems minutes went by before I think to ask what is it? It's a boy, Gabriela says. Another minute. I look in her eyes, is it all right? She laughs, yes. Yes, it makes no difference. This life, my baby. Our family. He's awake for six hours, looking at each person one by one. I can finally turn on my side and sleep. Labor: three hours and fifteen minutes.

JULY 31, 1975

"I'm living the strongest political statement I could make—that two women can take care of each other." G.R.

Who's the baby's other parent?

Every moment of the past nine months have answered this one for me. Who's the one who has worried, struggled, gone through her own personal and emotional changes being my lover, my provider, my support . . . who held me at night when I was sick and in pain and held back her own tears so mine could flow; who got up after a sleepless night caring for me and got in her car to drive to San Francisco at 7 A.M., work all day to earn money to feed me and our growing baby, pay for our home—who gets back broken from sitting, sitting, the endless driving, getting home at 8, 8:30 at the earliest, 10:30, 11 on late nights to collapse at dinner, go to bed, start it all over again, day after day . . . can there ever be any doubt as to the answer to that question, who is the parent of this baby?

NOVEMBER 9, 1975

I had this conversation with Gabriela after accompanying her to the clinic in Guerneville:

ME: I was thinking about those women at the River who don't have the money to get their babies what they need.

G: He's (Eden) a very privileged baby.

ME: I just want him to be conscious.

G: He will be. Because we both are. The important thing is for him to know the preciousness of human life. Then you don't have to fuck people over; and that he know the importance of his own life, as an individual. Some people never understand that.

NOVEMBER 17, 1975

My grandmother, the woman who raised me, left yesterday morning—the house today is as if she had never been here. A sunny still day in contrast to the rain and cold of her last day here. I long for a past that never existed, one in which Mama and I said I love you to each other, one in which she could walk well, could hear and see, one in which I could share with her what was really important to me, one which would defy death. She will not see my baby grow up. I saw her looking at him, playing with him. I am afraid to give him what I have, she said of her cold, but I want to kiss him, saying goodbye to him at the bus depot.

Oh mama, I have a file of all the photographs of your life that I have known, before time settled on you like a vise, stiffening your joints and your understanding—the vitality that was yours. It gives me strength to go on—still your past is my present—the life you lived simply, without question, continues to feed me in this time. Puddles of water from the weekend rain mirror the trees growing above them. Trees point out the birds and sky and tender mist, up, up, towards the bright hole of the sun.

Irena Klepfisz

Poland, 1944:
My mother is walking
down a road.

from Basshert*

My mother is walking down a road. Somewhere in Poland. Walking towards an unnamed town for some kind of permit. She is carrying her Aryan identity papers. She has left me with an old peasant who is willing to say she is my grandmother.

She is walking down a road. Her terror in leaving me behind, in risking the separation is swallowed now, like all other feelings. But as she walks, she pictures me waving from the dusty yard, imagines herself suddenly picked up, the identity papers challenged. And even if she were to survive that, would she ever find me later? She tastes the terror in her mouth again. She swallows.

I am over three years old, corn silk blond and blue eyed like any Polish child. There is terrible suffering among the peasants. Starvation. And like so many others, I am ill. Perhaps dying. I have bad lungs. Fever. An ugly ear infection that oozes pus. None of these symptoms are disappearing.

The night before, my mother feeds me watery soup and then sits and listens while I say my prayers to the Holy Mother, Mother of God. I ask her, just as the

---

* Bashert: Yiddish—(pre)destined, inevitable.

nuns taught me, to help us all: me, my mother, the old woman. And then catching myself, learning to use memory, I ask the Mother of God to help my father. The Polish words slip easily from my lips. My mother is satisfied. The peasant has perhaps heard and is reassured. My mother has found her to be kind, but knows that she is suspicious of strangers.

My mother is sick. Goiter. Malnutrition. Vitamin deficiencies. She has skin sores which she cannot cure. For months now she has been living in complete isolation, with no point of reference outside of herself. She has been her own sole advisor, companion, comforter. Almost everyone of her world is dead: three sisters, nephews, and nieces, her mother, her husband, her in-laws. All gone. Even the remnants of the resistance, those few left after the uprising, have dispersed into the Polish countryside. She is more alone than she could have ever imagined. Only she knows her real name and she is perhaps dying. She is thirty years old.

I am over three years old. I have no consciousness of our danger, our separateness from the others. I have no awareness that we are playing a part. I only know that I have a special name, that I have been named for the Goddess of Peace. And each night, I sleep secure in that knowledge. And when I wet my bed, my mother places me on her belly and lies on the stain. She fears the old woman and hopes her body's warmth will dry the sheet before dawn.

My mother is walking down a road. Another woman joins her. My mother sees through the deception, but she has promised herself that never, under any circumstances, will she take that risk. So she swallows her hunger for contact and trust and instead talks about the sick child left behind and lies about the husband in the labor camp.

Someone is walking towards them. A large, strange woman with wild red hair. They try not to look at her too closely, to seem overly curious. But as they pass her, my mother feels something move inside her. The movement grows and grows till it is an explosion of yearning that she cannot contain. She stops, orders her companion to continue without her. And then she turns.

The woman with the red hair has also stopped and turned. She is grotesque, bloated with hunger, almost savage in her rags. She and my mother move towards each other. Cautiously, deliberately, they probe past the hunger, the swollen flesh, the infected skin, the rags. Slowly, they begin to pierce five years of encrusted history. And slowly, there is perception and recognition.

In this wilderness of occupied Poland, in this vast emptiness where no one can be trusted, my mother has suddenly, bizarrely, met one of my father's teachers. A family friend. Another Jew.

They do not cry, but weep as they chronicle the dead and count the living. Then they rush to me. To the woman I am a familiar sight. She calculates that I will not live out the week, but comments only on my striking resemblance to my father. She says she has contacts. She leaves. One night a package of food is delivered anonymously. We eat. We begin to bridge the gap towards life. We survive.

Marilyn Hacker

Against Silence

for Margaret Delany

Because you are
my only daughter's only grandmother,
because your only grandchild is my child
I would have wished you to be reconciled

to how and what
I live. No name frames our connection, not
"in-laws." I hoped, more than "your son's ex-wife."
I've known you now for two-thirds of my life.

You had good friends,
good books, good food, good manners, a good mind.
I was fifteen. I wished this were my home.
(None of my Jewish aunts read *I. F. Stone's*

Weekly, or shopped at Saks
Fifth Avenue, none of them grew up Black
working poor, unduped and civilized.)
I know you were unpleasantly surprised

when, eighteen, we
presented you with the fait accompli
of courthouse marriage in one of two states
where no age-of-consent or miscegenat-

ion laws applied.
Your sister's Beetle—bumps knife thrusts inside
after a midnight Bellevue D and C—
brought me uptown. You took care of me,

a vomit-green
white girl in your son's room. Had I been
pregnant? Aborted? No. Miscarried? Yes.
You didn't ask. I didn't tell, just guessed

what you knew. You
asked my mother to lunch. I'd "had the flu."
She greeted me, "Your hair looks like dog shit.
Cut it or do something to it!"

I burned with shame
you saw what kind of family I came
from. Could you imagine me more
than an unacceptable daughter-in-law?

When, fortified,
I went home to the Lower East Side,
my new job, art school at night and my queer
marriage, you were, understandably, there.

For a decade's
holidays, there was always a place
set for me, if I was in New York.
Your gifts groomed me: a dark-green wool for work,

pinstriped Villager
shirts. I brought books, wine, an Irish mohair

shawl laced with velvet ribbons. I came back
from London with a kangaroo-pouch pack

containing your
exuberant golden granddaughter.
You never asked me why I lived alone
after that. Feast-day invitations

stopped—Iva went
with her father. Evenings you spent
with friends, but normal Sundays you'd be in.
I'd call, we'd come a little before noon.

Because you did
that, Sundays there'd be fried liver or shad
roe, or bacon, hot rolls, hash, poached eggs.
We ate while Iva tugged around our legs

the big plush bear
you gave her. From the pile beside your chair
I picked over, passed you the book reviews
in exchange for White Sales and the "News

of the Week in
Review." Your mother, ninety-eight, deep in
somnolent cushions, eighty years' baker of rolls,
wakened by child noise, called the child, and told

her stories
nine decades vivid, linking the rose-gold three-
year-old, British born, Black by law
and choice as she was, with diaspora

Virginia, Harlem;
linking me, listening beside them
with you. She died at one hundred and two
and I, childlike, took it for granted you

would certainly
be bad-mouthing Republicans with me
for two more decades' editorial page.
Seventy-four was merely middle age.

The question some
structuralist with me on a podium,
exalted past politeness, called *"idiote"*
(a schoolyard-brawl word) "For whom do you write?"

I could have answered
(although it wouldn't have occurred
to anyone to ask it after that),
"I write for somebody like Margaret"

—but I'd written
names for acts and actors which, by then,
reader, you'd read, and read me out, abhorred
in print lives you'd let live behind closed doors.

You wouldn't be
in that debate, agree to disagree.
We would need time, I thought. This can resume,
like any talk, with fresh air in the room

and a fresh pot
of coffee, in the fall. But it will not.
Some overload blocked silence in your brain.
A starched girl starts your syllables again.

You held your tongue
often enough to hear, when you were young,
and older, more than you wanted to discuss.
Some things were more acceptable, nameless.

You sometimes say
names amidst the glossolalial
paragraphs that you enunciate
now, unanswerable as, "Too late."

Baffled between
intention and expression, when your son
says, "Squeeze my hand, once for 'no,' twice for 'yes,' "
you squeeze ten times, or none, gratuitous.

A hemisphere
away from understanding where you are,
mourning your lost words, I am at a loss
for words to name what my loss of you is,
what it will be, or even what it was.

"five months" by Jean Weisinger

C.A. Griffith

Family Pictures

My family calls from EPA. They took the wrong exit from the freeway and got lost. I ask them where they are, and my mother laughs. "Well, we left the city, got on the 101 South, and now . . . well, it looks like we're back in East Oakland." She laughs again. "This sure don't look like the catalogue! We musta missed the exit, huh?" While she's looking for the name of the intersection to read me, I hear my great-uncle in the background, but he's not laughing. "Damn! Got Damn!"

I tease my mother and laugh with her, sharing the pain of what she sees before her eyes. I tell her to get back on University Avenue, follow it past the freeway overpass where it turns to Palm Drive, straight into the campus gates, and then follow the directions I sent them. Still, she's unsure.

"I keep asking folks which way to campus and I still get turned around." She says the street signs are too small. "And it just doesn't look right."

I tell her that when the road begins to smooth out, all the liquor stores, run-down buildings and Black folk disappear, when the street widens for magnolia trees and bike paths, the street signs change. The houses suddenly become large and grand, and when almost everyone looks too casual or too rich, then she's headed the right way.

"Lord, how far off are we?" she asks.

"Just a couple of miles, Mom. Just a couple of miles." Neither one of us has the strength to laugh anymore. I hang up the phone and wait.

In a few short minutes, my family will arrive and we'll try to bury all pain and loss with the joy of this moment. Still, I'm stunned by the irony of it all—that getting lost finally made them understand what I lacked the language and skill to explain for four years. I think of all the wasted time and the nights I'd cried, telling them it's a desert here. And they'd remind me how I'd blossomed in this desert. But there was precious little warmth here. Perhaps we were both wrong.

I will receive my degree from a university that was built on railroad money and dedicated to a dead son. I find myself transformed, canceled out, and feared in this place that struggled to contain me. The cold of this place has made me sharp, but it has also made me brittle. I tuck away the jagged edges and hold my mother, father and great-uncle tight, looking for signs of my former self in their eyes. They sense the shift, but say nothing. I try on my cap and gown and pretend not to notice when they talk about grandpa in the present tense. I pretend that he's here with us.

I am the good daughter. I don't tell them that I've deferred grad school. And I tell them almost nothing about Asani or the apartment she found for us in Brooklyn. My mother asks if I'm okay. "You look a good two or three thousand miles away." I smile and tell her that I'm fine. Really.

In a day, it's over. I tell my great-uncle that I'll stop by to see him on my way East. He wraps me in his arms, crushing me to his chest, and tells me how proud he is. But there's no hiding the pain in his hip, or that he seems more like a old, old man and not the Papa Bear I remember.

They give me an answering machine, a new pen stenciled with chili peppers, and two crisp, fifty-dollar bills for graduation.

"This is a magic pen," my father says. "And this is lucky money. Buy yourself something nice. No bills, ya hear?"

My great-uncle borrows my magic pen and slowly writes across Grant's face in big, fancy letters: "Fun $ from Mom and Dad," and then on the second one—"Fun $ from Papa Bear and Grandpa." I say that I miss him and we're all unable to speak. We nod our heads. Words will give us nothing more to say.

I thank them for their gifts and for being here with me. They apologize for not having more to offer and I remind them that they didn't raise me to think that way. They've been taken for a spin in my roommate's brand new car, and felt awkward and ashamed amid all this arrogance and opulence. Perhaps I've been here too long. I didn't prepare them for what I've become so accustomed to.

I long to tell them that this feeling of not belonging, not here in this cold place, not in the church that baptized me, not even at home, has become a shield, and a weapon. The streets which were once my neighborhood are now unforgiving of the words and intonation that betray me. My family loves a shadow in the shape of the smart one, the sensitive one, the good daughter they struggled to send to college. And my grandfather would have taken one look at those pictures of Asani and me, he would have taken one look in my impostor's eyes and understood. He would have found the magic words to fix things and make it safe for me to come back home.

I can't tell my family these things. So I tell them that this place hasn't changed me. Not that much. They know I've changed in some unnamed way, but let it go at that and fret about my moving to New York City. But until they call to tell me that they're safe at home in Oakland and Oklahoma, I'm uneasy.

I close my eyes and see Asani and me standing on the rooftop of her parent's apartment on Striver's Row. Looking out at the sun slowly sinking down, bright orange, swollen, and heavy into the city, we watch the lights come up across the East River and across the Hudson. Lights slowly spread out below us in Harlem and Washington Heights.

My fingers stroke the tar of the building. Soft ridges harden with the night. They're raised up against the limestone like a bas-relief, written in children scrawl, with backward R's and everything. Names like Jamin, Fiona O'Brian, Lola and Hanna. In spray paint, names like Johnny "Sweetman" Lewis, Roz, Manny, Alicía, Shaméqua, and Steel. And we wonder what all these Irish, Jewish, Puerto Rican, Dominican, and Black ghosts are saying to each other, if anything at all. A wind has kicked up, and suddenly it's too chilly. But we stay right where we are. We know that this moment is very special. She holds me close and the warmth of her body protects me from the chill of an unkind day.

They should have been home by now. I try to lay down and rest. I close my eyes and Asani is here with me again. I tell her I feel useless. And she tells me to hold her. She lays her head on my chest, scissors her leg between my thighs. I ask her if she can sleep like this.

"For a while," she murmurs.

But the pillow is nothing like Asani. And it doesn't comfort me. I can't sleep. I find myself walking along the railroad. I hear chain gangs and I feel iron, hot and heavy in my hands. Dirt deep into every single pore. Sweat burning in my eyes. Muscles aching. I hear the words, *Chinaman, Nigga, come here boy!* A sliver of a man on a horse. The one with the shade and the clean white shirt. The frail man, with the gun. Laughs.

The scent of death and heartache lingers, sweet and pungent among the honeysuckle. It waits with hot, shiny stones along the tracks. I see the Black porters, old men now, carrying bags and boxes that would break a young man's back.

I see my grandfather standing straight, and not smiling at all for the camera. Brotherhood of Sleeping Car Porters. 1936. I see my grandfather on the walls of an antique shop in town. "How much is that photograph?" *Two hundred dollars.* I finger the silver dollar he gave me when I was 'this high.'

"Josephine Baker gave me that dollar. Put a stack of 'em right in my hand. You're gonna grow up and look just like her."

It was our story, and we both knew it by heart, but I'd still ask him things, like "what was she like?"

"Oh, she was something marvelous. Strictly first class," he'd say. "Folks nearly died when she breezed into that station. And with all the fellas tripping over themselves to carry her bags, she asked me." Then he'd pause for effect and reach out to touch my arm. "She said, 'Do you mind lending me a hand?' She treated me with such kindness. Like she knew me. Just like you did the first time I saw you and held you in my arms. Just a little bitty baby you were! But you looked me right in the eye like the old souls do. And you smiled at me too, like a dear, old friend."

There he is, among friends I've heard about all my life. I recognize the man who my grandmother turned down to marry him instead. I recognize their best friend, Robert MacHenry. Here, finally, were all the faces from those stories and suddenly, they were too real. I've got to take him out of this place and bring him home, to family. It's just not right.

"That man, in the front row, with his hands on the woman's chair. That's my grandfather." The dried-up old woman who owns the store finally looks at me. *Well my, my. You look just like him. Palmer, come here and look at this girl.* Palmer looks at me over his half glasses and then looks at the photograph. *Which one, the Black one at this end or the Black one at the other end? Palmer! The tall gentleman at the left. Jesus, he looks just like her. I don't think so. Yes she does. Look at her eyes. I can't believe the resemblance.* "He always told me I'd look like Josephine Baker when I grew up." *Who's Josephine Baker?* "A woman before her time." *Oh, that's nice, honey. You go to college around here? The community college over the hill?* "No. Just up the road. Stanford. I just graduated." *Stanford. My, my. Your grandfather must be proud. That school was founded by a railroad man, you know.* "I know. My grandfather worked for Southern Pacific for thirty years and it ruined his back and his knees. But he loved that train. Couldn't stand to fly. . . . He died just outside of Tulsa. He was on his way to see his brother. Everyone on the train just thought he'd fallen asleep." *I'm sorry. Would you like the photograph?* "Where did you get it?" *Oh, I don't know, from a collector or an estate sale. Do you remember, Palmer?* "For two hundred dollars?" *No. Of course no! Well, we have to make a profit. Surely you learned about that at Stanford.*

She smiles. I leave—the words, and the bile and the fury—caged inside of me. The little bell dangling from the door rings in my ears long after I leave the cool darkness of the store. And I hear my grandfather's voice.

"Next stop. Paaalooow Altooow. Seven minutes to Paalooow Altoow, tickets, please, thank you, Ma'am. Next stop, Palo Alto. I could have said that. I could've punched and collected those tickets. I could have. You're gonna do anything, and I mean anything you want, girl. And I'll be up in heaven looking out for ya, baby gal. Me, grandma, and every colored man and woman who sweated, bled and died for those damned railroads. We'll be lookin' out for you."

I think about my history, my ancestors, hanging on display in stores for sale. And I think of my great-great grandparents. I picture their spirits swimming deep along the coastal waters, along the jagged edges of the east and south coasts, through the canal waters, beyond Panamá, and out to sea. Free from the weight of their bones on display in some museum, or crushed under the sagging foundation of some building, parking lot, or suburban tract home on some absurd cul-de-sac.

And I think about the gold embossed degree I'll get in the mail. ". . . Linden M. Jordan who has satisfactorily pursued the Studies and passed the Examinations required. Therefore the Degree of Bachelor of Science with all the Rights Privileges and Honors thereunto appertaining . . ." I know that I won't be able to put it up on my wall—like a grotesque trophy.

I walk the railroads, and lay my head to the steel, waiting. Waiting to hear the cries and moans and whispers of the dead. The thousands of hungry ghosts, languishing in unmarked graves. But has it been too long? I feel the thousands of Indian men, Mexican men, Chinese men, Irish men, Black men, all lined up where the cross beams should have been, hands gripping beams of iron, and the train, roaring over us, roaring over our long dead bodies.

I wait. And soon I hear the slow rustling of voices. I struggle to understand the soft, sickening feeling that wraps itself around me, fluttering, like dry leaves, whispering to my soul, "Welcome home, child. Welcome home." And then the cacophonous rush of words, furious and warm, in my own long forgotten, long bastardized tongues.

Beatrix Gates

Negotiations

for my parents

I

She called in the morning
to tell me, "This is the day,
he's going today." "All right"
I said or something—
I don't remember
asking anything at all
but I took in the trance-like
assuredness of her voice
accepting it fully
like breath
and joined her in the aloneness . . .
even as I hated the telephone
in my hand, the voice in my throat
and the distance closing.
I touched the hot cold
let my father   dying
in close   ears open   hearing
nothing more from him.

It was as she wanted
and I could only guess
he too wanted
The intensity
of her voice seemed to speak
to the approach   She was ready
to give him over
even as she counted,
heart beating in the stone-lined well,
the moments alive before her.
No fear allayed, she refused
to negotiate beyond
what was essential
"I just wanted to tell you,"
she said   her voice holding
all the proprietary calm
and fear of her solo watch
meeting the raw
truth of it
as usual.

Later telling me she thought
it was odd, when he packed
all his clothes for just a month
in the country, adding "I didn't say
anything." She didn't feel the
air leaving his lungs and
not coming back, at least
not then   Or the tightness
of his chest and shoulders
as he felt all his suits
and shoes slowly filling
with strangers
and walking away.

2

What strikes me now is
the weight behind the words—
her saying,   "I knew he was gone
when he hit the floor."
"What happened?" I asked.
"He fell out of bed."
She was there
in the same room
in the chair I had struggled
to speak from weeks before

as I sat trying to tell my father
the news of my life
the desires I had,
going back to school
and not knowing how to tell
him the clear facts of my life—
how much I loved him
and counted him the source
and foundation of any sanity,
gentleness or hope I had been able
to hold—   It was so simple.
I wanted to echo his greeting of the world,
but I wasn't as good,
prone to prideful resistance and fear,
I held on

I didn't hide
and I didn't speak,
the desire alive
the wordlessness
still and large—his sweet, interested face
craning forward, small breath
deepened by the line of oxygen
piped from the portable tanks

His own words had to be short,
his breath couldn't carry them,
so the words must have
started to accumulate
and then fallen
like stones in a crumbling well—
a few more falling each day
loosening the earth on the way down
until the depth of desire
could not be measured nor
the thousand expressions of it—
but the stones became the love
of holding the words inside
until they are just
the right ones
and match the conditions
perfectly—even the changing
and laughing, that kind of fluidity
and grace—

so when he fell,
he weighed every word
and then toppled, stone falling
before the open mouth of water

He fell beside my mother,
his witness, who had heard it all
before, but jumped up from the
listening chair, quick crouch,
alight in all the sounds
this body can utter.

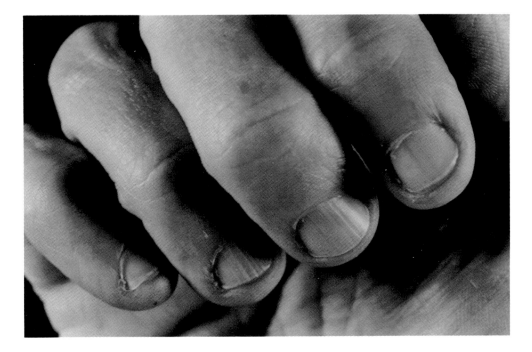

Untitled photograph by Betsy Crowell

Honor Moore

The Crimson Snake

The room on the top floor had silver light and silence. It was the first room I'd ever devoted entirely to my writing, and every object was a talisman— the old Chinese carpet, the French painted screen, the blue table on which I wrote, and, hanging on an exposed brick wall, her painting, *The Blue Girl*. Anger in the eyes and a bat wing black hat gave the lie both to the title's resonance with Gainsborough and the insouciance of the word "girl." This was no girl.

I was a girl, in my twenties, and a poet. I'd published one or two things well, and poems about my mother's death had become a play which had opened and closed. Now I was back at poems and this one was about her, my grandmother. I sat at the blue table, and, like objects in a still life, what she looked like gathered in my imagination: pale skin, phosphorescent blue eyes, long dark fingernails at her mouth hiding a laugh. I was afraid of my grandmother. She spoke like an actress, presenting rather than speaking. I can still hear the voice. Deep. A Boston Brahmin accent, an artist's ironic locution. I was afraid she'd catch me in a mistake, and the degree of her attention scared me. What could I say that could measure up to that intensity of listening?

Margarett Sargent wouldn't fit into a poem was how I put it later. I put her into a book instead. It would take ten years to tell the story, to express what reduced to five words: Painting. Madness. The family fear. Hers was a complicated story even before I knew much of it. An artist and my mother's bad mother. An artist and a woman. An artist who stopped painting and then went mad. Some said she went mad. I say she got mad.

What happened?

There is snow outside. I have moved to the country to write a biography of my artist grandmother.

Margarett Sargent began as a sculptor, then became a Modernist painter. She married my grandfather at twenty-eight. They lived in Boston. During the twenties, they had four children, spent part of each year in Paris. It was an unhappy marriage, and Margarett had many lovers, of both sexes. Between 1926 and 1931, she had nine one-woman shows. At forty-five, she stopped painting.

For two years in the city I could not write, and now, here I am in the quiet, the undistracted. Understand I have no idea what I'm doing.

It is cold. I have no friends here, or so I believe. I call my editor, and cry. Write about the snow, she says cheerily. I crawl back to the computer.

They say a biographer has an advantage if she has seen her subject move, but I never saw Margarett walk. I was late as usual. In my late twenties, I obsessively visited her. Not understanding I was a writer in pursuit of my material, I never asked a question or took a note.

I remember the salmon silk blanket cover draping the hospital bed with its silvery aluminum guardrails. I remember the red of her lipsticked mouth in motion: a crimson snake stretching in the sun, changing shape in a flash. Her tongue was once that quick.

How lonely she must have been all those years in bed, her window overlooking the city where she'd been a famous beauty, whose post office had once, in her youth, delivered a letter addressed simply, Margarett Sargent, Boston.

By now, after twenty years of shock treatments and five strokes, it was hard to understand what she said. I knew the story of my other grandmother, the one with silvery hair, whose pale salmon underwear lay perfectly folded in a tall mahogany bureau, whose lipstick was never crimson. Margarett's story had to do with sex, with doors slammed in the night, whispered telephone conversations, bottles hidden in the backs of closets, paint hardening on old palettes.

Every morning, a nurse applied crimson lipstick to the waiting canvas of my grandmother's mouth.

The light is different today. There is no snow on the ground, but all around me are piles of snow. It is summer and the snow is paper and open books. Scribbled-on paper and books open to certain pages. Crumpled paper and the storm of finishing a biography. Margarett has no more than seconds to live. I write her death, a sentence, drop my head to the table and weep. "She died alone in her room." What is peculiar is that I am still alive, still at my kitchen table, still surrounded by papers.

How did I presume I might come to understand her?

What I remember eating with her wasn't even a meal. Smoked salmon, capers, onion, crumbled eggs, red wine uncorked at the side of a hospital bed. She herself did not eat that evening—her mouth crippled by the stroke—but she watched me with a gleam of satisfaction in her eye. The salmon was Scottish, not oversalted or smoky. The egg was gathered in a small perfect mound, the capers were imported and minute, the wine dark red. I sat looking at what hung on the wall behind her head, at the flowers in the vase on the table that swiveled toward her. The light was dim and golden.

I was wanting.

I was wanting one of her paintings to hang on my wall, my garden to grow flowers like that, my bookshelves to hold the books hers did, books that told stories of a time, of suffering, of a certain dream, of art. She sat there, in her eighties, in her memories, looking at this granddaughter—all my possibility, all my youth. I came to believe I could not live my own life without justifying hers.

To whom?

I have not become a mother.

I have not become a married woman.

What brought me to write about Margarett was a wish for her real gift, the gift I was too tongue-tied to negotiate as I sat with her in that room. I have always been tongue-tied. I inherited her paintings, her passion for flowers, but what I wanted most from Margarett Sargent was the gift of an untied tongue.

The book I've written is a husk of all that living and thinking, of all that effort those mornings I sat at a keyboard surrounded on three sides by windows, sometimes shutting my eyes and letting my fingers move past the speed of thought to get down what I knew past my brain. I remember crying a lot. I remember laughing only once, laughing and kicking, laughing, banging my fists on the desk. I pushed her unruly life first into words, then into sentences, paragraphs. I pushed it to absorb and carry her colors.

The day she died on paper in my kitchen was a Friday. Saturday night I dreamed we were in Paris together in a hotel room hung with crimson and gold. Toward the end of the book in her real life, Margarett breaks down in Paris, but now, healthy and in possession of her beauty, she reclines on a bed in an elegant black sheath. As I watch, I can see that we are both laughing. I want to sleep forever if I can keep dreaming this, me asking, Margarett exclaiming, telling me all her answers.

"Fae Richards, by Kenny Long, 7, Philadelphia, 1940," from *The Watermelon Woman: The Fae Richards Photo Archive*, 1995, by Dunye/Leonard

Note: The archive of photographs was shot as a collaborative project by Cheryl Dunye (filmmaker) and Zoe Leonard (photographer) for the film *The Watermelon Woman*. Because the character, Fae "The Watermelon Woman" Richards, is fictional, her photographic past was created by staging private and public events from her illustrious life.

Jewelle Gomez

I Lost It at the Movies

My grandmother, Lydia, and my mother, Dolores, were both talking to me from their bathroom stalls in the Times Square movie theatre. I was washing the popcorn butter from my hands at the sink and didn't think it at all odd. The people in my family are always talking; conversation is a life force in our world. My great-grandmother, Grace, would narrate her life story from 7:00 A.M. until we went to bed at night. The only breaks were when we were reading, or the reverential periods when we sat looking out of our tenement windows observing the neighborhood—whose sights we naturally talked about later.

So it was not odd that Lydia and Dolores were talking non-stop from their stalls, oblivious to everyone except the three of us. I hadn't expected it to happen there. I hadn't really expected an "it" to happen at all. To be a lesbian is part of who I am, like being left-handed. It seemed a fact that needed no articulation. My first encounter with the word *bulldagger* was not charged with emotional conflict. When I was a teenager in the 1960s, my grandmother told me a story about a particular building in our Boston neighborhood that had gone to seed. She described the building's glorious past through the experience of a party she'd attended there twenty years before. The best part of the evening had been a woman she'd met and danced with.

Lydia had been a professional dancer and singer on the Black theatre circuit: to dance with women was part of who she was. They danced at the party, then the woman walked her home and asked her out. I heard the delicacy of my

203

grandmother's search for the right words, even in the retelling. She'd explained to the bulldagger, as she called her, that she liked her fine but was more interested in men. As she spoke I was struck with how careful my grandmother had been to make it clear to that woman (and, in effect, to me) that there was no offense taken in her attentions, that she just didn't "go that way." I was so happy at thirteen to have a word for what I knew myself to be. The word was mysterious and curious, as if from a new language that used some other alphabet. It left nothing familiar to cling to when touching its curves and crevices. Now a word existed, though, and my grandmother was not flinching in using it. In fact, she'd smiled at the good heart and dashing good looks of the bulldagger who'd liked her.

Once I had the knowledge of a word and a sense of its importance to me, I didn't feel the need to explain, confess, or define my identity as a lesbian. The process of reclaiming my ethnic identity in this country was already all-consuming. Of course, in different situations later on—some political, some not—I did make declarations. But not usually because I had to. Mostly they were declarations made to test the waters. A preparation for the rest of the world which, unlike my grandmother, might not have a grounding in what true love is about.

My first lover, the woman who'd been in my bed once a week through most of our high school years, married when we were twenty. After my writing started being published, I told her with my poems that I was a lesbian. She was not afraid to ask if what she'd read was about her and my love for her. So there, amidst her growing children and bowling trophies, I said yes, the poems were about my love for her. She did not pull back. And when I go home to visit my family I visit her. We sit across the kitchen table from each other, describing our lives and making jokes in the same way that we have for over twenty-five years.

During the 1970s I focused less on having a career than on how to eat and be creative simultaneously. Graduate school and a string of nontraditional jobs (stage manager, mid-town messenger, etc.) kept me so busy I had no time to think about my identity and its many layers. It was several years before I made the connection between my desire, my social isolation, and the difficulty I had with my writing. I thought of myself as a lesbian-between-girlfriends. Except the *between* had lasted five years.

After some anxiety and frustration I deliberately set about meeting women. Actually, I already knew many women. Including my closest friend back then, another Black woman who also worked in theatre. I tried opening up to her and explained my frustration at going to the parties we attended. I'd dance with men and keep up a good stream of patter, but inside my mind was racing, speculating on who might be someone I'd really be interested in. All the while I was too afraid to approach any women I was attracted to, certain I would be rejected because the women were either straight and horrified, or lesbian and terrified of being exposed. My friend listened with a pleasant, distant smile. Theoretical homosexuality was acceptable, and male homosexuality was even trendy. But my expression of the complexity and sometimes pain of the situation made her uncharacteristically obtuse. She became impatient and unsympathetic. I drifted away from her in pursuit of the women's community, a phrase that was not in my vocabulary yet, but I knew it was something more than just women. I fell into that community by connecting with other women writers, which helped me to focus on my writing as well as on my social life as a lesbian.

Yet none of these experiences demanded that I bare my soul. I remained honest but not explicit. *Expediency, diplomacy, discretion* are the words that come to mind now. At that time I knew no political framework through which to filter my lesbian experience. I was more preoccupied with the Attica riots than with Stonewall. Since the media helps to focus the public's attention with a proscribed spectrum, obscuring the connections between issues, I worried about who would shelter Angela Davis. The concept of sexual politics was remote and theoretical.

I'm not certain exactly when and where a theory converged with my reality. Being a Black woman and a lesbian blended unexpectedly for me like that famous scene in Ingmar Bergman's film *Persona*. The different faces came together as one, and my desire became part of my heritage, my skin, my perspective, my politics, and my future. I was certain that it had been my past that helped make the future possible. The women in my family had acted as if their lives were meaningful. Their lives were art. To be a lesbian among them was to be an artist. Perhaps the convergence came when I saw the faces of my great-grandmother, grandmother, and mother in those of the community of women I finally connected with. There was the same adventurous glint in their eyes, the same determined step, the penchant for breaking into song and for not waiting for anyone to take care of them.

I needed not to pretend to be other than who I was with any of these women in my family. Did I need to declare it? During the holidays when I brought home best friends/lovers, my family welcomed us warmly, clasping us to their magnificent bosoms. Yet there was always an element of silence in our neighborhood and in our home. It was disturbing to me, pressing against me more persistently each year. During visits to Boston, it no longer sufficed that Lydia and Dolores were loving and kind to the "friend" I had with me. Maybe it was just my getting older. Living in New York City at the age of thirty-two in 1980, there was little I kept deliberately hidden from anyone. Although the genteel silence that hovered around me when I entered my mother's or grandmother's apartments was palpable, I was unsure whether it was already there when I arrived or if I carried it home within myself. It cut me off from what I knew was a kind of fulfillment available only from my family. The lifeline from Grace to Lydia to Dolores to Jewelle is a strong one. We are bound by so many things, not the least of which is looking so much alike. I was not willing to be orphaned by silence.

If the idea of church weddings and station wagons holds no appeal for me, the concept of an extended family is certainly important. But my efforts were stunted by my family's inability to talk about the life I was creating for myself, for all of us. The silence felt all the more foolish because I thought I knew how my family would react. I was confident they would respond with their customary aplomb, just as they had when I'd first had my hair cut into an Afro (which they hated), or when I brought home friends who were vegetarians (which they found curious). While we had disagreed about issues, like the fight my mother and I had over Viet Nam when I was nineteen, always when the deal went down we sided with each other. Somewhere deep inside I think I believed that neither my grandmother nor my mother would ever censure my choices. Neither had actually raised me; my great-grandmother had done that. Grace had been a steely barricade against any encroachment on our personal freedoms, and she'd rarely disapproved out loud of any considered decision I'd made.

But it was not enough to have an unabashed admiration for these women. To have pride in how they'd so graciously survived in spite of the odds against them was easy. It was something else to be standing in a Times Square movie theatre faced with the chance to say "it" out loud and risk the loss of their brilliant and benevolent smiles.

My mother had started reading the graffiti written on the wall of the bathroom cubicle. We hooted at each of her dramatic renderings. Then she said (not breaking rhythm, since we all know timing is everything), "Here's one I haven't seen before—DYKES UNITE." There was that profound silence again, as if the frames of my life had ground to a halt in a projector. We were in a freeze-frame, and options played themselves out in my head in rapid succession: Say nothing? Say something? Say what?

I laughed and said, "Yeah, but have you seen the rubber stamp on my desk at home?"

"No," said my mother, with a slight bit of puzzlement. "What's it say?"

"I saw it," my grandmother called out from her stall. "It says Lesbian Money."

"What?"

"LESBIAN MONEY," Lydia repeated loudly over the water running in the row of sinks.

"I just stamp it on my big bills," I said tentatively, and we all screamed with laughter. The other women in the restroom had only been a shadow for me in these moments, but they came into focus as I felt each one press more closely to her sink, trying to pretend that the conversation was not happening.

Since that night there has been little said on the subject. Yet. There have been some awkward moments, usually in social situations where Lydia or Dolores felt uncertain.

A couple of years after our Times Square encounter I visited my grandmother for the weekend with my lover. One of the neighbors in her building dropped by, and when she left, my grandmother spoke to me in low tones while my lover was in another room. She said we should be careful about being so open in front of other people because they weren't necessarily as fair-minded as she. I was flooded, momentarily, with shock and disappointment. But before I could respond, she heard the words and their incongruity with who she was. She grabbed my arm and demanded, "Forget I said that. Nobody pays rent around this apartment but me."

We have not explored "it," but the shift in our relationship is clear. I feel free to be an adult, and my family has the chance to see me as such.

I'm lucky. My family was as relieved as I was to finally know who I am.

V
Praisesongs
Community & Legacy

"Barbara Deming" by JEB (Joan E. Biren)

Judith McDaniel

Love Is a Struggle, Too

Barbara Deming was a peace activist and an advocate for nonviolent change. During her lifetime she struggled against the building, testing, and use of nuclear weapons; she struggled for equal rights for black people and for women; and in 1969 she was beginning to struggle openly for her own right to live as a lesbian with the woman she loved.

In her poems written that year, Barbara asks,

> Each night I cling to you—
> A floating spar,
> Do we drift landward?

After a few weeks, the sense of drifting with life is replaced by the struggle:

> My love is water,
> I swim in her arms,
> Struggling toward what new land?
> Visions of it catch at my mind
> As, buffeted, sustained,
> I change, I change.

The following letter to fellow writer and lesbian feminist activist Rita Mae Brown was written in 1972. It refers to that difficult period in 1969 when Barbara and her partner, Jane Gapen Verlaine, were fighting to keep custody of Jane's children after a contested divorce in which Jane's husband named Barbara as the reason Jane was unfit to raise her own children. She wrote in a letter to her friend Dave Dellinger that Oscar told Jane "right in front of the kids" that he "forbids them to have any more contact with her Bull Dike [sic] friend."[1]

At the time Barbara Deming wrote this letter, she was recovering from nearly fatal injuries she received in a car accident on her way to deliver a talk at the War Resisters' League national conference in 1971. Both lungs collapsed, her pelvis and both legs broken, Barbara was in a body cast for nearly a year and she never fully recovered from the physical trauma. As she said to Rita Mae Brown, "finding words takes . . . energy." But she did take the time and the energy to write this long letter about the most important thing in her life—her love for Jane and her desire to live openly as a lesbian. Her excruciating honesty (counting and recounting the times she might have lied about her sexuality), her willingness to test each boundary, especially those like the class status that privileged her, and her strong sense of reality and what is possible, make this letter an important addition to lesbian history. Two years later, in 1974, Barbara published her book *We Cannot Live Without Our Lives* with a dedication "To all those seeking the courage to assert 'I am'—and especially to my lesbian sisters."

December 1, 1972

Rita Mae, dear sister—

I hear that you have a new book of poems out. Could you tell me (just on a postcard if you are rushed) what its title is and whether I can get it from a regular bookstore or whether I have to send for it to some special place?[2]

I keep wanting to write to you—but also keep lacking the full energy to write to you as I would really like, talking of many things. Finding words takes more energy, for me, than anything anything, and that kind of energy is returning to me very slowly. But let me today just *begin* to respond to your long ago letter—which I've just hunted for and reread, and thank you for again.

About my being white and middleclass (which of course I was born; it wasn't a matter of my choice)—I'm glad that you say, at least, that you find no class-supremacy in my writing. God knows I believe that I feel none. I do feel more and more that as long as there are class differences, anyone born into *any* class will be disadvantaged—in terms of ability to be the human beings that we should be. Each of us wounded in a different way because of it. Though some, God knows, wounded *most painfully*. Our job is, yes, to reach out toward each other, constantly, trying to find ways to destroy these differences. Now my words begin to run out. To be continued.

And I want to turn to something else that you wrote:"Here you were willing to take risks, deprivation, pain for the sake of peace and black people—will you do it for yourself and for me and other Lesbians/women? I think until you do I will think of you as a kind of Lady Bountiful bestowing your energies and passions on the other oppressed and sidestepping your own oppression and that of other Lesbians. It's the most dangerous one to face. I can't really blame you but until you do face it, I can't really trust you."

All I can answer is that though I have far *far* to go in the struggle against my own oppression—our oppression—it is a struggle I entered as best I knew how many many years ago. I chose to live with women (first fought within myself the struggle to trust my own instincts about what was a good life for me), and I lived with them openly, never trying to pretend that the woman I lived with was anything but the very dearest person to me in the world. I never wore a button, naming myself a Lesbian, and I talked of my nature rarely, and for the most part (though not entirely) only when another person brought up the subject. (Then I did not lie. No—once I remember lying, or avoiding an answer actually, but only once. Ha—but now I remember another time, too.) But I didn't marry—to have a shield; or make a point of being seen often with men; or live separately from the woman I loved—or anything of that sort. Many many people knew me for what I am. (I know it well, because one old family friend who loves to talk about people, talked a great deal about me always, and has often reported to me a variety of responses from others.)

As the years went by I wanted more and more—even before gay liberation—to be more open still, but always the woman I lived with wanted very much *not* to be open, was deeply afraid of being. It is hard to drag someone else into battle—especially the person one loves. If I were the only one to have to suffer, you would find me standing fully in the open now. I still have to find my way there. And I intend to. My spirit wrestles with the problem. Trust me to that extent.

When Jane and I decided to live together (this was in 1969), her exhusband, who wanted still to have power over her, threatened a custody suit—on the grounds that I was a Lesbian (for he was one of many who had heard that I was)

and the grounds, too, of my "long criminal record." This was in the South, too—
where you know what the courts are like. If we'd not both been ready to fight
for our rights, we would have kissed each other very quickly goodbye. But we
fought him as best we knew how. And are still living together, and the children
are with us. We didn't say openly in that struggle that we loved one another, because if we had there would have been no chance at all to keep the children—
who desperately wanted to be with their mother and not with their father.

Again the terrible problem of dragging others into danger. It was neverthe-
less taken for granted by everybody. How right you are that one's own oppression is the hardest to face. I have never felt as bled and bled and bled by any other
struggle. Above all by the sense that we stood utterly alone in our struggle. What
her exhusband was asking for was outrageous, and he should have been able to
find no allies at all. Though his threat was, his clout was, that Jane could be found
unfit to have the children, he actually was content enough to have them live
with us, for he is too lazy to want to have the care of them himself, and he never
really worried about our "bad influence" upon them, just saw at once that by
raising this issue he could be in a position to bully her. He wanted the settle-
ment to be that the children would be in Jane's care, with it understood that I
would support them (as I do—though he makes lots of money), but he was to
have legal power to take them away from us at any time he wanted. What could
be fairer? Yet he knew that society would back him up as he made this shame-
less demand, just because of the nature of our love.

Yes, we were on our own. Even Jane's lawyer treated us with contempt. And
as for his—he was obscene. Almost every friend or relative who knew of our
struggle was leery about it all—clearly felt that the right thing for us to do was
to part. But we refused to part. And refused to sign his agreement. And refused
to lose the children. And we won, finally. Too long a story to tell here. We had
to plot it out day by day by ourselves. Struggling against the lawyer's bullyings,
too. (He wanted us to sign!) We probably couldn't have won without money,
though. Class again. I am very aware of this. I do understand well the anger of
those women who have not that resource at least.

This is getting to be a long letter. Where am I? I am walking—limping—in
your direction, the direction of complete frankness, as fast as I am able to.

Jane's son, who is 17 now, has, I reckon, one more year to live with us. She
has told him about us and he took the news better than I expected him to. (I
was, I should confess, in deep fear about what his response would be.) (Her
daughter, who's 15, took it with utter equanimity.) But he cares terribly terribly
about public opinion, and if we were more open than we already are—were po-

litically open—I'm afraid it would be almost unbearable to him. I find this hard to treat lightly. And so of course does Jane. But once he has finished school and can if he likes seek his own fortune—it will be difficult still but I am determined at that point to take a further step. . . .

I do now talk frankly with other people in the Movement. No, no great risk in that. And yet it has been very much more difficult than I could have believed.

And again I thank you with all my heart for being out there first. But there can never be thanks enough for the people who have done that—and taken the *BRUNT.*

With strong love,
Barbara Deming

[1] Letter to Dave Dellinger, August 30, 1969.
[2] Deming is probably referring to Rita Mae Brown's second book of poems, *Songs To A Handsome Woman,* published by Diana Press in 1973.

Alicia Gaspar de Alba

Descarada/No Shame:

An Abridged Politics of Location

My work is about resistance, about the legacy of resistance that flows through my veins as a Chicana lesbian/butche/tortillera feminist from the border. In that list of appositions that define me, which came first? I became a Chicana at twenty. I became aware of myself as a fronteriza at twenty-two. Although I wasn't formally a feminist until I reached high school and fought for the rights of female athletes in my editorials, I had always gotten in trouble for being the wrong kind of girl: the kind that talked back, disobeyed, and wasted time. As far as my lesbianism—well, I think I always loved girls, even when I didn't want to be one, even when I thought butche was better than femme any day, never mind that femmes gave me the kind of dreams that tortillas are made of.

Back talk and disobedience were outward manifestations of my resistance to both my family's and the school's patriarchal domination, dogmatically enforced by my grandmother at home and the nuns at school. Wasting time, or rather, reading stories and writing in my journal rather than cleaning the house and memorizing the Act of Contrition, was my inward resistance. In my journal, I used English—a language foreign to my family, and the medium through which I talked back most forcefully—, I used English to curse at the injustices of my young female life, and to construct fictions in which the protagonists defied the social codes by engaging in, for example, interracial relationships, masturbation, and Mother Superior matricide. In my reading, I solved crimes with Nancy

Drew, stirred cauldrons with Morgan le Fay, jousted with Sir Lancelot, saved Jane from alligators and snakes, joined Dracula in his nightly forays for fresh blood.

I married for the first time at six years old; the neighbor girl who was my wife wasn't allowed to walk on her own; in other words, I didn't let her walk; I wanted to carry her everywhere. In my innocent domination of her, I was acting out what I saw—my uncles' and grandfather's oppression of their wives. Her lack of agency was precisely what I, growing up as a girl, unconsciously resisted.

At twelve (probably as a result of the witchcraft kit I had hidden in my closet through which I learned to channel the wisdom of powerful women), proving Simone de Beauvoir's theory that "one is not **born** a woman,"[1] and foreseeing Monique Wittig's notion that lesbians aren't women,[2] I chased after my friend Giselle, frightened her constantly with my insistence that she look under my uniform to see that I really wasn't a girl.

At sixteen, I opened my legs to my boyfriend and kissed a woman, both for the first time. In my journal of that period, I called the former, which I now realize was date rape, "the most beautiful and fulfilling experience of my life, the immortal sacrifice." I called the other event a trap, a nightmare, a morbid web of lesbian love in which I had been inadvertently caught (notice the passive voice). The truth is, the immortal sacrifice bled like hell, and I couldn't walk without pain, or piss without it burning, or play basketball for nearly a week. The morbid web of lesbian love had been spinning in *my* innocent mind for years.

The truth is, she excited me. Her gentleness, her aroma, the way she blushed whenever I stared too hard. I liked sitting next to her in her car, listening to our favorite song, "It's Magic." I liked teaching her to swim in the pool of the Ridgemar Apartments, at sunset, when there was hardly anyone around to see me stroke the wet skin of her arm. And, the night of our first kiss, on our way to the Circle K to buy ice and cigarettes for the party going on at my house, she confessed that she loved me, that she had never felt that way before, that she was afraid. I held her in my sixteen-year-old arms and felt carnations exploding in my chest. I remember how the car zigzagged down the dark street, an orange Love Bug climbing onto curbs, floating past stores and houses. No memory of ice or cigarettes or time. Just that warm, wild drifting into the night.

Three months after my wedding to the white man who performed the immortal sacrifice on me in the backseat of his father's car, I started a story set in a gay bar. I had never been to a gay bar, and wrote such an outrageously ridiculous description of the place, that my husband suggested I go to a real gay bar with one of the "girls" he worked with who was bisexual. (For that, I shall always be indebted to him.) She and I went to the Old Plantation in El Paso and ended up staying, dancing, talking, until last call. Afterwards, we went to her apartment, and I spent the night. I remember after making love to her, opening my eyes and seeing that it was dawn: both a literal and a symbolic awakening. From then on, I knew consciously that I loved women, and wanted, more than anything, to make my life with a woman. Not that it was easy to leave my husband, to come out to my family (my grandmother didn't speak to me for two years), to label myself a lesbian. Despite what I knew about myself and what I desired, homophobia was still informing my existence. As Gloria Anzaldúa says, homophobia in many ways is "the fear of going home. And of not being taken in. We're afraid of being abandoned by the mother, the culture, *la Raza*. . . ."[3] Crossing the sexual border of my identity wasn't like driving over the Córdoba bridge into Juárez. "The awakening of consciousness," says Adrienne Rich, "is not like crossing a frontier—one step and you are in another country."[4] My awakening as a lesbian was more furtive than that. More like wading across the river in the dark, heart pumping loud as the migra helicopters patrolling the line. More like being caught wet and deported several times.

It wasn't until my husband started to censor my writing that I knew I could no longer hide in the safety and privilege, in the fairy tale, of a heterosexual marriage.

I didn't actually call myself butche. I just knew I was. I knew I liked going to El Noa Noa on Alameda, where the women wore stockings and mascara, and the dykes wore boots and tejanas. I liked standing at the bar with my arm around *my* woman. I liked her to watch me shoot pool. I liked feeling her close to me on the dance floor, my right hand pressing at the back of her waist, guiding her to the rhythm of the ballad or the ranchera or the salsa pounding out of the speakers. If any other butche wanted to dance with her, I expected to be asked; she was my woman, after all. I liked ordering her drinks, lighting her cigarette, making her come. I felt like Midas with the golden touch. Any time I brought a woman to orgasm, both of us glowed. I always came after she did, or during, but not before. Ladies first. But when it was my turn, I wanted the same treatment. My breasts, my feet, my armpits, my cunt—everything wanted to be touched, turned to gold.

Now, how, you may ask, did I go from a butche to a tortillera?

I remember it was a Saturday in September, Iowa City, 1985, the day I was invited to my first party of "maricones and tortilleras." I had never heard the term tortillera in a different context than tortilla-maker; all I could see was la señora del mercado sitting by her tin tub of masa clapping tortillas into shape. It took a Cuban-identified Irish-American lesbian to explain to me that *tortillera* also meant "lesbian," not only to the Latino/a gay community of Iowa City in 1985, but to America Latina at large. What's the connection? I asked, between a *tortillera* and a lesbian? Something to do with the sound, they said, the kneading of *masa* and palms rubbing together, the clapping of tongues, the intersection of good taste and the golden touch. Thus this Chicana dyke from El Chuco, Texas, was indoctrinated into *tortillerismo.*[5] I knew that part of the reason that gravity had pulled me to the Midwest had been revealed; I would have to write a poem about this new label, this new identity that smelled of warm, moist corn, that sounded of my tía Suky's hands patting *gorditas* in the kitchen. Like **lesbian** and **Chicana,** *tortillera* was originally a derogatory term. But we take it in our mouths, taste the truth of it, and change the meaning. In this way, we begin to own our own names.

MAKING TORTILLAS

My body remembers
what it means to love slowly,
what it means to start
from scratch:
to soak the maíz,
scatter bonedust in the limewater,
and let the seeds soften
overnight.

Sunrise is the best time
for grinding masa,
cornmeal rolling out
on the metate like a flannel sheet.
Smell of wet corn, lard, fresh
morning love and the light
sound of clapping.

       Pressed between the palms,
   clap-clap
         thin yellow moons—
   clap-clap
         still moist, heavy still

                              from last night's soaking
              clap-clap
                              slowly start finding their shape
              clap-clap.

              My body remembers
              the feel of the griddle,
              beads of grease sizzling
              under the skin, a cry gathering
              like an air bubble in the belly
              of the unleavened cake. Smell
              of baked tortillas all over the house,
              all over the hands still
              hot from clapping, cooking.

              Tortilleras, we are called,
              grinders of maíz, makers, bakers,
              slow lovers of women.
              The secret is starting from scratch.[6]

    I don't know what's worse for my family: that I'm a lesbian or a Chicana. Both terms are equally shameful in their eyes, equally scandalous and worthy of ostracism and oppression. My Chicana self is ridiculed, criticized, invalidated because, according to the people who love me, this is Mexican blood in my veins, and how can I call myself a Chicana if I love la cultura mexicana so much, if I was brought up as a mexicana, if I was never allowed to associate with prietos or pochos, cholos or pachucos, if I was swatted on the head every time I mixed Spanish with English? When my grandmother received my book of poems, she was very proud, until one of my uncles took it upon himself to act as translator. What a disgrace, what a pity, what a waste of education, they said, that I had the nerve to publish a book and announce, in black print, in English and Spanish words mixed together, that I am "the first Chicana fruit of the family." Needless to say, my grandmother was very upset about my book. That lady who does not know the meaning of political activism, who has never heard of Martin Luther King, Jr., or César Chávez, organized a family boycott so powerful that it nearly catapulted my relationship with the family into oblivion. Again, she refused to talk to me; her silence lasted over a year. My aunt was angry at me for having sent her the book in the first place, but I explained that I had two motivations: I wanted my grandmother to see that what she had called wasting time, the hours I spent hunched over my desk, had produced a body of work worthy of being published, and I didn't want her to say, later, when she found out about the book through somebody else, as she inevitably would, that I hadn't sent her a copy of the book because I was ashamed of my life. To have her or anybody think that I was ashamed of being a lesbian and a Chicana was nothing short of self-betrayal.

Among the many things my grandmother called me was the epithet **descarada**. In Mexican culture, to have no shame is the equivalent of having no honor, no dignity, no face. To have no face is to be invisible, to be even more devalued than the Mexican peso.

> The world knows us by our faces [says Gloria Anzaldúa in *Haciendo Caras*], the most naked, most vulnerable, exposed and significant topography of the body. When our *caras* do not live up to the "image" that the family or community wants us to wear and when we rebel against the engraving of our bodies, we experience ostracism, alienation, isolation, and shame.[7]

Like Sor Juana Inés de la Cruz, whose story I'm telling through my Chicana lesbian/butche/tortillera feminist fronteriza voice and vision,[8] I both resisted the making of my face in my family's/my culture's image, and made my own face, several faces, *más caras,* through my writing. A través del silencio y de la pluma, me descaré y me hice la cara.★ When I stood at the foot of Niagara Falls, another tourist on the *Maid of the Mist,* the boat was like my consciousness, weighed down by so many contradictions, but at the same time slipping easily through the rainbows that splash out of that relentless cascade; and I realized that, as always, I was in between two countries, and that, like the river, my resistance, my identity would continue to flow.

★ Translation: Through silence and the pen, I both bared and created my face.

Notes

1. See Simone de Beauvoir, *The Second Sex.* (New York: Alfred Knopf, 1952).

2. See Monique Wittig, "One Is Not Born a Woman," *Feminist Issues* 2 (Winter 1981): 47–54.

3. See Gloria Anzaldúa, *Borderlands/La Frontera: The New Mestiza.* (San Francisco: spinsters/aunt lute, 1987): 20.

4. See Adrienne Rich, "When We Dead Awaken: Writing as Re-Vision," *Adrienne Rich's Poetry,* ed. Barbara Charlesworth Gelpi and Albert Gelpi. (New York: W. W. Norton, 1975): 90.

5. For a review of work done by *tortilleras* Chicanas since 1981, see *"Tortillerismo:* Work by Chicana Lesbians," *Signs: Journal of Women in Culture and Society.* Vol. 18, no. 4, "Theorizing Lesbian Experience," (Summer 1993): 956–963.

6. See Gaspar de Alba, *Three Times a Woman: Chicana Poetry.* (Tempe: Bilingual Review/Press, 1989): 44–45.

7. See "Haciendo caras, una entrada/an introduction," *Haciendo Caras/Making Face, Making Soul: Critical and Creative Perspectives by Women of Color,* ed. Gloria Anzaldúa. (San Francisco: aunt lute, 1990): xxiii.

8. See Gaspar de Alba, "Excerpts from the Sapphic Diary of Sor Juana Inés de la Cruz," *Tasting Life Twice: Literary Lesbian Fiction by New American Writers,* ed. Ellen Levy. (New York: Avon Books, 1995): 182–190.

See also Gaspar de Alba, "Juana Inés," *Growing Up Chicana/o,* ed. Tiffany Ana López. (New York: William Morrow & Co., 1993): 67–85.

"Audre Lorde and friends" by Jean Weisinger

Kate Rushin

Praisesong for the Poet

for Audre Lorde

Drummers are always like that
Take it in Put it out Use it
Before she lose it

Drummers are always like that
Flashy Dazzling Cool
Cool not too cool to
Get hot
Get down
Sounds
Her axe
Sounds her creation
Sounds her life
Plangent and sweet sweet
Vibrations   pounding   resounding
Strikes the sweet spot sweating
Eyeing us over her symbols trembling
Audre Audre
Leaves her body

Her body
This body this body
Lay down bloodbed
Stretch out restbed
Arch up lovebed
Cool sheets for your sickbed
Witness witness
Witness your deathbed this body
This body
Honey brass bell tongue
Kettle of flame
This body this body
Won't come by here again
Leaves her books her words
Her sisters her children her lovers
Her poetry emotion

Audre   Audre
Gives us bottom
Keeps Time
Audre Audre
Got to
Give the
Drummer
Some

Ninia Leilani Baehr

Sharing the Spirit of Aloha:
Baehr v. Lewin and
Responsible Tourism

Once upon a time Hawai'i was a nation, and in this nation people used chants and *hula* to tell stories and transmit history. Many legendary tales revolved around love among both gods and mortals, and sexual relationships not only between men and women but also among members of the same sex were part of everyday life. So were *māhūs*, people whom we might now call transsexuals but whom in Hawai'i were accorded the status of a third gender.

Christian missionaries of European ancestry (those early proponents of the "missionary position") arrived in Hawai'i intending to convert the local population. Despite the existence of the strong *'ohana* system—the Hawaiian version of "family values" that ensured that all members of society were cared for—these missionaries were happy neither with the sexual freedom in evidence nor with the *hula* dances in which bare-chested men and women used their bodies to convey spiritual history that was very different from what was recorded in the Bible. They advised Hawaiian women to wear the modest *mu'u mu'us* that Hawai'i is ironically now famous for. They also tried to get each member of the populace to have sex with only one person, to whom he or she must be married, and who must be of the opposite sex—*māhūs* were nowhere in the equation.

The missionaries considered not only sexual freedom but also *hula* to be dangerous to their new moral order, and when their views gained sufficient influence, *hula* was outlawed for many years—although underground *hula* teachers (many of them *mahus*) kept the traditional chants and dances alive. *Hula* was eventually reintroduced in a new form, one in which female breasts were not bared and history was not passed on. Now, foreigners were entertained and money was spent at establishments that were not owned by Hawaiians.

Of course, less and less *was* owned by Hawaiians and eventually even the nation of Hawai'i itself came under foreign rule when the U.S. military took over 'Iolani Palace by force and imprisoned Queen Lili'uokalani. Roughly half a century after being occupied, Hawai'i was added to the United States as a state. By that time, the rich legacy of *āikane* (male consorts to royal men) and *māhūs* and others who would now be called "queer" was deeply buried in Hawaiian history.

Needless to say, I didn't know any of this history when I was born in Honolulu on June 6, 1960. Neither did Genora, when she was born four days later and five miles away. In fact, as Genora and I grew up, we each believed that we would never find other women like ourselves in the islands. If Genora and I had met as toddlers, or even as budding baby dykes, our lives would have been much easier, but that was not the case. Genora grew up in neighborhoods where others of Filipino, Hawaiian, and Chinese ancestry lived. She graduated from public high school, got a technical degree and took two full-time jobs as a television engineer—she was the first female engineer at both stations. Working the day shift at one job and the night shift at another, Genora put in a minimum of eighty hours each week to help buy a home in which she and her parents could live; in nine years she racked up nearly two decades of work experience. Despite their age and shifting health status, her parents did nearly the same.

I, meanwhile, traveled with my *haole* (foreign/Caucasian) teacher parents, moving from one island to another, one state to another, and then one country to another, until they got divorced. By then, I was old enough to keep moving on my own, which I did until I completed an MA in Women's History and returned home to Hawai'i with the intention of continuing my education.

And then I met Genora.

Actually, my mother introduced us. One day in the parking lot of the television station where she worked, she pointed out a beautiful woman about my age and said, "That's my wonderful friend Genora. I've heard she's a lesbian, and I'd be happy if she was your friend, too . . ." To this day my mother swears that she didn't have anything romantic in mind, but she must have understood that I was lonely. For years I had known that one of the things I most wanted to accomplish in my life was to love another person very well for a very long time— and be loved long and well by that person in return. During the past few years, I had come in contact with thousands of eligible women through my work on abortion rights, sexual assault and sexual freedom—I had even worked at Eve's Garden—but none of my encounters evolved into the relationship I craved. After years of becoming both more deeply lonely and simultaneously more severely annoyed with myself for being lonely, I came to the conclusion that I was not going to meet my "Ms. Right" and that I had better make a plan for my life as a single person. I returned home to pour my energy into my studies.

I did study feverishly—for about three weeks—and I barely looked up from my books until the moment my mother pointed to Genora. And then I never looked at my books again, because from the first time I saw her I could think of nothing but this incredible woman. I said to myself, "No wonder I didn't meet Ms. Right in New York or Michigan or Georgia—she was right here all along!" She was adorable. She was perfect! But was she gay? Was she single? Would she go out on a date with me—soon?

Fortunately for me, the answer to all three questions was yes. I fell in love with Genora the instant I laid eyes on her, and although her reaction wasn't quite so immediate, we did become very involved quite quickly. But of course, things weren't simple. For one thing, Genora was not "out" to her family, her coworkers or even her friends. Back then she had never been to a lesbian bar or a gay community center. She was absolutely isolated; even the women she had dated up until then had insisted that they would eventually marry men.

It's true we were unlikely plaintiffs—perhaps even an unlikely couple, coming as we did from different racial, economic, educational and experiential backgrounds. But the intense emotional connection between us overcame these differences (at least initially) and in addition to having a fantastic sexual attraction to one another, we both felt an urgent desire to care for and be cared for by the other. In time we got in contact with the local Gay Community Center to see whether we could leave our life insurance to one another and to ask if there were any domestic partnership policies we should be aware of. The man we spoke to told us that while there were no domestic partnership benefits available to us, he believed we ought to be able to get legally married. He told us that one or two other couples were thinking about applying for a marriage license, too.

This was a huge decision for us, especially for Genora. In the heat of passion in the middle of the night she had been saying, "Let's get married," or "Let's have a commitment ceremony," but neither one of us ever imagined that legal marriage might be possible. At that time in Hawai'i there was no protection against discrimination in the workplace, and there was every possibility that Genora would be fired from both her jobs and not be able to pay her mortgage if she became involved in an effort that made our relationship public. With so much of the hard-won economic security she had worked to build on the line, I knew this had to be her decision. And she decided she wanted to marry me legally.

Genora and I had already accepted many of the responsibilities of marriage. We were committed to supporting one another financially and to caring for each other in sickness or in health, for better or for worse. While we shared the responsibilities of married couples, however, we didn't enjoy the benefits. The legal benefits of marriage, such as the ability to visit one another in the hospital, cover one another on health insurance plans, or convey entitlements such as social security payments to one another in the event of death, are most important in times of crisis. We wanted to plan ahead.

On December 17, 1990, Genora and I drove to the Honolulu Gay Community Center where we joined two other couples we had never met; we six walked downtown to the Department of Health to apply for our marriage licenses. Our applications were denied, and we three couples hired a lawyer and sued the State of Hawai'i. Our case was filed on May 1, 1991. The plaintiffs were listed in alphabetical order and the suit became known as *Baehr v. Lewin.*

The day we applied for a marriage license the local news media showed up in droves and our privacy vanished literally overnight. Fortunately, even though Genora had never told her mother and father that she was gay—much less that she was about to show up on their television in an effort to marry another woman—they stood by her, and me. My mother did the same. Outside our families and our lawyer, Dan Foley, we had no allies that we knew of, but Genora immediately took it upon herself to generate support where she could. First, she talked with people at her workplace. Next, she made dates to speak to elementary and high school classes. Then she moved on to radio and television interviews and finally to lecturing to college classes.

Genora had always wanted to go to college, but she had envisioned going as a student, not as a proponent of a controversial subject. A brown-skinned woman of mixed ancestry with total command of Pidgin English, she was able to connect with local students who took one look at my white face and barely made eye contact with me again. She excelled at engaging "difficult" high school crowds and was amazed at how many outwardly rough-and-tough teenage boys sought her out after her talks to ask for her number. Physically, Genora is not a large woman, but once a college class, made up mostly of football players trying to fulfill their academic requirements, voted her the most powerful speaker of the semester. In the coming years, Genora spoke to thousands of people in person and reached millions via the print and electronic media.

Meanwhile, she continued to work two full-time jobs and I served as half-time Co-Director of the University of Hawai'i Women's Center and also worked half-time grooming horses at a stable. From our kitchen table we were organizing our effort to get married and were always behind in our payments to our lawyer. Our early fundraisers were held in gay-friendly bars and restaurants and each one was put together painstakingly. We hand-addressed invitations, got our families and friends to help us cater and asked everyone we could think of to donate imaginative door prizes. Most of our supporters were working-class men and women we did not know—drag queens, butch/femme couples and transsexuals. These were people who were not in evidence in the more enfranchised circles of gay activists that were not initially enthusiastic about our case. Some of the people who came to parties and gave us money had had Holy Union ceremonies, and many of those had actually thought that they were getting legally married. Once they found out that the State didn't honor the status their church had conferred on them, they worked for equal rights.

The composition of early supporters reflected the composition of the plaintiffs on the whole. In our tiny group the majority of plaintiffs were women, the majority were of color, and the majority had been born in the islands. Most were not college-educated, some were supporting children and/or other family members, and all earned at or below median income.

Then on May 5, 1993, the Supreme Court of the State of Hawai'i issued an opinion that attracted national attention to *Baehr v. Lewin* and augmented our base of support. The decision was so remarkable that suddenly even the national gay and lesbian organizations that had shown no interest in this issue began to take note. In its 1993 decision, the High Court indicated that the Health Department was indeed discriminating against the plaintiffs in *Baehr v. Lewin;* the Health Department will now have to issue each plaintiff a marriage license unless it can prove a "compelling state interest" in continuing to discriminate. This "interest" will be held up to the strictest scrutiny under the law. The Court noted that the Hawai'i State Constitution prohibits discrimination on the basis of sex, and because we were all denied marriage licenses solely because we and our partners are of the same sex, the State is in violation of the Constitution (this decision is a legal step forward not only for same-sex couples but also for women as a class). In essence, the State will have to stop discriminating unless it can prove that if we same-sex couples get married something truly terrible will happen and that the only way to avoid this calamity is to prevent our marriages.

The State will have its chance to prove its case in lower court in 1996. Whichever side loses at that level will almost certainly appeal back to the Hawai'i Supreme Court. At this writing, most legal observers agree that the State will not be able to meet the burden the High Court has put upon it. But of course the wheels of justice grind slowly. By the time we do get married, Genora and I already will have devoted nearly a decade not only to our work for equal marriage rights but also to each other. After such a long engagement, our wedding gathering will be somewhat like an anniversary party. We will be able to celebrate all the things we have accomplished in our relationship in the past, and we will enter into a legal contract that will increase our ability to provide for one another in the future.

If and when we plaintiffs in *Baehr v. Lewin* do win the right to get married, there will be legal ramifications for couples like us in the other forty-nine states and beyond. Hawai'i is a major honeymoon destination. Every day, opposite-sex couples fly to the islands to have a wedding on the beach, enjoy the sun and surf and then return home—where their marriages are legally recognized under the Full Faith and Credit Clause of the U.S. Constitution. We believe that same-sex couples ought to be able to do the same thing.

Of course other state governments may not agree—not to mention the federal government. We anticipate a backlash on the North American continent when marriage rights are equalized in Hawai'i. To get ready to protect our victory so that everyone can benefit, we need to start preparing our own community and our political allies now.

Genora and I know that many people have mixed or even out-and-out negative feelings about working for equal marriage rights, because marriages frequently don't work out happily (true); or that marriage historically has been oppressive to women (true); or that it traditionally has been about property (true); or that perpetuating the institution of marriage while denying other definitions of family is oppressive to everyone (true). We recognize the mixed feelings people have about supporting equal rights within the context of an institution they believe is inherently wrong. Having been raised in the pacifist Religious Society of Friends, I had similar sentiments about the issue of gays in the military. And I would never want people who have alternative visions of loving and living to give those up. But I do not believe that my relationship with Genora will become oppressive to us if we are granted equal rights. I believe that it will become more secure. Marriage isn't for everyone, but it's what we want. (Perhaps we and couples like us will even help improve the institution.)

Civil rights supporters who want to organize on the continent of North America can contact national organizations such as Lambda for guidance. People who want to help me and Genora and the other plaintiffs pay our legal fees can contact the Hawai'i Equal Rights Marriage Project through the Lesbian and Gay Community Center for the island of O'ahu. And to couples who have the money and desire to travel to Hawai'i in the event that they can marry there, Genora and I have a request to make: Have a great time!—and keep in mind that Hawai'i is unique. At present, there is no place (not even Denmark or Sweden, which have broad domestic partnership policies) where same-sex couples can get legally married. In recognizing our relationships, Hawai'i will be recognizing what is rightfully ours. Our hope is that we, as same-sex couples, will extend the same recognition to the people of Hawaii.

Over the years, the islands have become home to a huge variety of ethnic groups. These groups have developed their own way of living—speaking, cooking, loving, looking—that is simply called "local." And, to a degree, each of these groups has also maintained its own identity. Hawai'i is not the harmonious melting pot of the American dream, but there is a style of tolerance that has not always been operative on the mainland. When Genora and I were little girls, interracial couples—even those of opposite sexes—could not get married in many states on the North American continent; this situation was finally corrected via the lawsuit *Loving v. Virginia,* despite the objection of lawyers who insisted (as our opponents do in this case) that God did not intend the plaintiffs to marry one another and therefore the government should not allow it. In Hawai'i, interracial marriage is common. In fact, all of Genora's siblings married, as did mine, and not one of our brothers or sisters married strictly within their race.

The islands are also home to an ever-growing sovereignty movement that seeks self-determination for the people of Hawai'i. Different sovereignty groups have different specific blueprints for independence, but increasing numbers of residents agree that the people of Hawai'i in general and the people of Hawaiian ancestry in particular need to have greater control over their land, culture and economy. More and more people are learning the native language, restoring hidden history, recovering ancient *hula,* returning to traditional diets and finding ways to fish, farm and produce goods according to the methods of the ancestors. Native Hawaiians lead and define the sovereignty movement, but even *haoles* are growing respectful of the concept. Not long ago a locally prominent network of Christian churches marked the one hundredth anniversary of the U.S. takeover of Hawai'i by publicly apologizing for the church's historical contribution to imperialism. (Given what Christianity has meant in Hawai'i, it should come as no surprise that some local residents are less than enthusiastic when, once again, groups such as the Christian Coalition—an outside organization of Christians from far away—attempt to tell the people of Hawai'i that same-sex marriage is wrong.)

Today native Hawaiians are at the bottom of the socioeconomic ladder in Hawai'i, yet the Hawaiian culture is used to lure tourists to spend dollars in hotels not owned by locals built on land not controlled by locals (much less native Hawaiians). Some sovereignty groups believe that tourism should be ended. Other groups agree that the tourism industry as it currently operates is economically, culturally and environmentally exploitative, but they also believe that at present the local economy is dependent on tourism. At least for now they favor "responsible tourism." Neither Genora nor I endorse one sovereignty blueprint over another, but as supporters of both sovereignty and equal marriage rights for same-sex couples, we feel strongly that if through our involvement in *Baehr v. Lewin* we are to play a role in bringing visitors to Hawai'i, we also must at the very least play a role in promoting responsible tourism.

There is no infrastructure yet whereby visitors can ensure that their dollars go to local businesses or that the tourist activities they engage in—attending *lū'aus,* watching *hula,* or seeing a historic site—convey the realities of life for local people. Genora and I hope that such an infrastructure will be established before our case is resolved, but in the meantime we suggest that any same-sex couple traveling to Hawai'i to get married first get in touch with *Na Mamo O Hawai'i,* a gay and lesbian organization of native Hawaiians, Asian and Pacific islanders and their friends, or with a similar group. Talking with residents can be great for finding the way to sights that are breathtaking, history that is affirming and people who possess the spirit of *aloha*—a Hawaiian word that means "hello," "good-bye" and "love." To me, *aloha* also connotes hospitality and generosity. But, despite what the travel ads may say, *aloha* is not something that can be bought—*aloha* must be shared. In becoming the first to recognize our individual worth and the worth of our relationships in the area of marriage, Hawai'i will be extending its *aloha* to members of same-sex couples. In accepting Hawaii's offer of respect and *aloha,* we must respond in kind. And in this way, each of us will show how much we appreciate being able to dance *hula* at our legal same-sex wedding.

"Joan Nestle and Mabel Hampton" by Morgan Gwenwald

An Interview by Kate Rushin

Mabel Hampton:
"Cracking Open the Door"

Mabel Hampton *was born in Winston-Salem, North Carolina, in 1902. After her mother, and then her grandmother died (when she was about six years old), Mabel's aunt came and took her to New York City, where she lives now. Unhappy living with her aunt and minister uncle, Mabel left home early and made a life on her own. She's done many things in her life, including singing, dancing, and domestic work. In 1979, she helped found the Lesbian Herstory Archives with Joan Nestle, donating her own books to begin the collection.*

Here are excerpts of Mabel's story (she is eighty-five years old at this writing) as told to local writer and poet, Kate Rushin.

I always said to myself, wherever I went and whatever I did, I always do what my mother says. I dare to say that my mother took care of me all through my life up until I was a grown woman. . . . I believe that. All through life. Didn't matter what I did or where I went, Mother was with me to show me the right path. Lot of people don't believe that, but I believe it. If someone says something to me, I don't want to do it, I says, well, my mother will tell me what to do. The dead takes care of me . . . and also the living. . . .

I never got into too much trouble. When I got to New York, when Grandma died, my aunt put me in school down in the Village [Greenwich Village], and when I ran away, I also went to school. Disappeared into thin air for fourteen years, so don't tell me children can't hide. I got along nicely. People took me in. . . . They sent me to school in New Jersey, but I never told them why I left.

I did housework; I did show work. A little bit of everything. The reason I jumped into housework was at least nobody bothered me. I got my money and I got my food and nobody messed with me. I just dabbled around like I was crazy. . . . I had myself a ripping good time. In the twenties, I went on stage for a while, and everybody seemed to like me. Nothing bothered me. I seemed to grow along with the times. I had all women friends. I never bothered with the men, because, on account of my uncle, I was scared of them. He was a minister, but he was fresh, and I didn't like 'im. . . . There were plenty of clubs I lived in, and I made friends with different women in the clubs and in the theater. Everything came natural to me. . . .

We had [social] clubs that other women would come and join; we'd have parties and things like that to meet each other. If you knew somebody they might introduce you to a friend who would say, "Come down and spend the night." We'd have a few friends in, have food, spend a couple of days and then go home. You'd have a place to stay and something to eat, and a place to meet other women.

I had a small club. Four or five people would come and stay the weekend, and meet other girls. Then they would bring somebody else and they would bring somebody else, and that's the way it went on. Mabel's club house in Harlem—122nd St. near Fifth Ave. I had four or five rooms, and it was only my girlfriend and me.

I never had "rent" parties, because you had to be careful. I went to parties that were "rent" parties. People would come and bring food and give the girl ten or fifteen bucks, and they'd have drinks and stay all night long to dance. That's the way we carried on. All women now—there weren't any men tangled in there. Mostly all black too; very seldom did I have whites.

Some of the girls were married, but they wouldn't let you know they were married. You'd have to squeeze it out of them. But now it seems like so many of them were married that you were surprised. You had to be careful with the women you had with you because they'd talk. They'd get in bed with their husbands and talk up a dream. And then there were other women whose husbands, if you said their wives did anything at all, why they'd beat you up.

I had one girlfriend whose boyfriend worked on the road. Somebody told him something. Said, "Old man, your old lady's a bulldagger." He said, "Oh, no!" So he came in one night. . . . I happened to be there, and I heard the key and went to the head of the stairs and looked down; they had a glass in the front door, and I saw this man with this key. So I turned right around and went back to the room and said, "I think Pop is coming." She said, "Oh, no." I said, "You'd better believe he's coming."

He was up those stairs before I could say boo! He said, "Hello, Mabel." I said, "Hi, Sweetie. How are you?" I put my arm through his arm and said, "What are you doing here?" To give 'em a chance to get their selves together, I said, "Maud is sleeping. If you want, I'll wake her up."

"Oh, no, don't wake her. I didn't have to work tonight."

I said, "She's all right. Come on downstairs, and we'll have some soda or some champagne on ice."

So we went on down the back stairs. That gave her a chance to come out of the room and come down the front stairs. So we set down at the table and he said, "Is that some fried chicken?" I said, "Yeh, we were expecting some people maybe around twelve or one, but they called and said they couldn't come." He said, "That's all right. I'll take a piece of chicken and some potato salad." And I offered him some chitlins. I know all the men love chitlins. So I fixed his plate, and I fixed a little plate for myself, and we sat there and talked, and later she came struttin' on down the stairs. "Why Pops, what are you doing here?" He says, "Now I didn't have to work tonight, so I thought I'd come home and see what you chicks were doing." She says, "Just what you see us doing. What do you think we're doing?" He says, "I know you weren't doing anything. I'm going out to the bar and I'm going to beat up Sam."

"You're going to beat up Sam? Who is he?"

"Oh, some old S.J. tried to tell me something I didn't want to hear." And he bet me money. I'll win my money. I said, "Good! And when you win it bring it back here." Anyhow, after he ate and drank, and he went on there, we set down and laughed! We had a ball!

Now the young generation is stepping in, and they're taking over. They'll take somebody today, and turn around and boom, boom, boom, take somebody else tomorrow. But we didn't do that. We didn't mess around like that. That's why I don't know too many people, because I stuck right with one person and that was my person: Lillian [Foster]. We were together 42 years. We met in 1932, and she died in 1979.

I didn't mix in with too many people. I fed everybody, most of them, with a long-handled spoon. Because I didn't want them to know my business, and I didn't want to know theirs. . . . I had no family. I never bothered nobody. Nobody bothered me. I had a lot of [Black women] friends. . . . We didn't use the term gay. We were just lovers . . . something like that.

I loved all my friends, like Ethel Waters, and all them big people. I loved them and got along with them. I was little Mabel, that's all. Little Mabel run like hell,

I'm telling you. I knew Alberta Hunter very well. I knew all those women. They were young women. I got in next them, you see. I would dance at the Garden of Joy. Then just before I met Lillian, I took up concert singing. I sang at the World's Fair. I was in Jersey City with Lillian then. I got along nicely.

I have my own religion. I don't mix up with nobody else's. I was Catholic and that's that. If Father Jeffries doesn't like what I do that's his business. "Miss Hampton, why don't you come to confession?" I say, "What am I gonna confess? What am I gonna confess?" I'll do the same thing as long as I live. And I'm positively sure that God knows all about it. So why should you worry?

Right now the most important thing to me is living here [at the Lesbian Herstory Archives in Joan Nestle's apartment in New York City]. I never figured on being in a place like this. . . . Hundreds of women come to visit; I want to live and see more, more, more. . . . I met Joan [Nestle]'s mother in 1958; Joan was a young girl of seventeen then. I went to work for her mother. I was like one in the family. Anything happened to Joan, her mother would get on the phone and call me.

I'm glad I started the Archives. I gave Joan the first books I had. All about the gays. That's all I lived for—to see that something comes to generations that I had been longing to see.

I didn't think anything of the civil rights movement at the time, because I didn't think it would come out like it is now. It's right out in full force, and you can't stop it. It's no stopping now. We've got the front seat, and we're going to hold onto that seat, even if we have to take everyone down with us.

When the women's movement came along I thought that the doors began to crack open. When the door begins to crack open, it won't be too long before there'll be another crack and another crack and then before you know it, the door will be wide open.

And when the gay movement really came out, I said, "Here it comes! Here it comes! Whoopie!" I was in the Gay Pride Parade a few weeks ago. I had a buddy push me in a chair. All the flags were behind me. I had a lovely time. One of the women who was something [a liaison] to the mayor was right there by my side. I thought, "This is just what the doctor ordered."

People should come out of the closet and stay out. Try to fight to do whatever you can to make our life a beautiful life to live.

Adrienne Rich

For Memory

Old words: *trust fidelity*
Nothing new yet to take their place.

I rake leaves, clear the lawn, October grass
painfully green beneath the gold
and in this silent labor thoughts of you
start up
I hear your voice: *disloyalty betrayal*
stinging the wires

I stuff the old leaves into sacks
and still they fall and still
I see my work undone

One shivering rainswept afternoon
and the whole job to be done over

I can't know what you know
unless you tell me

there are gashes in our understandings
of this world
We came together in a common
fury of direction
barely mentioning difference
(what drew our finest hairs
to fire
the deep, difficult troughs
unvoiced)
I fell through a basement railing
the first day of school and cut my forehead open—
did I ever tell you? More than forty years
and I still remember smelling my own blood
like the smell of a new schoolbook

And did you ever tell me
how your mother called you in from play
and from whom?   To what?   These atoms filmed by ordinary dust
that common life we each and all bent out of orbit from
to which we must return simply to say
this is where I came from
this is what I knew

The past is not a husk   yet change goes on

Freedom. It isn't once, to walk out
under the Milky Way, feeling the rivers
of light, the fields of dark—
freedom is daily, prose-bound, routine
remembering. Putting together, inch by inch
the starry worlds. From all the lost collections.

1979

"Alice Molloy" by Jean Weisinger

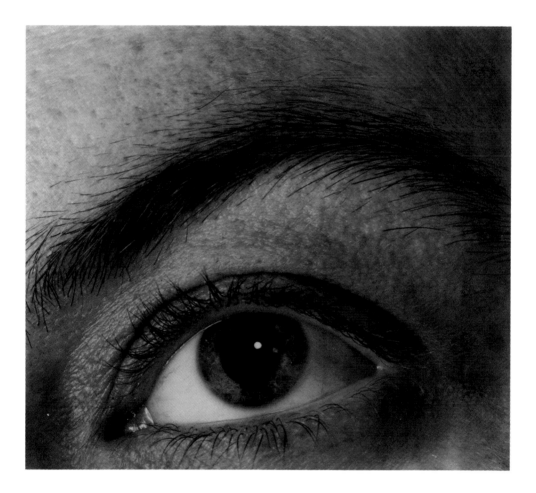

"Supersight, Muriel Rukeyser's Eye, New York, c. 1940,"
by Berenice Abbott/Commerce Graphics Ltd, Inc.

Note: This image appeared as the author photograph on Muriel Rukeyser's book
about the pioneering scientist, *The Traces of Thomas Harriot* (Random House, 1970).

Jan Heller Levi

I am staring at an eye . . .

I am staring at an eye. Or is it staring at me? It is severe, specific, and, deep in the iris, somehow, kind. It is the eye of genius. And in its genius, passes stern judgment. Also, because this is what genius does, forgives.

That high arched brow, that flurry of stiff hairs that define. Every eyelash particular. Turn it upside down: it is the glare of a crow. Turn it back: it swoops into the book jacket's white spine: in nonserif lowercase, the words *the traces of;* in chiseled capital letters, *THOMAS HARIOT;* then her name, in red, no it's more orange than red, her name, Muriel—the sounds "a little like Mortal and More and Endure/and a word like Real, a sound like Health or Hell . . ." (the lines are hers, from the poem "Then I Saw What the Calling Was"), her name, known to us too little, lost to us too long: *Muriel Rukeyser.*

The photograph was taken by Berenice Abbott. A friend muses, what went on between those two women that day? Or the days before, the days after? Were they lovers? Was this author photo a gift of love, in something of the same way that, as Rukeyser wrote, writing is: "only another way of giving—a courtesy, if you will, and a form of love." My courtesy: to leave alone what I cannot know.

Have I been too discreet? Was she? If she were alive today, would she declare? Declare herself? From her poem "Despisals":

Among our secrecies, not to despise our Jews
(that is, ourselves) or our darkness, our blacks,
or in our sexuality   wherever it takes us
and we now know we are productive
too productive, too reproductive
for our present invention—never to despise
the homosexual who goes building another
with touch with touch (not to despise any touch)
each like himself, like herself each.
You are this.

You are this. This woman, who lived with this photograph for years in her apartment. The actual print, I think. Tragically frayed at the edges, from long incarceration in a manila envelope too small to contain it. Bent. Creased. I found it years after her death, after I cleaned out her apartment in Westbeth and stored the boxes and boxes of papers in the damp basement of a cathedral. Finally, those papers found their way to the Library of Congress. Save for the one or two boxes that ended up in the back of my closet. And when I found those boxes, I found, in that too-small envelope, her eye.

Oh, I know she had been watching me. Has been watching me. Through the destruction of a marriage, the reckless flight into a woman's arms. Oh but I loved her. Don't misunderstand me. But him, I loved him too.

No, this isn't what I meant to write at all. Though for a long time I have wanted to apologize to Muriel Rukeyser, or to someone anyway, for that too-small envelope. (I'm not the one who put the photo in it; and I suspect it was done years before I came along, but facts like that have so little to do with long-term, free-floating guilt . . .) What I am trying to do is report on the pity of all our too-small envelopes, that cannot accommodate the largeness of our experience.

Do you think she was a lesbian, people ask. *Certainly she was.* But do I think she would turn her back on a man? *That flirt?,* I say, laughing. *Certainly not.* What it comes down to is this: She was always a great opener of doors.

Mab Segrest

Les*Beijing

"Gays Don't Have Fun" read the headline on the back page of the daily newspaper of the Forum on Women. I guess whoever wrote the article wasn't at the disco last night, I reflected with what was left of my brain. Late the evening before in a disco packed with lesbians from many countries, with young Chinese couples (not all of them straight), and green-clad Chinese police, a Black woman and a white woman had climbed up on the small stage and begun a lithe dance together to a slow, bluesy song. I'd thought, "Well, here's where we get to see the inside of Chinese jails. Harry Wu, where are you?" But, remarkably, the crowd was receptive, charged like we were with the music and the movement.

"The meaning of our love for women is what we have constantly to expand." The phrase kept floating through my head, the title of an Adrienne Rich essay circa 1977, as I negotiated the muddy but vibrant scene at the conference site at Huairou. This China experience at a conference of 25,000 women had me flashing back to when lesbian/feminism was declared "a whole new force in history," its goal "not equality but utter transformation"; and Adrienne had urged us not to withdraw from the "immense, burgeoning diversity of the global women's movement" that moved vibrantly now around me. Beijing sounded again for me the lesbian and feminist ground note. It was remarkable to be in a place where global sisterhood and global community were not an abstraction but something to see each day on the streets.

It reminded me of the days (far enough back that Rita Mae was political) of "woman identification," when we lesbians considered ourselves the "rage of all women condensed to the point of explosion." The days when, fresh from her first breast surgery, Audre Lorde electrified us: "Your silences will not save you," she said, and started to teach us about honoring differences.   Then the differences hit.

"With such grace, such blind faith the commitment to women in the [U.S.] feminist movement grew to be exclusive and reactionary." Cherríe Moraga lamented the grief I myself came to feel as I saw too close the power of racism and class biases explode "lesbian community." I felt the tremors in Durham when the Lesbian Sex Mafia brought their determination to organize "for our sexual desire as strongly as for our sexual defense" into the Barnard Conference in Sexuality in 1982, and former lesbian/feminists fought the "sex wars" to a draw over pornography and censorship. A more complex understanding of lesbian sexuality emerged as lesbians publicly claimed sexual practices and identities such as butch/femme and SM that had been formerly derided as "male identified" but were now explored by working-class lesbians as "shaped in large part by class." "I will give up nothing. I will give up no one," Dorothy Allison, in the thick of the Barnard dispute, declared.

With other dykes, I felt this new openness about lesbian sexuality and the growing tragedy of AIDS create new alliances with gay men. ACT UP, Queer Nation, and Lesbian Avengers brought new models of militance. "Queer" theory blossomed, located too exclusively within universities for my tastes. A resurgent Right Wing increasingly contracted the space of "normalcy" through the Bush and Reagan years—of Hardwick, Oregon, Colorado, the Christian Coalition, a deepening racism, and a restructuring of the global economy that I fear will bring a full-blown fascism in this decade in this country. Faced with the growing threat from the Right and no longer convinced that lesbian/feminism by itself would bring "utter transformation," I relocated myself politically in the anti-racist, anti-fascist movement, like many other lesbians who went to the ground in a range of progressive movements in the 1980s.

Turkey baster in hand, I also joined the ranks of Lesbian Moms as my lover Barbara gave birth to our daughter, Annie, who would change our lives forever (less time for meetings, more capacity for love). My understanding of gender shifted as I read Leslie Feinberg's *Stone Butch Blues,* and I realized that I care less about people's plumbing than their hearts and Attitude. I watched with amazement as kd cavorted on *Austin City Limits* in her chopped-off farmers boots and gender fuck, and lesbians finally became chic, and Dorothy got a great review for *Bastard Out of Carolina* in the *New York Times,* and lesbians began to pull in six-figure book contracts. With many, many women and men I mourned Audre Lorde, whose death called us to take up her life's work more maturely as we ourselves aged.

In Beijing last month, I felt all this history was there with me as the lesbian tent took its place among ten "diversity tents," across from a lively grassroots women's tent, near the older women's tent and a shamefully inaccessible disability tent. There were open lesbians (myself included) on the plenary programs that framed the NGO conference; lesbian regional meetings and panels; and daily caucus meeting at five P.M. Five hundred women marched for lesbian rights. A post-Crusades alliance of Islamic fundamentalists and the Vatican struggled to keep the word "gender" altogether out of the proposed Platform for Action at the parallel UN conference in Beijing, and "family" monolithic and singular. "Sexual orientation" was mentioned four times in the draft Platform, the first time the issue was ever debated on the floor of the UN. Although these disputed passages were removed, near dawn in the final hour, thirty countries rose to speak against discrimination on the basis of sexual orientation. What did pass was a statement on "the human rights of women . . . to have control over and decide freely and responsibly on matters relating to their sexuality." All of this lesbian organizing (the meaning of our love for women that we must constantly expand) will open up more space for gay men, and for other sexual minorities.

One of the Asian lesbians in The Tent had a T-shirt on that said, "QUEER BABE." But it reminded me of the moment at the Black Nations/Queer Nations Conference in New York last spring when Simon Nkoli, the first person in the African National Congress to come out (at his treason trial), asked—"We are calling ourselves queer now?"

In this international context, I realized that I'm not so sure about this "Queer" thing anymore, if it's what we should be exporting. Why reinscribe our alienation? I don't have the illusions I had twenty years ago. But what I want these days as a lesbian and a human being is an acknowledgment of my beloved place within multiple and relating communities, at a time when the forces driving this country (fear, greed, competition, and meanness) are out to destroy community altogether. The South Africans call what I want *Ubuntu*—to be "born to belonging." But it must be a community in which we "give up nothing and no one"—to the drive for profits, narrow ideology, or rigid community norms. After all, it's the South Africans who have sexual orientation, for now at least, in their constitution.

For us to be all together there in China, talking and dancing and marching, bringing our particular histories, all our broken silences, it changed me; or maybe just brought me back around. Or maybe it was the Filipina group, Inang Laya ("Mother Freedom"), who had us holding hands together and singing in the Grassroots Tent that last Wednesday, as someone translated the lyrics from Tagalog: "Will it be enough to love you and all other women forever?" There seemed to be a good many of us there willing to give it a try.

"Lesbian Rights March, September 1995, People's Republic of China" by Ann Meredith

"Lesbian Rights March, September 1995, People's Republic of China" by Ann Meredith

Muriel Rukeyser

Waking This Morning

Waking this morning,
a violent woman in the violent day
Laughing.
                      Past the line of memory
along the long body of your life
in which move childhood, youth, your lifetime of touch,
eyes, lips, chest, belly, sex, legs, to the waves of the sheet.
I look past the little plant
on the city windowsill
to the tall towers bookshaped, crushed together in greed,
the river flashing flowing corroded,
the intricate harbor and the sea, the wars, the moon, the
    planets, all who people space
in the sun visible invisible.
African violets in the light
breathing, in a breathing universe.   I want strong peace, and
    delight,
the wild good.
I want to make my touch poems:

to find my morning, to find you entire
alive moving among the anti-touch people.

                    I say across the waves of the air to you:
today once more
I will try to be non-violent
one more day
this morning, waking the world away
in the violent day.

"Saguaro Scape" by Margaret Randall

Notes on Contributors

Berenice Abbott (1898–1991) began her career as an apprentice to Man Ray in 1923. Her WPA-sponsored project, "Changing New York," recorded the arrival of the city's skyscrapers. She devised the Projection-Supersight system of photography, which utilizes a specially designed camera to take larger-than-life images on 16″ × 20″ sheet film. A Supersight photograph of Muriel Rukeyser's eye is included in this anthology, and apparently, Abbott and Rukeyser had imagined collaborating on a book of Supersight photographs and poems. Abbott marketed and patented many of her inventions, and published three books of science photography in the sixties before relocating to Maine. During her lifetime, retrospective exhibits were held at the Smithsonian, the Museum of Modern Art and the New York Public Library. Abbott had her last exhibition at the Portland Museum of Art in 1991, the same year she died.

Donna Allegra writes poetry, fiction and essays. Her work has been most recently anthologized in *SportsDykes; Lesbian Erotics; All the Ways Home: Short Stories About Children and the Lesbian and Gay Community; Out of the Class Closet—Lesbians Speak;* and *Dyke Life.*

Dorothy Allison is at work on a new novel, *Cavedweller.* Her books include the poetry collection *The Women Who Hate Me,* and the novel *Bastard Out of Carolina,* nominated for the National Book Award. She lives in northern California with her partner and her son.

Madelyn Arnold is the author of *Bird-Eyes* (Seal Press, 1988) and has published stories in a number of literary and feminist journals and anthologies. She lives in Seattle, Washington, where she is at work on a new novel.

Ninia Leilani Baehr has a strong background in feminist activism and is the author of *Abortion Without Apology: A Radical History for the 1990s.* She makes her living as a grant writer and is most proud of her work with urban youth.

JEB (Joan E. Biren) is the author of two volumes of lesbian photography: *Eye to Eye* (1979) and *Making a Way* (1987). She has also produced videos, including *A Simple Matter of Justice,* the official record of the 1993 March on Washington.

Beth Brant is a Bay of Quinte Mohawk. She is the author of *Mohawk Trail, Food & Spirits* and *Writing as Witness.* She is the editor of *A Gathering of Spirit* and *I'll Sing 'Til I Die: Conversations with Tyendinaga Elders.*

Mi Ok Song Bruining is a Libra Rat, born in Korea and adopted when she was five years old. She holds an MSW and is currently writing a book on international adoption issues. Her poetry has been published in many anthologies.

Pat Califia, the unofficial poster dyke for lesbian S/M, is a prolific writer of fiction and nonfiction and an authority on contemporary sexual issues. She lives in San Francisco, and has published *Melting Point* and *Macho Sluts* with Alyson Publications, among other titles.

Canyon Sam's book *One Hundred Voices of Tar: Tibetan Women Speak* will soon be published. Her nationally acclaimed solo show, *The Dissident,* is being made into a film by Academy Award–nominated filmmaker Elizabeth Thompson. Canyon's writing appears in *Lesbian Words: State of the Art, Amazon All Stars,* and elsewhere.

Shu Lea Cheang is a filmmaker and installation artist whose multichannel video installations, *Color Schemes* and *Those Fluttering Objects of Desire,* were both exhibited at the Whitney Museum of American Art. *Fresh Kill* was her first feature film, and in 1995 she developed a cybernetic bowling tournament, *Bowling Alley,* for Walker Art Center. She is now developing a web feature as a one-year performance/installation.

Chrystos, born off-reservation of a Menominee father and a euro-immigrant mother, is self-educated. She has published five books of poetry, received an NEA grant and an Astraea's Sappho Award of Distinction, and works actively on Native Rights and many political issues.

Cheryl Clarke has published four widely praised books of poetry: *Narratives: Poems in the Tradition of Black Women, Living As a Lesbian, Humid Pitch* and *Experimental Love*. One of the longest serving editors on the "Conditions" collective (1981–90), she works at Rutgers University.

Tee A. Corinne is a writer and artist whose work has been published in the feminist and lesbian press since 1974. Her books include *The Cunt Coloring Book, The Sparkling Lavender Dust of Lust, Family, Lovers, Dreams of the Woman Who Loved Sex* and *Yantras of Womanlove*.

Betsy Crowell grew up in Wyoming and worked as a teacher, a mother and an administrator of services for the disabled before she became a photographer. She lives in New York City with the painter Louise Fishman.

Diana Davies is an anarchist documentary photographer living in Massachusetts. Davies's work has been published in the *New York Times, WIN Magazine, Life* and the *Village Voice*. She has exhibited widely, and her photographs are in collections at the Smithsonian Institution, Howard University, the Special Collections of the New York Public Library and the Swarthmore Peace Library.

Barbara Deming's (1917–84) papers are housed at the Radcliffe College Schlesinger Library and are open to researchers. Poet, essayist, fiction writer and tireless activist, her book *Prisons That Could Not Hold* was recently reprinted by the University of Georgia Press, and her collected poems, *I Change, I Change,* was published by New Victoria Press in 1996.

Alexis De Veaux is a poet, writer and activist whose work is widely known. The author of several books, her short stories have appeared in the anthologies *Midnight Birds* (1980), *Memory of Kin: Stories About Family by Black Writers* (1991), and *Children of the Night* (1995). She holds a doctorate in American Studies and teaches Women's Studies at SUNY, Buffalo.

Cheryl Dunye is the driving force behind the feature film *The Watermelon Woman*. Her previous work includes *Greetings from Africa* and the experimental videos *The Potluck and the Passion* and *She Don't Fade*. Dunye's work has been featured at the Sundance Film Festival, International Berlin Film Festival, Toronto International Film and Video Festival and the New York Lesbian and Gay Film and Video Festival (1995 Victor Russo Award).

Elsa E'der is one of nineteen granddaughters descendant from Filipino/Chinese/Portuguese plantation laborers of Hawaii. A resident of San Francisco since 1982, she has been involved in numerous lesbian, women of color and Asian American projects and events. Currently, she is revising a screenplay entitled *Venus in Gemini.*

E.T. Baby Maniac (Ela Troyano, Jane Castle and Shu Lea Cheang) collaborated on the video *Sex Fish, 6:00* in 1993.

Kleya Forté-Escamilla has published two novels and a short story collection; she is writing a new novel about women in community and a nonfiction book about her lifetime spiritual journey. The former Astraea Award–winner instructs nonnative, English-speaking writers, currently Croatian women, in writing.

Alicia Gaspar de Alba, a native of the Juárez/El Paso border and a founding faculty member of the César Chávez Center in Chicano/Chicana Studies at UCLA, holds a Ph.D. in American Studies. Author of *The Mystery of Survival and Other Stories,* she has published fiction and poetry in numerous anthologies.

Alvia Golden's writing can be found in *The Crimson Edge: Older Women Writing* (Chicory Blue Press), *The Arc of Love: An Anthology of Lesbian Love Poems* (Scribner), and *The Hudson Review.*

Jewelle Gomez is the author of these Firebrand Books: *The Gilda Stories, Forty Three Septembers, Oral Tradition* and *Bones and Ash: A Gilda Story* (performed by Urban Bush Women); and she is the coeditor with Eric Garber of *Swords of the Rainbow,* from Alyson Publications.

Luz Maria Gordillo, born in Mexico City, received a Masters in Media Studies from the New School for Social Research, and has had exhibits at Parsons School of Design and a one-woman show at the New School entitled *Mi México.* She is working on *Thighs with Neon Lights,* and has produced many cultural events promoting Latin American artists in New York.

C. A. Griffith is a writer and independent video/filmmaker. Currently residing in Santa Barbara, she is pursuing a career in teaching. As cameraperson and cinematographer, her credits include *Eyes on the Prize II, Juice* and *Audre Lorde: A Litany for Survival. Family Pictures* was the centerpiece of her MFA video/installation project. Her writing can also be found in *Calyx, Herotica 4* and *Cultures of Resistance: Black Women Film and Video Artists.*

Elisabeth Griggs is a photographer living in New York City.

Morgan Gwenwald has been an activist photographer for more than twenty years, documenting events and actions. She also creates fine art portraits and lesbian erotica. Her work has appeared in many groundbreaking books, including *Coming to Power, The Persistent Desire* and *No Thing But the Girl,* as well as in many community publications in the U.S., Europe and Australia.

Marilyn Hacker, winner of the National Book Award, a Lambda Literary Award and the Lenore Marshall/*Nation* Award for Poetry, has published eight books of poetry—most recently, *Winter Numbers* and *Selected Poems* from W. W. Norton. She lives in New York and Paris.

Barbara Hammer, lesbian/feminist experimental film/video artist, has made over fifty films and twenty-seven videos. Her two feature documentaries, *Nitrate Kisses* and *Tender Fictions* (1995), played at Sundance and Berlin Film Festivals to much acclaim. She received the Polar Bear Award at Berlin for a lifetime contribution to lesbian filmmaking.

Gale Jackson, a poet, storyteller, librarian and cultural education worker, has appeared in *Black American Literature Forum, Callaloo, Ploughshares* and *The Kenyon Review.* Her books include the collaborative *We Stand Our Ground* (New York: Ikon, 1988) and a forthcoming folktale adaptation, *Rattlesnake's Tale.*

Melanie Kaye/Kantrowitz is the author of *The Issue Is Power* and *My Jewish Face & Other Stories,* coeditor of *The Tribe of Dina,* and former editor of *Sinister Wisdom.* She is codirector of "Jews for Radical & Economic Justice" in New York City and has taught all over the country.

Kathryn Kirk is a documentary photographer living and working in New York City. Her photographs have appeared in *Sinister Wisdom, The Blatant Image, Zeit Magazine* and the *New York Times.*

Irene Klepfisz, author of *A Few Words in the Mother Tongue* (poetry) and *Dream of an Insomniac* (essays), was a founding editor of *Conditions* magazine and currently serves as editorial consultant for the Jewish feminist magazine *Bridges*. She is also a member of *Hemshekh: Feminist Institute for Secular Jewish Cultural Community*.

Lisa Kron, a solo performer and founding member of the Obie Award–winning company The Five Lesbian Brothers, was nominated for a 1994–95 Drama Desk Award for *101 Humiliating Stories*. Kron's *2.5 Minute Ride* will be produced by International Productions Associates and the La Jolla Playhouse in September 1996.

Joan Larkin's collections of poetry include *Housework, A Long Sound* and *Cold River*. She coedited the anthologies *Amazon Poetry, Lesbian Poetry* and *Gay and Lesbian Poetry in Our Time*. A 1996 NEA grant recipient in poetry, she lives and writes in New York City.

Zoe Leonard has exhibited internationally, in many one-person and group exhibitions. A founding member of "Fierce Pussy," her work is in the collections of the Ghent Museum, Belgium; the Museum of Fine Arts, Houston; Staad Museum, Germany; and the Whitney Museum of American Art in New York City.

Jan Heller Levi is a poet and the editor of *A Muriel Rukeyser Reader* (W. W. Norton). She lives in New York City and works at the *New York Times*.

Cynthia Lollar received a 1995 grant for fiction from the Maryland State Arts Council and is completing an MFA in creative writing at American University. She lives with her partner of ten years in College Park, Maryland.

Audre Lorde's inspiration (1934–92) is legion—calling on us to do our work. New York State Poet and NEA grant recipient, she published sixteen books of poetry and prose, including *The Black Unicorn, Sister Outsider, The Cancer Journals, Zami: A New Spelling of My Name, Undersong* and *The Marvelous Arithmetics of Distance*.

Judith McDaniel is a writer and activist who lives in Tucson, Arizona. Her most recent book is *The Lesbian Couples Guide* (HarperCollins, 1995). She is working on *The Life of Barbara Deming* and is the literary executor of Barbara Deming's estate.

Colleen McKay lives and works in New York City. She is primarily a portrait and documentary photographer with special affection for Mexico and Latin America.

Hawk Madrone: "At fifty-six, my home is my sanctuary, a women-only hilltop in southern Oregon. With my animal companions always nearby, I am a woodworker, gardener, photographer, baker, knitter, teacher, woodsman, writer, who purposes to do Tai Chi as a way of life."

Ann Meredith, internationally acclaimed photographer, curator and arts activist, has chronicled women's, Lesbian and Gay culture for the last twenty-six years. Her work is in the Library of Congress, the New York Public Library and the Smithsonian Institution.

Honor Moore published *The White Blackbird,* a biography of her painter-grandmother, Margarett Sargent, in March 1996 (Viking). *Memoir* (poems) appeared in 1988 (Chicory Blue Press). She teaches writing workshops at her home in Connecticut and is completing a new book of poems.

Lisa Morphew is a writer/photographer living in Asheville, North Carolina, where she is editor of *Community Connections,* the gay and lesbian newspaper. Her photographs have been exhibited nationally and in France, and are housed in numerous collections. She received a North Carolina Fellowship in Photography in 1989.

Eileen Myles has lived in New York City since 1974. Her latest books are *Maxfield Parrish/early and new poems, Chelsea Girls* and *The New Fuck You,* coedited with Liz Kotz. Currently she's writing a fiction trilogy, the first of which is called *Cool for You.*

Carol O'Donnell lives in Brooklyn and spent her childhood in the coalfields, factories and ethnic strongholds of northeast Pennsylvania. She is a teacher of glorious children at Manhattan Country School, and is an educational activist. She graduated from Sarah Lawrence and has a collection of stories ready.

Margaret Randall's most recent book is *The Price You Pay: The Hidden Cost of Women's Relationship to Money* (Routledge, 1996). She lives with her lifetime companion, the artist Barbara Byers, in Albuquerque, New Mexico.

M.C. Randall lives in Oakland and is a member of *Salmon Run,* a lesbian writing group. She has previously published in *Sinister Wisdom* and *Prosodia,* and has recently completed the Master of Poetics Program at New College in San Francisco.

Bessy Reyna was born in Cuba and raised in Panama. Her work appears in anthologies in the U.S. and Latin America, including *In Other Words: Literature by Latinas in the U.S.* (R. Fernandez, ed., Arte Publico, 1994) and *The Arc of Love: An Anthology of Lesbian Love Poems* (C. Coss., ed., Scribner, 1996).

Adrienne Rich has published sixteen books of poetry and four books of prose—most recently *Dark Fields of the Republic* and *What Is Found There*. She has been honored with many awards, from the Yale Younger Poets Prize in 1951 to the Lenore Marshall/*Nation* Prize for Poetry (for *An Atlas of the Difficult World*) and a recent MacArthur Award.

Marian Roth is a self-taught photographer, and has been making pictures for twenty-five years. She lives, makes art and teaches photography in Provincetown, Massachusetts. Roth has received grants from the Barbara Deming Foundation and the Massachusetts Artists Council for "The Working Women of Provincetown," and her book, *Album,* has been published by Cosmos Press.

Muriel Rukeyser (1913–79), the visionary and uncategorizable poet, is the author of seventeen books of poetry, three plays, five children's books, a novel and a documentary screenplay. A partial and excellent sampling of her legacy is gathered in *A Muriel Rukeyser Reader,* and *The Life of Poetry* will be reprinted in the near future.

Kate Rushin's first book of poetry is the acclaimed *The Black Back-Ups,* and she collaborated on the play *Sanctuary: The Spirit of Harriet Tubman.* From 1982–92, she was a member of the New Words Book Store Collective. Currently, she is Director of the Center for African American Studies and Visiting Writer at Wesleyan University.

Saskia Scheffer was born in Almelo, the Netherlands, and studied language and literature at the University of Amsterdam. She is primarily self-taught in photography, taking a few courses at ICP and studying with independent teachers.

Ruth L. Schwartz, author of *Accordian Breathing and Dancing* (Pittsburgh, 1996), has received grants from the NEA and the Astraea Foundation. She lives in Oakland, California, with her lover, Gladys, to whom she donated a kidney on May 11, 1995.

Maureen Seaton is the author of *The Sea Among the Cupboards, Fear of Subways* and *Furious Cooking* (University of Iowa Press, 1996), winner of the Iowa Prize for Poetry. She is the 1994 recipient of an Illinois Arts Council grant and an NEA Fellowship.

Mab Segrest is a forty-seven-year-old writer and organizer who lives in Durham, North Carolina, with her partner, Barbara, and their nine-year-old daughter, Annie. She is the author of *My Mama's Dead Squirrel: Lesbian Essays on Southern Culture* and *Memoir of a Race Traitor.*

Vita C. Shapiro has sought meaning and connection in her life through teaching, gardening, healing, photography and music. At fifty, she is studying to become a physical therapist and lives in a hand-built home in the woods of Ulster County, New York.

Alix Kates Shulman's memoir, *Drinking the Rain,* was nominated for a 1995 *Los Angeles Times* Book Prize. She is the author of ten books, including *Memoirs of an Ex-Prom Queen* and two books on the anarchist Emma Goldman. Her work has been translated into ten languages.

Chea Villanueva, of Filipino/Irish heritage, grew up on the streets of Philadelphia hanging with her homegirls. Throughout her life she has written about Butch/Femme relationships, gang girls and women in prison. She is the author of *The Chinagirls* and *Jessie's Song* and is currently writing *Bulletproof Butches.*

Jean Weisinger is based in San Francisco and has exhibited nationally and internationally. Her photographs have been featured in many books, magazines and journals as well as in several films, including Marlon Riggs's *Black is . . . Black Ain't* (Signifying Works) and Sweet Honey in the Rock's *A Priority* (Earthbeat).

Lucy Winer (Wildlight Productions) is an independent filmmaker currently in production on *Golden Threads,* a documentary, about ninety-year-old Christine Burton, founder of a global networking service for older lesbians. Credits include *Rate It X,* a controversial feature about sexism; *Silent Pioneers,* about lesbian/gay elders; and the groundbreaking series "Positive: Life with HIV."

Shay Youngblood is author of the plays *Shakin' the Mess Outta Misery* and *Talking Bones* (Dramatic Publishing Company), and of the short-story collection *The Big Mama Stories* (Firebrand Books). She is the recipient of numerous awards including a Pushcart Prize for fiction, the Lorraine Hansberry Playwriting Award and an Astraea Lesbian Writers' Award.

Acknowledgments
of Copyright